It was a time of pleasure,
to be riding in the early morning air,
to feel the drumming earth come upward
through the pony's legs and enter
his own flesh. Yes, the earth power
coming into him as he moved over it.
And a thing of the air, like a bird.
He breathed deeply of the bird-air,
and that was power too. He held his head high,
a being in flight. And he sang,
as his people sang, of the gray rising sun
and the shadows that were only emerging
from the night.

D'Arcy McNickle
Wind From An Enemy Sky

NAVAJO COMMUNITY COLLEGE PRESS

Earth Power Coming

Short Fiction in Native American Literature

EDITED BY SIMON J. ORTIZ

Navajo Community College Press gratefully acknowledges the reprinting of the following:

NEEK: News of the Native Community, "Egg Boat" by Nora Dauenhauer, reprinted with permission.

Blue Cloud Quarterly, "Hawk's Flight" by Gerald Haslam, reprinted with permission.

Pacific Quarterly Moana, "Amen" by Linda Hogan, reprinted with permission.

Sinister Wisdom, "New Shoes" by Linda Hogan, reprinted with permission.

Wilma Elizabeth McDaniel: A Collection of Short Stories, Day Tonight, Night Today Press, "A Dream of Grand Junction" and "Return of a Native Dreamer" by Wilma Elizabeth McDaniel, reprinted with permission.

Malahat Review, "She Keeps The Dance Turning Like The Earth" by Duane Niatum, reprinted with permission.

Title of the book and prefatory passage: From p. 106 in *Wind From An Enemy Sky* by D'arcy McNickle. Copyright © 1978 by the estate of D'Arcy McNickle. Reprinted by permission of Harper & Row, Publishers, Inc.

Published by Navajo Community College Press
Navajo Community College
Tsaile, Arizona 86556

Designed by Linnea Gentry, Santa Fe

International Standard Book Number 0-912586-50-8
Library of Congress Catalog Card Number 83-060959

Contents

Introduction

THE FOLLOWING works of short fiction by Native American writers presented in this volume sing forth in the morning, feeling "the earth power coming," singing for the people as do the words of D'Arcy McNickle whose passage from *Wind From An Enemy Sky* prefaces this book.

There have always been the songs, the prayers, the stories. There have always been the voices. There have always been the people. There have always been those words which evoked meaning and the meaning's magical wonder. There has always been the spirit which inspired the desire for life to go on. And it has been through the words of the songs, the prayers, the stories that the people have found a way to continue, for life to go on.

It is the very experience of life that engenders life. It is the act of perception that insures knowledge. For Indian people, it has been the evolvement of a system of life which insists on one's full awareness of his relationship to all life. Through words derived from one's thoughts, beliefs, acts, experiences, it is possible to share this awareness with all mankind. Included in this volume is a small measure of some of those words.

There is a wide variety of styles, themes and topics presented in the fiction of this collection of thirty authors. Their stories are evidence of the commitment made by Native American writers to express themselves in this genre of literature. It is not only a commitment to literature and writing but it is something more serious than that. I believe it is to make sure that the voice keeps

singing forth so that the earth power will not cease, and that the
people remain fully aware of their social, economic, political,
cultural, and spiritual relationships and responsibilities to all things.

I shall say only one thing in general about the stories in *Earth Power
Coming*.

Most of the fiction is grounded in the oral tradition and its varied
aspects. Humor is exemplified by Gerald Vizenor's and Peter Blue
Cloud's stories of storytellers. Blue Cloud's "Waterbugs" explains
"verbatim" as one true style of storytelling and Vizenor's
"Reservation Café" bitingly reflects that Indians have always
offered knowledge but "No one believes in tribal stories... Few
people believe what we have been telling about the earth."

There is an aspect of the oral tradition which relates directly to
the significant place that myths, legends, stories have in our lives.
Linda Hogan's story, "Amen," expresses this poignantly in her
telling of the night of the ancient fish. "It grew large. It was older
than all of them. It had hooks in it and lived." The fish survived all
those years and it is a symbol of the survival of oppressed people.

The creation of the mythic story, which states the human
condition and experience, is a means of dealing with the world.
Elizabeth Cook-Lynn and Joe Bruchac tell about this in their
respective stories, "The Power of Horses" and "Turtle Meat."
When we learn in Anna Walter's story, "The Warriors," that "It's
more than just repeating words," we realize it is creative expression
which brings about realization and regeneration. This then is the
way that people deal with the world, especially when times and
events prove difficult and harsh.

All of the stories, which range from stark realism to surrealism,
are good. Should there be any criticism about the selection of the
stories in *Earth Power Coming*, let the editor bear it. Without
sacrificing quality, I wanted the book to be as representative as
possible. Some years ago when the only other Native American
fiction collection was published, the editor remarked that he
concentrated on Southwestern Indian stories because the cultures of
the Southwest were older and more firmly established—and the

climate was good. I never did like that remark. Indian people are everywhere across this nation and beyond, throughout the Western hemisphere in fact, and their voices are strong. This major collection of short fiction is a significant indication of the voice that is singing of "the earth power coming." Listen, the earth and its power and people are singing!

Simon J. Ortiz, Editor
June, 1983

Earth Power Coming

New Shoes

Linda Hogan

E VEN SHAKING the folds out of the sheet, Sullie formed questions in her head about the shoes. She looked as if she might divine answers from the whiteness of afternoon light in the fine weavings of cotton. The way an old woman might read the future inside a porcelain teacup.

Manny came in quietly, leaving her cart out on the balcony walkway of the motel. "Up where I come from, people read the newspapers instead of the sheets," Manny said, and then she went out the door, her legs two shadows inside her thin skirt.

Sullie tucked the sheets beneath the mattress and smoothed the worn green bedspread across them. It was the color of algae, mossy and faded. New motel guests would arrive soon to sleep between the sheets and the cotton was fragrant with the odor of laundry soap and the smell of scorch from the big mangle. Sullie's short hands tightened a wrinkle away. She watched herself in the dresser mirror as she folded a blanket. Some hair had fallen down the back of her neck. She pinned it up. Her dry and darkened elbows bent toward the ceiling and the pale blue smock rose up away from her hips. She watched the reflection of herself push the soiled bedclothes deep into the canvas bag that hung on the side of the metal cart. In the loneliness of the room, in the mirror with its distortion right at Sullie's forehead and another at her thighs, she saw herself the way others probably saw her, too serious, dark-eyed, her shoulders too heavy, but alive and moving, filling up the room that had never known a permanent tenant.

In the storeroom the black hands of the clock on the wall said 3:00.

3

Already too late for the bus and Donna would be home ahead of her,
sitting on the sofa listening for the sound of her mother's shoes,
lazily turning the pages of an old magazine. Or perhaps she would
have opened the metal wardrobe and stepped into one of Sullie's
outdated dresses and stood before the mirror, turning herself this
way and that, sticking her chest out a little too far, piling her own
dark hair upon her head. With the one tube of dimestore lipstick
Sullie bought and once treasured, Donna would paint little smudges
on her cheekbones and smooth them out, darken her full lips that
were still rosy from childhood. And she would step, barefooted, into
the new shoes and stand in the full-length mirror inside the door of
the wardrobe and look at the narrow lines of her hips curving out
beneath the small of her back.

Sullie unsnapped the blue smock and hung it on the coathook. On
its pocket in red thread were embroidered the words, "The Pines
Motel." The words hung there in the sky blue cloth like writing
from an airplane.

"There's only one pine in this entire vicinity," Manny said, "and
it's that half-dead straggler over there across the street. Behind the
white house."

Manny had already replaced her unused sheets on the shelves, had
dropped the canvas bag of soiled linens into the corner for the
laundry. "You going to walk?" she asked Sullie. "You ought to take
the bus. How much money you figure you save walking those two
miles?"

"I only walk in the morning."

"When your feet are still good?" Manny removed the safety pin
from between her teeth and pinned her shirt from the underside.
"Does it show?" She smiled and the rich gold of her eyes warmed
Sullie. Manny with skin the color of earth, black hair straightened
only enough to look smooth on the surface, like water where the
undercurrents twist and pull beneath a seamless and leaden skin.
Manny's voice was slow, not full of fast chatter like the other maids,
not talking about boyfriends and children, about whether to go
dancing or save money for a car.

Manny made thirty-five cents an hour more than Sullie because she was colored instead of Indian. When Sullie got the nerve up to ask the manager about money, he said, "Don't gossip. I don't keep people on when they gossip. And take that chip off your shoulder."

The house with the pine stood alone and surrounded by a few shrubs, a small area of lawn, a remnant of farmland cut through with new streets and clouds of exhaust rising up from buses. In front of the house was a diner and Sullie's bus stop. It was all visible from the second floor balcony of the motel. The dying tree bent by an invisible wind, shaped like a tired old woman reaching down to touch children.

Sullie seated herself on the bench that advertised used cars.

Manny gestured with her head toward the diner. "Want some coffee?" But Sullie shook her head. "Suit yourself," said Manny and she walked toward the diner, slowly, as if she were wearing green silk and gold bracelets instead of the thin printed shirt and skirt. She went into the diner, a converted house trailer that had an extra room on the back side of it. The windows were slightly yellow from the grease of cooking. Behind them Sullie could see Manny sliding down into a seat behind the brown oilcloth and the little mustard jar vases with plastic flowers.

Sullie sat outside in the whirl of traffic, thinking of home, of large and slow-moving turtles migrating by the hundreds across the dirt roads, of silent nights when frogs leapt into water and the world came alive with the sounds of their swelling throats.

The wind began to blow off the street. With her hand Sullie covered her face from the dust and grit. Other women held down their skirts, their red and gold hair flying across their faces. A motion caught Sullie's eye. Up in the sky, something white was flying like a large bird. In spite of the blowing sand, she looked up but as she squinted at the sky, the bird lengthened and exposed itself as only a sheet of plastic churning and twisting in the wind. It stretched out like a long white snake and then lost its air current and began falling.

On the bus two elderly women sat in front of her. They were both speaking and neither one listened to the other. They carried on two different conversations the way people did in the city, without silences, without listening. Trying to get it all said before it was too late, before they were interrupted by thoughts. One of the women had steel blue hair. The other one fanned herself with a paper as if it were hot and humid, talking to her own face in the window about her children, one in San Diego in the navy, one in Nevada running a gas station. She put the paper down on her lap and powdered her nose, squinting into the little circle of mirror that was caked pink with powder.

A man with dark hair in front of the women puffed hard on his cigarette. The powdered woman fanned away the smoke. Sullie watched it rise, nearly blue, into the light of the windows, drifting like a cloud in the air currents, touching the hair oil spot on the glass. It was like mist rising off a lake in the early morning. Steam from a kettle of boiling vegetables, squash, tomato, onion. It smelled good, the sweet odor of burning tobacco.

Buildings blurred past the window. The early shift men carried lunch pails to their cars and buses, all gliding past the window as if Sullie were sitting still and watching a movie, a large fast-moving film of people disappearing into the south. Even those people walking north were swept into it, pulled finally backwards across the window and gone.

Sullie stood and pulled the narrow rope. She felt exposed, the people behind her looking at her tied-back hair with its first strands of white, at her cotton dress wrinkled from sitting on the plastic seat, at the heaviness of her arm, bare and vulnerable reaching upward to ring the bell. She stepped out the door and it hissed shut behind her.

Donna was not there. Her notebook was on the table and there was a dirty glass sitting beside the shiny new dishdrainer Sullie had bought with her last paycheck. Sullie rinsed the glass and placed it, upside down, in the orange plastic drainer, then wiped the glass and the drainer both with a towel. Her shoes creaked the gray linoleum where it was bulging.

Donna's sweater was on the floor beside the sofa bed. Sullie picked it up and then, once again, she reached beneath the sofa and pulled out one of the sleek black shoes. New shoes. They were shiny, unworn. Patent leather with narrow pointed heels and a softly sculptured hole in each toe. Sullie brushed the dust from them with her skirt. She saw her face reflected in the shiny leather, her wide forehead in the roundness of leather. Her heart jumped in her chest again as it had when she first found the shoes.

They were prettier than the shoes Anna May had worn that summer when she came from Tulsa on the back of a man's motorcycle. And Anna May had worn them, dust-ridden, red leather, all the way from the city down the dirt roads, over the big gullies that washed into the soil. She wore them home, wearing also a red and blue dress flying out on the back of a motorcycle.

What a big to-do the family made, admiring the bright dress and shoes even before they welcomed Anna May and her thin-faced boyfriend. Sullie had polished the buckles of her sister's shoes, walked around the floor in the red shoes that were too big and wobbly, her dry and dirty legs rising out of them like old sticks and her ankles turning.

Sullie put Donna's new shoes back under the sofa. She lined them up and put them where they couldn't be seen from the table.

It was dark when Donna returned. Sullie's eyes wandered from Donna's face down the small shoulders held too high, the large hands that were always out of place, looking right down at her feet in the run-over saddle shoes. She glanced again at Donna's light-skinned face. "I've been worried," she said.

"I was at a friend's," Donna said.

"Hungry?"

"We ate."

Sullie opened the refrigerator and stood in the light. Steam rolled out the door and surrounded her. She took out the bologna and, sitting at the table, made herself a sandwich.

Donna looked at the window, watching their reflections on the glass. A woman and a girl like themselves sitting in the dark square of glass.

"What did you eat?"

"Meatloaf and potatoes." With her finger Donna traced the pattern of the black matrix in the gold-colored plastic table. "Look, this one is shaped like a hawk. See? There's its wing. See its beak? It's saying, 'The train is about to come by.'"

"I haven't had meatloaf in a hundred years," Sullie said. She reached across the table to touch Donna's arm. Donna pulled away, got up and filled the glass with water from the faucet. The water clouded and cleared.

"What do you really think a hawk would say, mom?"

Sullie was quiet. She stood up and went over to fold the quilt Rena had made. She was careful with the quilt, removing it from the sofa back. Each patch was embroidered with stories of Sullie's life. If Rena had lived long enough, there would have been more stories to stitch, Sullie's life with Donna's father. That one would have contained a car and a man smoking cigarettes. There would have been a patch for the birth of Donna, the little light-skinned Indian who would someday wear black patent leather pumps on her bony feet. There would be a square containing the Pines Motel with Sullie standing on the balcony looking out at the yellowing pine tree that had lost most of its needles and looked like an old woman weeping. What else? A small coffin containing her dead son. Sullie taking the bus to Denver with little Donna crying and snuffling next to her. It was all like the great stained glass window, the quilt colors with light behind them. There was a picture for every special event of Sullie's childhood, a picture of Sullie's birth, the swarm of bees, little circles of gold, flying across the pale blue cotton, the old people all standing on the front porch of the old house. One of them, an old woman named Lemon was wearing a yellow dress and holding the dark infant up to the sun. Her legs were red. There were indigo clouds.

The last patch had never been finished. Rena was working on it the summer she died. On it was the lake with golden fish stitched down across the quilted waves. And there were the two glorious red mules whose backs were outlined in yellow thread as if the sun shone down on them. Men in rafts and boats. A group of women sitting at a table and gossiping were just outlined in ink. Nothing solid to them. Nothing filled in or completed. They were like shadows with white centers.

Sullie folded the quilt and put it on the table beside the couch. "Help me pull out this sofa, will you, honey?" She looked at Donna. "You know, I really think the hawk would say, 'It shall come to pass that all the world will be laid bare by the doings of men.'"

Donna looked at the quilt. "Can we sleep under it?"

"I'm saving it," Sullie told her once again.

"What for? When you get old and die?"

"No, honey, I just want to keep it nice. When you grow up, I'll give it to you."

Donna laid down between the sheets. Sullie sat next to her and ran her fingers down a loose strand of Donna's hair.

Saving things for old age. The very idea. Sullie reprimanded herself. Saving things when the girl wanted something pretty to hold now and to touch. No good. A mother and daughter alone in the city, no good. It was what happened when you married a man who drove up in the heat of summer after being gone two years and you had to tell him about the death of his son and then you wept and went away with the man, going anywhere just to get out of that desolate place and the heat. Just to get out of that place where your uncle had come home drunk and shot his wife, the place where your cousin sold off everything you owned one day just to buy a bottle and then tried to kiss your neck. Not that it was much to look at, but he sold it off to a young couple in a pickup truck that looked like they came from back east. And you went away with the white man and he went into the army. So the hawk would say.

It was better with him gone, with her husband gone. Even trying to earn a living. To mend socks and underwear for only two people. To not have to listen to that man bragging about what he used to be when he sang in bars or when he played baseball with some big team or other. Better to not even get anymore of his letters or snapshots, the shiny snapshots he sent of himself and his army friends sitting it out in bars with pretty oriental women smiling behind him. Still, Donna was growing up different. Like a stranger. She was going to be a white girl. Sullie could already see it in her. In her way of holding tension, of shaking her foot. In the hair she kept cutting. She was growing up with the noise of buses and cars, of GI's and red-dressed women laughing outside the window at night. She wasn't growing in the heat of woodstoves that burned hot even in the summer and the fireflies with their own little lanterns going on and off. Well, she wouldn't be picking cotton for the Woodruffs either like Sullie had done, feeling mad because Mrs. Woodruff was half Indian herself and spending that cotton money on silk dresses and luncheons at fancy places while Sullie was out there picking it from the dusty fields with her eyes watering. And she wouldn't be growing up laying down with men on the road at night like Anna May had done.

It must have been the quilt that moved her to dream of walking in the big lake at home. The water was warm against her legs. Silent except for the sound of water dripping off her, touching up against the shores in a slow rhythm like maybe it loved the land. And suddenly she was standing in the street by the diner, cars bearing down on her and she was paralyzed, unable to save herself.

Sullie woke up. It was cool. She covered Donna with her own half of the blanket and got up. They sky was growing lighter outside the window, beginning to light up the white cotton curtains with the rose colors of sunrise. Traffic picked up. Standing in her pale gown, her long hair loose and down around her waist, Sullie opened the curtains while the coffee water boiled. She called softly into the other room. And then she went over to pull back the covers. "Time to get up."

Outside, Donna stood at the end of the bench, waiting for the bus. Two young GI's slouched down on the bench. They wore olive drab, one with his military hat pulled down as if he were sleeping, one leg crossed over the other. His hands were folded loosely in his lap. Donna stood almost at attention.

A train passed over. It clattered and thundered along the trestle and it seemed to blow open Donna's tightly held sweater. It blew her hair in a blur of heat and exhaust, the heat waving up like a mirage, a summer field or highway. The soldier who sat straight up waved at an invisible conductor leaning off the platform between cars, and then he glanced at Donna. His eyes took in her thin body and chest. Under his gaze, she was stiff and unmoving. She stared straight ahead, but her body tightened inside her blue-gray sweater.

The train hurried past, carrying coal in the sweating black cars and speeding east on the vibrating track.

Donna was still. In the center of all the motion, the automobiles filled with people, the gold and red plastic streamers that waved and twisted about the used car lot, she was still, and then the train was gone.

Indoors, Sullie wiped the black shoes with a dish towel. She set them down on the table, on the speaking hawk laminated into plastic. She dried the dish drainer. It was pretty, the color of wildflowers at home. Bright orange like children's new toys and painted Mexican salt shakers, city swingsets. In the morning light, the entire kitchen shone, each item clear and full of its own beauty. The cereal bowls were dragonfly blue. The coffee cup was deep rich brown. It sat on the table beside the black shoes.

The shoes were small. Donna's size. Inside, in the place where Donna's delicate arch would touch and rise when she walked, were the words, "Montgomery Wards." Monkey Wards, as Sullie's cousins called the large white department store on Broadway, the store with the wires going through the ceiling, across the desks, the little tubes of money sliding through air and stopping.

Sullie's own shoes were flat and worn, scuffed. The soles were worn down at the heels. Last week a nail had pushed into the heel of her foot.

Suppose Donna had stolen them, she wondered, standing back and

looking at the new shoes. She sipped her coffee. Suppose Donna had
stolen these woman shoes? Or stolen Sullie's money. Sullie picked up
her handbag and unzipped the money compartment. Eighteen
dollars and twenty-nine cents. It was all there.

Sullie imagined the fancy shoes on Donna's little horse legs. With
the pink toes and jagged toenails protruding through the sculptured
holes. Donna's thin calf muscles flexed above the high heels.
Destitute and impoverished thin legs the color of cream and with
fine and scraggly hairs and big knees all looking so much worse
above the shining black shoes. And there were those young soldiers
already looking at the little breasts and at the red-black hair moving
unevenly across her shoulder blades. What would they think when
they saw the girl walking at a slant, wearing them? Surely they
wouldn't want to touch those pitiful small legs and thighs or cup
their big hands over the bulges of her breasts.

Someone must have given them to her. The meatloaf friend.

Donna could not count money and she was shy with salesclerks,
holding her handful of pennies too close to her own body and
waiting for the clerks to reach over and count out what they needed
from the moist palm. Donna's schoolteacher, Miss Fiedler, had
herself told Sullie that Donna couldn't count money. She had visited
their place and all the while Miss Fielder spoke, her blue eyes darted
around the room, never resting on Sullie who believed the woman
was looking for bugs and dust. Those cornflower blue eyes looking
at the nailholes in the bare walls, at Donna's drawings taped on the
kitchen wall next to the window, at the quilt with its needlework
pictures of Sullie and her own mother standing surrounded by a field
of green corn with a red turtle floating in the sky like a great sun and
a yellow frog and curled scorpion in each corner.

"What's that?" Miss Fiedler pointed at the turtle and the scorpion.
"Oh, a red turtle. It looks like it's swimming."

"The sky turtle. From an old story my father used to tell."

Miss Fiedler kept her feet square on the floor and her knees
together. Sullie was aware of her own green blouse. It was ironed
but growing thin beneath the arms. Sullie remembered to lean

forward as she had seen other women do, to look at the teacher's face and occasionally at the pale yellow sweater and its softness and at the blonde curled hair. The teacher sat like a gold light in the center of the sofa that day, like a madonna in a church surrounded by a quilt of stained glass pictures.

Finally Miss Fiedler looked right up at Sullie. "I was passing by and thought I might as well stop in. I thought it would be better than a letter."

"Oh?"

"Donna isn't ready to go on to seventh grade. It's out of the question. She doesn't even count money." She added, "She doesn't get along with the other girls."

And in a long silence following the words, the room brightened as the red turtle sun came out from behind a cloud. The teacher's hair lit up like brass. She expected Sullie to say something. Sullie watched the woman's face brighten. Then she said to the teacher, "She's good at art though, don't you think?" And Sullie went over to open the drawer and remove the collection of pictures she kept there. "See here? This is Lucy Vine. It looks just like her." And there was old Lucy wearing some plants in a sling of cloth on her back. She was bent, nearly white-headed, leaning over a fire. Behind her was a metal tub for washing and some men's shirts hanging along a fence like scarecrows and a raven flying overhead, its blue-black wings spread wide.

"Nice. That is nice."

Sullie looked up at the teacher and repeated, "She's good at art," and the teacher looked back at Sullie and said nothing.

Even remembering this Sullie felt ashamed and her face grew warm. She removed her apron and hung it on the doorknob that was heavy and crystal. The color of larva, with light pouring through it. Sullie lifted the apron and looked again at the doorknob, the room reflected in it a hundred times, herself standing upside down and looking at the tiny replicas of the motel-apartment. She left it uncovered. She put the apron over the back of the kitchen chair. The door knob was the nicest thing in the room besides the quilt and

Donna's pictures. The pictures were lovely. There was one Donna had sketched of Sullie from the back, her shoulders soft and round-looking, the hair unkempt, the heavy face just visible in profile. And there was a picture of women dancing in a row. They wore gathered skirts over their heavy hips, dresses with the sewn patterns, the Diamondback sign, the Trail of Tears, the Hand of God. They were joined hand to elbow. Their white aprons were tied in neat bows at the back. "Funny dresses," Donna commented when she completed the picture.

Pretty as a picture postcard, Mrs. Meers was standing at the door with her arms folded, the red and gold streamers flying behind her in the car lot. There were flags on the antennae of a used Chevy that said $250 in white soap on the windshield. Mrs. Meers, the manager, fidgeted with her hair, one arm still crossed in front of her stomach. Sullie opened the door.

"You got a phone call from the motel. They say you're mighty late coming in today."

"The Pines? I'm not going in." Sullie didn't look surprised at the message.

"You don't look sick to me." Mrs. Meers dropped both hands to her hips. They were slim in white pants.

"I didn't say I was sick. Just tell them I'll be there tomorrow."

Mrs. Meers looked more seriously at Sullie. Like a doctor might do when he discovered you were not just entertaining yourself by sitting in his examining room. She squinted and sucked in her cheeks. "I don't mean to step into your business, but to tell the truth I'm not good at lying. You tell them. And tell them to quit calling me. Tell them you'll get your own phone."

Sullie shrugged. "It's not lying." Only the hint of a shrug, so slight that Mrs. Meers did not notice. And Mrs. Meers continued talking, more softly now. "What's so important that you can't go in? What's worth losing your job over?"

"Look there!" Sullie was pointing toward the street. "Look there. Is that your little cat?"

Mrs. Meers looked impatient. "You know I don't keep cats."

"It'll get run down."

Mrs. Meers tucked in her red shirt. "Look, I know I ain't supposed to be looking out for you tenants."

"Show's through," Sullie said.

"What?"

"Your shirt. It shows through your pants."

The landlady waved her hand in exasperation. "Listen to that. You worry about my shirt."

Sullie half-listened. She nodded. She was still watching the kitten stumble away from the wheels of one car and toward another.

"Okay. Okay, I'll tell them." Mrs. Meers went off grumbling, saying how it was these people could buy fancy black shoes like those on the table and not ever go to work. Must be government dole or something. She herself could not afford shoes like those and she was running this place. She waved her arm as if to clear her mind, to get rid of Sullie and that sneaky quiet kid of hers. Deserves to lose her job, she mumbled. And all the while Sullie was out there in the street calling to the kitten, a scrawny little cat with greasy fur. "No pets!" Mrs. Meers yelled at Sullie. "No pets allowed. We don't even let goldfish in."

After the cat coiled up on the sofa, Sullie washed her hands and returned her attention to the shoes. If they were stolen, they would have to be taken back. That would be the right thing to do, to hand the shoes to the salesclerk. She might be one of those older, efficient types who wore maroon suits and shirts that tied in bows at the neck. Pearl earrings. Or one of the tall ones in the thin dresses. If she were a young clerk, she would be nervous and call the manager. The managers were tight about the rules. They stuck with the rules. They might call in the police.

Sullie had never stolen anything. Just the thought of it sent her heart racing and made her knees weak. She had no courage against teachers, clerks, police, managers, and even now the fear came flying into her.

She put the shoes back where she found them.

It was a quiet day. Early afternoons were quiet. The traffic died down. The red and gold streamers were lifeless. A good day just for walking.

Sullie stepped across the railroad ties that smelled of creosote and the penny smell of oiled metal. She went across the vacant lot filled with weeds and a few spears of green that were irises. Behind the rows of houses, there was a lake, a few elm trees. She heard the doves in the mornings from her kitchen and she was hungry to look at the water, the blue sky lying down on its surface.

Two ducks swam there. The bright-colored male was showing off. He shook himself, ruffled his feathers and paddled his orange feet. The female ignored him, diving under water with her backside exposed. Dipping and surfacing. A plane flew over and Sullie caught its light on the water.

An old man with a cane tipped his dark hat. He wore a heavy coat as if it were still winter and he had not noticed the change of seasons, the warm sun and the green dusty leaves on the few elms. A woman sat on a swing, her two children pushing at one another. The woman stared at the ducks. Her face looked bored and vacant, the look of mothers with young children. She would have spoken to Sullie if Sullie were thinner and looked different. If Sullie had worn a pair of slacks and a flowered blouse. The woman wanted to speak to someone. She greeted the old man.

When Sullie headed back, she had to wait at the tracks for a train to pass. It was a passenger train and the faces in the windows rushed past. One small boy waved at her. The wheels clattered, metal on metal. A man and woman stood on the platform, the wind in their hair and faces. His arm around her waist. The sounds roared in Sullie's ears and the earth beneath her feet rumbled and shook and then the train grew smaller in the distance, growing lighter and she picked her way over the tracks and through the weeds of the field, out of the heat and cement and into the fresh smell of the grocery store. Cool. The banana odor, the laundry soap fragrance. There were cartons of eggs on the rack, tan and perfectly smooth and oval, red meats with their own fleshy odor. "How much?" she asked, pointing at the ground beef.

The man in the white cap gestured to the marker. Sullie ordered a pound and he scooped it and wrapped it in white butcher paper, wrote .31 on the top with black crayon.

Sullie left the store, walking slowly, her arms full of the large bag, her face to one side of it watching for cracks and settlings in the sidewalk. Carrying milk and a small bag of flour, a half dozen eggs, an apple for Donna, two potatoes. And there was a small container of cinnamon inside the bag. A gold and green shaker holding in the sweet red of the other countries, of islands with their own slow women carrying curled brown bark in baskets. The metal box was the color of their dresses, water green and sunlight color.

Sullie would make bread pudding out of it and fill the apartment up with the odors of islands and Mexico, warmth and spice and people dancing in bright colors and with looseness in their hips, at least as far as she imagined.

When Sullie arrived, there was another smell in the apartment, the wax and perfume smell of the lipstick Donna was wearing. The rouged cheeks and red lips made her look younger, against the girl's intentions. Her big dark eyes were innocent in contrast with the crimson lips. The lipstick paled her skin. All of her weaknesses were revealed by the rosy cheeks and the painted lips, as if her plainness normally strengthened her, camouflaged the self-consciousness of her expression and the awkwardness of her movements, the pensive bend of her shoulders. She looked away when people spoke to her and she did not look up into Sullie's eyes now while Sullie stood, her arms full of the brown paper bag. Sullie stood one moment before putting the groceries down on the table, and she said, "So." Nothing more or less, simply, "So."

The kitten slept in the child's lap. Its paws were twitching slightly. Down in the quick of it, beneath the smell of transmission fluid, the kitten was dreaming of something pleasant. Cream, perhaps. Or of stalking brilliant green flies. Lord, Lord, Sullie breathed, what things we put in our heads. All of us. Filling ourselves up with hopes. Looking out for an extra dollar or good job. Putting on these faces. Even the cats. And here it was, the kitten, all comfortable while Mrs. Meers over there was plotting how to get rid of it. No pets. All these dreams and hopes, and nothing out there but rules and laws. Even in the churchyards. Even in the big homes, the ones that smell like paint and god-fearing Sunday dinners. Even in the motel rooms, a sign on the door saying when to move on. A bible full of do and don't. A boss clocking you in. Red lights. And there was a girl with red lips whose eyes do not meet yours and her head filled up with pretty things and men who would someday love her right out of her loneliness for a few hours. Her head filled up with pearls, silk dresses, shining hair. Evening in Paris perfume in the pretty blue bottles. All those thoughts flying around in there like crows circling over something down on the road.

Sullie was quiet as she put away the groceries. She removed her shoes and walked on the gray linoleum, her feet with a soft animal sound against the floor. She struck a match against the stove. The odor of sulphur and then of gas as she held it to the little hole inside the dark oven. All at once, as the fire took, there was the sound of burning, of the box-like oven opening up. She was going to cook meatloaf. Donna, holding the kitten, stood by the table and traced the black marbled patterns with her finger. "It's a monkey."

"Does it talk?"

"It says you got fired for missing work today."

Sullie put down a fork. "Who says that?"

"The monkey says Mrs. Meers told him."

"Monkeys lie. Besides, what's he doing hanging around women with black roots in their hair?"

"Did you ever hear of television? It's new. It's like a radio, only with pictures. And they move like in a movie." She was filled up with amazement and the magic of it. Her eyes darkened. "I saw one."

"How do they get the pictures."

"They come in the air."

"Pictures? You mean they are in the air?"

"Even in here and if we could turn on a button they'd show up. Yes, they would." And Donna saw the apartment peopled with men and women, animals, new places, all around her the black and white pictures of the rest of the world.

"I'll be. They think of everything, don't they? They just sit back up there in Washington with old Eisenhower and they think of everything." Sullie rubbed on the soap bar while she spoke and the bubbles foamed up in the dishwasher. She smiled down at Donna. She dried her hands. "Sit there. Stay there." She went over to the couch. "Don't move." Donna remained at the table while her mother bent and reached underneath the couch for the shoes. Donna's hands tightened.

"Child," Sullie said, standing up. "I don't know where they come from but they are about your size."

Donna was still. The light from the ceiling was on her hair and behind her, the small lamp burned an outline about her, like a small fire, like a burning match. Her delicate face was soft-looking even with the red lips.

"I found these. Here, put them on."

Donna stood and balanced herself by holding on to Sullie and then to the chair back. She put one small foot inside a shoe and then the other. She stood taller and thinner than before. She looked frail. The leg muscles tightened. She wobbled.

Sullie went to the wardrobe cabinet and opened the door to reveal the picture inside. "Look," she said and she was almost breathless. "Look. You're pretty."

Donna looked herself up and down. She looked into the depths of the mirror for the moving pictures of men who were flying through ordinary air, for the women selling Halo shampoo on the television. She heard their voices. She looked at the black patent leather shoes. She lifted one foot and polished the shoe against the back of her leg. She stood, turning herself in front of the mirror. Her skin looked moist, childlike in its warmth and lack of pores.

Sullie stood, her bare feet quiet, rocking a little, swaying in place. Donna could see her mother in the back of the mirror behind her, a dark woman, plain and dark and standing way back in the distance with her hair tied, her feet bare, a heaviness in the way she stood there in that air, that very air all the perfect white kitchens floated through, all the starched blonde women drifted into like ghosts. Sullie moved more fully into the mirror, her darkness like a lovely shadow beside the pale girl, her hand on the girl's narrow shoulder. "Pretty," she said, "You sure look pretty."

Private Property

Leslie Marmon Silko

ALL PUEBLO TRIBES have stories about such a person—a young child, an orphan. Someone has taken the child and has given it a place by the fire to sleep. The child's clothes are whatever the people no longer want. The child empties the ashes and gathers wood. The child is always quiet, sitting in its place tending the fire. They pay little attention to the child as they complain and tell stories about one another. The child listens although it has nothing to gain or lose in anything they say. The child simply listens. Some years go by and great danger stalks the village—in some versions of the story it is a drought and great famine, other times it is a monster in the form of a giant bear. And when all the others have failed and even the priests doubt the prayers, this child, still wearing old clothes, goes out. The child confronts the danger and the village is saved. Among the Pueblo people the child's reliability as a narrator is believed to be perfect.

Etta works with the wind at her back. Sand and dust roll down the road. She feels scattered drops of rain and sometimes flakes of snow. What they have been saying about her all these years is untrue. They are angry because she left. Old leaves and weed stalks lie in gray drifts at the corners of the old fence. Part of an old newspaper is caught in the tumbleweeds; the wind presses it into brittle yellow flakes. She rakes the debris as high as her belly. They continue with stories about her. Going away has changed her. Living with white people has changed her. Fragments of glass blink like animal eyes.

21

The wind pushes the flames deep into the bones and old manure heaped under the pile of dry weeds. The rake drags out a shriveled work shoe and then the sleeve torn from a child's dress. They burn as dark and thick as hair. The wind pushes her off balance. Flames pour around her and catch the salt bushes. The yard burns bare. The sky is the color of stray smoke. The next morning the wind is gone. The ground is crusted with frost and still the blackened bones smolder.

The horses trot past the house before dawn. The sky and earth are the same color then—dense gray of the night burned down. At the approach of the sun, the east horizon bleeds dark blue. Reyna sits up in her bed suddenly and looks out the window at the horses. She has been dreaming she was stolen by Navajos and was taken away in their wagon. The sound of the horses' hooves outside the window had been the wagon horses of her dreams. The white one trots in the lead, followed by the gray. The little sorrel mare is always last. The gray sneezes at their dust. They are headed for the river. Reyna wants to remember this, and gets up. The sky is milky. Village dogs are barking in the distance. She dresses and finds her black wool cardigan. The dawn air smells like rain but it has been weeks since the last storm. The crickets don't feel the light. The mockingbird is in the pear tree. The bare adobe yard is swept clean. A distance north of the pear tree there is an old wire fence caught on gray cedar posts that lean in different directions. Etta has come back after many years to live in the little stone house.

The sound of the hammer had been Reyna's first warning. She blames herself for leaving the old fence posts and wire. The fence should have been torn down years ago. The old wire had lain half-buried in the sand that had drifted around the posts. Etta was wearing mens' gloves that were too large for her. She pulled the strands of wire up and hammered fence staples to hold the wire to the posts. Etta has made the fence the boundary line. She has planted morning glories and hollyhocks all along it. She waters them every morning before it gets hot. Reyna watches her. The morning glories and hollyhocks are all that hold up the fence posts anymore.

Etta is watching Reyna from the kitchen window of the little stone house. She fills the coffee pot without looking at the level of water. Reyna is walking the fence between their yards. She paces the length of the fence as if she can pull the fence down with her walking. They had been married to brothers, but the men died long ago. They don't call each other "sister-in-law" anymore. The fire in the cookstove is cracking like rifle shots. She bought a pick-up load of pinon wood from a Navajo. The little house has one room, but the walls are rock and adobe mortar two feet thick. The one who got the big house got the smaller yard. That is how Etta remembers it. Their mother-in-law had been a kind woman. She wanted her sons and daughters-in-law to live happily with each other. She followed the old ways. She believed houses and fields must always be held by the women. There had been no nieces or daughters. The old woman stood by the pear tree with the daughters-in-law and gave them each a house, and the yard to divide. She pointed at the little stone house. She said the one who got the little house got the bigger share of the yard. Etta remembers that.

Cheromiah drives up in his white Ford pick-up. He walks to the gate smiling. He wears his big belly over his Levi's like an apron. Reyna is gathering kindling at the woodpile. The juniper chips are hard and smooth as flint. She rubs her hands together although there is no dust. "They came through this morning before it was even daylight." She points in the direction of the river. "They were going down that way." He frowns, then he smiles. "I've been looking for them all week," he says. The old woman shakes her head. "Well, if you hurry, they might still be there.". They are his horses. His father-in-law gave him the white one when it was a colt. Its feet are as big around as pie pans. The gray is the sorrel mare's colt. The horses belong to Cheromiah, but the horses don't know that. "Nobody told them," that's what people say and then they laugh. The white horse leans against corral planks until they give way. It steps over low spots in old stone fences. The gray and little sorrel follow.

"The old lady said to share and love one another. She said we only make use of these things as long as we are here. We don't own them. Nobody owns anything." Juanita nods. She listens to both of her aunts. The two old women are quarreling over a narrow strip of ground between the two houses. The earth is hard-packed. Nothing grows there. Juanita listens to her Aunt Reyna and agrees that her Aunt Etta is wrong. Too many years living in Winslow. Aunt Etta returns and she wants to make the yard "private property" like white people do in Winslow. Juanita visits both of her aunts everyday. She visits her Aunt Etta in the afternoon while her Aunt Reyna is resting. Etta and Reyna know their grandniece must visit both her aunts. Juanita has no husband or family to look after. She is the one who looks after the old folks. She is not like her brothers or sister who have wives or a husband. She doesn't forget. She looked after Uncle Joe for ten years until he finally died. He always told her she would have the house because women should have the houses. He didn't have much. Just his wagon horses, the house and a pig. He was the oldest and believed in the old ways. Aunt Reyna was right. If her brother Joe were alive he would talk to Etta. He would remind her that this is the village, not Winslow, Arizona. He would remind Etta how they all must share. Aunt Reyna would have more space for her woodpile then.

Most people die once, but "old man Joe he died twice," that's what people said, and then they laughed. Juanita knew they joked about it, but still she held her head high. She was the only one who even tried to look after the old folks. That November, Uncle Joe had been sick with pneumonia. His house smelled of Vicks and Ben-Gay. She checked on him every morning. He was always up before dawn the way all the old folks were. They greeted the sun and prayed for everybody. He was always up and had a fire in his little pot belly stove to make coffee. But that morning she knocked and there was no answer. Her heart was beating fast because she knew what she would find. The stove was cold. She stood by his bed and watched. He did not move. She touched the hand on top of the blanket and the fingers were as cold as the room. Juanita ran all the way to Aunt Reyna's house with the news. They sent word. The nephews and the clansmen came with picks and shovels. Before they went to dress him for burial, they cooked the big meal always prepared for the gravediggers. Aunt Reyna rolled out the tortillas and cried. Joe had always been so good to her. Joe had always loved her best after their parents died.

Cheromiah came walking by that morning while Juanita was getting more firewood. He was dragging a long rope and leather halter. He asked if she had seen any sign of his horses. She shook her head and then she told him Uncle Joe had passed away that morning. Tears came to her eyes. Cheromiah stood quietly for amoment. "I will miss the old man. He taught me everything I know about horses." Juanita nodded. Her arms were full of juniper wood. She looked away toward the southeast. "I saw your gray horse up in the sandhills the other day." Cheromiah smiled and thanked her. Cheromiah's truck didn't start in cold weather. He didn't feel like walking all the way up to the sand hills that morning. He took the road around the far side of the village to get home. It took him past Uncle Joe's place. The pig was butting its head against the planks of the pen making loud smacking sounds. The wagon horses were eating corn stalks the old man bundled up after harvest for winter feed. Cheromiah wondered which of the old man's relatives was already looking after the livestock. He heard someone chopping wood on the other side of the house. The old man saw him and waved in the direction of the river. "They were down there last evening grazing in the willows." Cheromiah dropped the halter and rope and gestured with both hands. "Uncle Joe! They told me you died! Everyone thinks you are dead! They already cooked the gravediggers lunch!"

From that time on Uncle Joe didn't get up before dawn like he once did. But he wouldn't let them tease Juanita about her mistake. Behind her back, Juanita's cousins and in-laws were saying that she was in such a hurry to collect her inheritance. They didn't think she should get everything. They thought all of it should be shared

equally. The following spring, Uncle Joe's wagon horses went down
Paguate Hill too fast and the wagon wheel hit a big rock. He was
thrown from the wagon and a sheepherder found him. Uncle Joe
was unconscious for two days and then he died. "This time he really
is dead, poor thing," people would say and then they'd smile.

The trouble over the pig started on the day of the funeral. Juanita
caught her brother's wife at the pig pen. The wife held a large pail in
both hands. The pail was full of a yellowish liquid. There were bones
swimming in it. Corn tassels floated like hair. She looked Juanita in
the eye as she dumped the lard pail into the trough. The pig switched
its tail and made one push through the liquid with its snout. It looked
up at both of them. The snout kept moving. The pig would not eat.
Juanita had already fed the pigs scraps from the gravediggers' plates.
She didn't want her brothers' wives feeding the pig. They would
claim, they had fed the pig more than she had. They would say that
whoever fed the pig the most should get the biggest share of meat.
At butchering time they would show up to collect half. "It won't eat
slop," Juanita said, "don't be feeding it slop."

The stories they told about Etta always came back to the same thing.

While the other girls learn cooking and sewing at the Indian
School, Etta works in the greenhouse. In the evenings the teacher
sits with her on the sofa. They repeat the names of the flowers. She
teaches Etta the parts of the flower. On Saturdays while the
dormitory matrons take the others to town, Etta stays with the
teacher. Etta kneels beside her in the garden. They press brown dirt
over the gladiola bulbs. The teacher runs a hot bath for her. The
teacher will not let her return to the dormitory until she has cleaned
Etta's fingernails. The other girls tell stories about Etta.

The white gauze curtains are breathing in and out. The hollyhocks
bend around the fence posts and lean over the wire. The buds are
tight and press between the green lips of the sheath. The seed had
been saved in a mason jar. Etta found it in the pantry behind a veil of

cobwebs. She planted it the length of the fence to mark the boundary. She had only been a child the first time, but she can still remember the colors — reds and yellows swaying above her head, tiny black ants in the white eyes of pollen. Others were purple and dark red, almost black as dried blood. She planted the seeds the teacher had given her. She saved the seeds from the only year the hollyhocks grew. Etta doesn't eat pork. She is thinking about the row of tamarisk trees she will plant along the fence so people cannot see her yard or house. She does not want to spend her retirement with everyone in the village minding her business the way they always have. Somebody is always fighting over something. The years away taught her differently. She knows better now. The yard is hers. They can't take it just because she had lived away from the village all those years. A person could go away and come back again. The village people don't understand fences. At Indian School she learned fences tell you where you stand. In Winslow, white people built fences around their houses, otherwise something might be lost or stolen. There were rumors about her the whole time she lived in Winslow. The gossip was not true. The teacher had written to her all the years Etta was married. It was a job to go to after her husband died. The teacher was sick and old. Etta went because she loved caring for the flowers. It was only a job, but people like to talk. The teacher was sick for a long time before she died.

"What do you want with those things," the clanswoman scolded, "wasting water on something we can't eat." The old woman mumbled to herself all the way across the garden. Etta started crying. She sat on the ground by the hollyhocks she had planted, and held her face. She pressed her fingers into her eyes. The old woman had taken her in. It was the duty of the clan to accept orphans.

Etta tells her she is not coming back from Indian School in the summer. She has a job at school caring for the flowers. She and the clanswoman are cleaning a sheep stomach, rinsing it under the mulberry tree. The intestines are coiled in a white enamel pan. They are bluish gray, the color of the sky before snow. Strands of tallow

branch across them like clouds. "You are not much good to me
anyway. I took you because no one else wanted to. I have tried to
teach you, but the white people at that school have ruined you. You
waste good water growing things we cannot eat."

The first time Etta returned from Winslow for a visit, Reyna
confided there was gossip going on in the village. Etta could tell by
the details that her sister-in-law was embroidering stories about her
too. They did not speak to each other after that. People were jealous
of her because she had left. They were certain she preferred white
people. But Etta spoke only to the teacher. White people did not see
her when she walked on the street.

The heat holds the afternoon motionless. The sun does not move. It
has parched all color from the sky and left only the fine ash. The
street below is empty. Down the long dim hall there are voices in
English and, more distantly, the ticking of a clock. The room is
white and narrow. The shade is pulled. It pulses heat the texture of
pearls. The water in the basin is the color of garnets. Etta waits in a
chair beside the bed. The sheets are soaked with her fever. She
murmurs the parts of the flowers—she whispers that the bud is
swelling open, but that afternoon was long ago.

Ruthie's husband is seeing that other woman in the cornfield. The
cornfield belongs to her and to her sister, Juanita. Their mother left
it to both of them. In the morning her husband walks to the fields
with the hoe on his shoulder. Not long after, the woman appears
with a coal bucket filled with stove ashes. The woman follows the
path toward the trash pile, but when she gets to the far corner of the
cornfield she stops. When she thinks no one is watching she sets the
bucket down. She gathers up the skirt of her dress and steps over the
fence where the wire sags.

Ruthie would not have suspected anything if she had not noticed
the rocks. He was always hauling rocks to build a new shed or
corral. But this time there was something about the colors of the
sandstone. The reddish pink and orange yellow looked as if they had

been taken from the center of the sky as the sun went down. She had never seen such intense color in sandstone. She had always remembered it being shades of pale yellow or peppered white-colors for walls and fences. But these rocks looked as if rain had just fallen on them. She watched her husband. He was unloading the rocks from the old wagon and stacking them carefully next to the woodpile. When he had finished it was dark and she could not see the colors of the sandstone any longer. She thought about how good-looking he was, the kind of man all the other women chase.

Reyna goes with them. She takes her cane but carries it ready in her hand like a rabbit club. Her grandnieces have asked her to go with them. Ruthie's husband is carrying on with another woman. The same one as before. They are going after them together-the two sisters and the old aunt. Ruthie told Juanita about it first. It was their mother's field and now it is theirs. If Juanita had a husband he would work there too. "The worst thing is them doing it in the cornfield. It makes the corn sickly, it makes the beans stop growing. If they want to do it they can go down to the trash and lie in the tin cans and broken glass with the flies," that's what Reyna says.

They surprise them lying together on the sandy ground in the shade of the tall corn plants. Last time they caught them together they reported them to the woman's grandmother, but the old woman didn't seem to care. They told that woman's husband too. But he has a job in Albuquerque, and men don't bother to look after things. It is up to women to take care of everything. He is supposed to be hoeing weeds in their field, but instead he is rolling around on the ground with that woman, killing off all their melons and beans.

Her breasts are long and brown. They bounce against her like potatoes. She runs with her blue dress in her hand. She leaves her shoes. They are next to his hoe. Ruthie stands between Juanita and Aunt Reyna. They gesture with their arms and yell. They are not scolding him. They don't even look at him. They are scolding the rest of the village over husband-stealing and corn that is sickly. Renya raps on the fence post with her cane. Juanita calls him a pig. Ruthie cries because the beans won't grow. He kneels to lace his work shoes. He kneels for a long time. His fingers move slowly. They are not talking to him. They are talking about the other woman. The red chili stew she makes is runny and pale. They pay no attention to him. He goes back to hoeing weeds. Their voices sift away in the wind. Occasionally he stops to wipe his forehead on his sleeve. He looks up at the sky or over the sand hills. Off in the distance there is a man on foot. He is crossing the big sand dune above the river. He is dragging a rope. The horses are grazing on yellow rice grass at the foot of the dune. They are down wind from him. He inches along, straining to crouch over his own stomach. The big white horse whirls suddenly, holding its tail high. The gray half-circles and joins it, blowing loudly through its nostrils. The little sorrel mare bolts to the top of the next dune before she turns.

Etta awakens and the yard is full of horses. The gray chews a hollyhock. Red petals stream from its mouth. The sorrel mare watches her come out the door. The white horse charges away, rolling his eyes at her nightgown. Etta throws a piece of juniper from the woodpile. The gray horse presses hard against the white one. They tremble in the corner of the fence, strings of blue morning glories trampled under their hooves. Etta yells and the sorrel mare startles, crowding against the gray. They heave forward against the fence, and the posts make slow cracking sounds. The wire whines and squeaks. It gives way suddenly and the white horse stumbles ahead tangled in wire. The sorrel and the gray bolt past, and for an instant the white horse hesitates, shivering at the wire caught around its forelegs and neck. Then the white horse leaps forward, rusty wire and fence posts trailing behind like a broken necklace.

Reservation Café: The Origins of American Indian Instant Coffee

Gerald Vizenor

S HAMAN TRUTH LIES, tribal trickster and mixedblood master of socioacupuncture, interrupted an academic assessorization conference to proclaim a modest reservation economic development scheme that would corner and control international coffee markets.

The college deans at the conference were neither surprised nor displeased with the unusual proclamation. Tricksters were well known in high education circles for exploiting familiar forums of instruction, revealing unnatural visions and banal dreams.

The shaman trickster earned his nickname from a television interview: "Truth lies in tribal dreams," he said, emphasizing the word *lies,* and then he concluded that "white histories are nothing more than word piles," emphasizing the last word. Reminded of these ironies, he allows that it is "better to be known as Truth Lies than as Word Piles."

Truth Lies told the assessorization conferees that "great spirits offered coffee to the tribes, and now we have the first proud word and the best beans, enough to take back the world markets from the word pilers." The deans sat in neat rows, stout fingers bound over their stomachs, like woodchucks waiting at the roadside for the racial traffic to clear before making a move.

The trickster had been invited to the conference to express a short tribal benediction, not a diatribe on coffee fascism. The invitation was a throw back to frontier mission romances and racial overcompensations, but the urban shaman was not a native speaker of a tribal language so he told a few short stories, seven in all, about the mythic world in the tribal mind where the white man is tricked from his illusions of power and dominance and then taught to walk backwards in dreams, backwards right out of the country.

Truth Lies unfurled a small birch bark scroll. He gestured with his lips, in the tribal manner, toward the scroll, while he circled his right fist, which held seven dark red coffee beans, around the microphone, an uncommon benediction. The trickster consulted the scroll from time to time as he told stories to the deans about the tribal origin of coffee, and as he talked he pinched the seven red beans into a fine instant powder over a cup of hot water.

First pinch:
In the beginning there was the word and the first word was coffee, or *makade mashkiki waaboo,* a black medicine drink, in the *anishinaabe* oral tradition. It was a time when *naanabozho,* one of the first humans on the earth, a super trickster who dreamed in different forms and languages, spoke the same tongue as the plants and animals.

Well, several weeks after the famous flood, the first trickster noticed that when his earthdiver friends, the otter and muskrat and beaver, ate some red berries from an evergreen shrub, they danced and sang with such ecstacies that *naanabozho* invented loneliness to protect himself from the shared pleasures of others. He asked the animals to explain but there was no language then for their pleasures. The trickster, an empiricist of sorts, ate some of the red berries, and as he ate he interviewed the evergreen shrub about the meaning of pleasure. The shrub shrugged his inquiries at first, but then, when *naanabozho* began to snap his fingers, roll his head and eyes, and wriggle his enormous toes in the shrubbery, the shrub revealed that she was named coffee, or *makade mashkiki waaboo,* the first word in the creation of the world.

Second pinch:

Great spirits created the species *coffea anishinaabica,* the frost tolerant low altitude pinch ground coffee which, until now at this telling, has been a tribal secret. *Coffea anishinaabica* thrives along the shores of Algoma, the Sea of the Algonquin, or Lake Superior. Later, much later, two other important species were created, *coffea arabica* and *coffea robusta,* in other parts of the world, but these species, as you know, are pinchless and sensitive to frost.

There are two simple methods to prepare *coffea anishinaabica* beans. The first and the most traditional method is to do nothing. You heard it right, *nothing.* The shrubs flower in the spring and then red berries appear in summer. Late in winter under a whole moon the berries are harvested by shaking the shrubs. Sometimes the shrubs shake back and tell stories like this one. The berries are stored in birch bark containers with a fresh cedar bough. Some traditionalists tell that one should pick and pinch no more than one bean at a time. Storage, according to the static fundamentalists who talk backwards far enough to lock the past into the present, welcomes evil admirers.

The second method is sacred, a ceremonial preparation shared by some women of the tribe. Vision berries, as the beans are named one at a time, are picked with ritual care from sacred shrubs grown at Michilimackinac, or Turtle Island. Tumbled for several nights in red cedar water, the beans are separated and bound in birch bark balls and suspended in cedar trees over the winter. In the spring, the beans are pinched into a ceremonial brew, and the hallucinogenic alkaloids released from this ritual process cause one to feel the summer in the spring, from tribal coffee no less.

Third pinch:

You must wonder how could such a fantastic coffee bean, pinched into a rich nuance without roasting, be held a secret for such a long time? Well, the answer is simple: No one believes in tribal stories. We have hundreds of herbal cures for various diseases but who has listened? What the tribes have told the white man has passed through their ears with little attention; some are impressed with mythic form but not with content. Few people believe what we have been telling about the earth: Rivers are dead, fish are poisoned, and the air is evil with pollution, evil enough to drive the cockroaches to the mountains for a rest.

Twice, however, we almost lost the secret to enterprising white men. Bishop Frederic Baraga, a small man with compulsive historical missions, tried *makade mashkiki waaboo* on several occasions. Stories are told about how he drank a cedar blend of *coffea anishinaabica* in place of sacramental wine during services.

Bishop Baraga, in one respect at least, became a tribal person: His superiors did not believe his stories about pinch coffee from the woodland lakeshores in the new world. Notes on his experiences with the sacred *miskwaawaak,* cedar blend, disappeared from his memorabilia.

Then, a few years ago, three white shoguns who had cornered the wild rice market, heard about *coffea anishinaabica* and attempted to shake all the shrubs for personal profit. Well, the shrubs shook back and spoke in the voices of their white mothers. The three exploiters were lost in a snow storm, misdirected by the talking shrubs, never returned.

Fourth pinch:

Little does the white man know that once we shared the secret of *coffea anishinaabica* with the whole world. It was during the war, the great war, a time when coffee production of the most common species, *arabica* and *robusts,* was cut short and instant coffee appeared for use in the field. Well, we supplied the instant coffee from pinch beans, one more tribal contribution to the white man during his endless wars. Tribal children shook the shrubs during the war and pinched the beans for distribution as instant coffee to the soldiers on the front.

Fifth pinch:

You smile, surprised, a mask of derision, no doubt. Well, listen to this: The code talkers during the war spoke in tribal languages over the radios to confuse the enemies at home and overseas. While winning the word wars, these tribal code talkers maintained an elaborate pinch coffee exchange in military units throughout the world. Now you know why that coffee tasted so good on the front lines.

Sixth pinch:

Following the war, we saved our pinch beans and then with new economic schemes in the sixties we traveled with the elders to the International Coffee Conference. But the conferees from coffee producing countries would have nothing to do with our claim to a percentage of the market, even after our efforts during the war. So, with a sense of evertribal humor, we war danced, a dance we created for the moment, at the entrance to the United Nations. While we danced we offered free pinches of coffee to the public, a sort of tribal war dance coffee break. The hippies were impressed, so impressed by the effects of the sacred brew that they promised a brisk sale of our pinch beans to weird friends in communes on the coast.

Seventh pinch:

There is a notion that coffee fosters radical political discussions. Well, the world should consider the tribes as one enormous reservation café, more ominous with pinch beans than the Oxford Club in England or the Café Foy in France. The pinch bean *coffea anishinaabica* is the beginning of an international revolution.

Since we were shunned at the conference and denied a place in the international coffee market, we have harvested and stored billions of birch bark bundles of *coffea anishinaabica* on the reservation. More berries are waiting to be shook, and soon, in a few months time, we plan to saturate the world markets with pinch beans, a paraeconomic disruption of coffee supplies.

How, you ask, can we establish these markets? Well, it all started with the hippies, believe it or not, who shared some tribal economic values and introduced new methods of distribution. In the late sixties, like the code talkers during the war, the hippies spoke a peculiar patois and started selling our beans to romantic liberals all over the world. Europeans became our best customers for secret pinch coffee. Karl May Red Roast, for example, is cut and sold to tourists for more than a thousand times the original value on the frozen shrub.

There you have it, pinch seven *coffea anishinaabica* beans once a day into hot water, drink while looking at a tree, and your delusions of progress and domination through power will dissolve and you will feel a new sense of acceptance with the world.

Shaman Truth Lies pinched his last bean and then he announced a ceremonial coffee break, time enough to sip his cedar brew and dance backwards through the auditorium holding out his cap.

The deans at the conference on academic assessorization were so pleased with the entertaining benediction that they voted to name the trickster an honorary dean of a college of his choice.

The trickster returned the gesture, he named all the deans honorary tricksters, members of an urban reservation of their choice.

The Warriors

Anna L. Walters

IN OUR YOUTH, we saw hobos come and go, sliding by our faded white house like wary cats who did not want us too close. Sister and I waved at the strange procession of passing men and women hobos. Just between ourselves, Sister and I talked of that hobo parade. We guessed at and imagined the places and towns we thought the hobos might have come from or had been. Mostly they were White or Black people. But there were Indian hobos too. It never occurred to Sister and me that this would be Uncle Ralph's end.

Sister and I were little and Uncle Ralph came to visit us. He lifted us over his head and shook us around him like gourd rattles. He was Momma's younger brother and he could have disciplined us if he so desired. That was part of our custom. But he never did. Instead, he taught us Pawnee words. "*Pari'* is Pawnee and *pita* is man," he said. Between the words, he tapped out drumbeats with his fingers on the table top, ghost dance and round dance songs that he suddenly remembered and sang. His melodic voice lilted over us and hung around the corners of the house for days. His stories of life and death were fierce and gentle. Warriors dangled in delicate balance.

He told us his version of the story of *Pahukatawa,* a Skidi Pawnee warrior. He was killed by the Sioux but the animals, feeling compassion for him, brought *Pahukatawa* to life again. "The Evening Star and the Morning Star bore children and some people say that these offspring are who we are," he often said. At times he pointed to those stars and greeted them by their Pawnee names. He liked to pray. He prayed for Sister and me and for everyone and every tiny

37

thing in the world, but we never heard him ask for anything for himself from *Atius,* the Father.

"For beauty is why we live," Uncle Ralph said when he talked of precious things only the Pawnees know. "We die for it too." He called himself an ancient Pawnee warrior when he was quite young. He told us that warriors must brave all storms and odds and stand their ground. He knew intimate details of every battle the Pawnees ever fought since Pawnee time began, and Sister and I knew even then that Uncle Ralph had a great battlefield of his own.

As a child I thought that Uncle Ralph had been born into the wrong time. The Pawnees had been ravaged so often by then. The tribe of several thousand at its peak over a century before were then a few hundred people who had been closely confined for over a century. The warrior life was gone. Uncle Ralph was trapped in a transparent bubble of a new time. The bubble bound him tight as it blew around us.

Uncle Ralph talked obsessively of warriors, painted proud warriors who shrieked poignant battle cries at the top of their lungs and died with honor. Sister and I were very little then, lost from him in the world of children who saw everything with children's eyes. And though we saw with wide eyes the painted warriors that he fantasized and heard their fierce and haunting battle cries, we did not hear his. Now that we are old and Uncle Ralph has been gone for a long time, Sister and I know that when he died, he was tired and alone. But he was a warrior.

The hobos were always around in our youth. Sister and I were curious about them and this curiosity claimed much of our time. They crept by the house at all hours of the day and night, dressed in rags and odd clothing. They wandered to us from the railroad tracks where they had leaped from slow-moving box cars onto the flatland. They hid in high clumps of weeds and brush that ran along the fence near the tracks. The hobos usually travelled alone, but Sister and I saw them come together, like poor families, to share a tin of beans or sardines they ate with sticks or twigs. Uncle Ralph watched them from a distance too.

One early morning, Sister and I crossed the tracks on our way to school and collided with a tall haggard whiteman. He wore a very old-fashioned pin-striped black jacket covered with lint and soot. There was fright in his eyes when they met ours. He scurried around us, quickening his pace. The pole over his shoulder where his possessions hung in a bundle at the end bounced as he nearly ran from us.

"Looks just like a scared jackrabbit," Sister said as she watched him dart away.

That evening we told Momma about the scared man. She warned us about the dangers of hobos as our father threw us a stern look. Uncle Ralph was visiting but he didn't say anything. He stayed the night and Sister asked him, "Hey, Uncle Ralph, why do you suppose they's hobos?"

Uncle Ralph was a large man. He took Sister and put her on one knee. "You see, Sister," he said, "hobos are a different kind. They see things in a different way. Them hobos are kind of like us. We're not like other people in some ways and yet we are. It has to do with what you see and feel when you look at this old world."

His answer satisfied Sister for awhile and he taught us some more Pawnee words that night.

Not long after Uncle Ralph's explanation, Sister and I surprised a Black man with white whiskers and fuzzy hair. He was climbing through the barbed wire fence that marked our property line. He wore faded blue over-alls with pockets stuffed full of handkerchiefs. He wiped sweat from his face and when it dried he looked up and saw us. I remembered what Uncle Ralph had said and wondered what the Black man saw when he looked at us standing there.

"We might scare him," Sister said softly to me, remembering the whiteman who had scampered away.

Sister whispered, "Hi," to the Black man. Her voice was barely audible.

"Boy, it's shore hot," he said. His voice was big and he smiled.

"Where are you going?" Sister asked.

"Me? Nowheres, I guess," he muttered.

"Then what you doing here?" Sister went on. She was bold for a seven-year-old kid. I was a year older but I was also more quiet. "This here place is ours," she said.

He looked around and saw our house with its flowering mimosa trees and rich green, mowed lawn stretching out before him. Other houses sat around ours.

"I reckon I'm lost," he said.

Sister pointed to the weeds and brush further up the road. "That's where you want to go. That's where they all go, the hobos."

I tried to quiet Sister but she didn't hush. "The hobos stay up there," she said. "You a hobo?"

He ignored her question and asked his own, "Say, what is you all? You not Black, you not White. What is you all?

Sister looked at me. She put one hand on her chest and the other hand on me, "We Indians!" Sister said.

He stared at us and smiled again. "Is that a fact?" he said.

"Know what kind of Indians we are?" Sister asked him.

He shook his fuzzy head. "Indians is Indians, I guess," he said.

Sister wrinkled her forehead and retorted, "Not us! We not like others. We see things different. We're Pawnees. We're warriors!"

I pushed my elbow into Sister's side. She quieted.

The man was looking down the road and he shuffled his feet. "I'd best go," he said.

Sister pointed to the brush and weeds one more time. "That way," she said.

He climbed back through the fence and brush as Sister yelled, "Bye now!" She waved a damp handkerchief.

Sister and I didn't tell Momma and Dad about the Black man. But much later Sister told Uncle Ralph every word that had been exchanged with the Black man. Uncle Ralph listened and smiled.

Months later when the warm weather had cooled and Uncle Ralph came to stay with us for a couple of weeks, Sister and I went to the hobo place. We had planned it for a long time. That afternoon when we pushed away the weeds, not a hobo was in sight.

The ground was packed down tight in the clearing among the high weeds. We walked around the encircling brush and found folded cardboards stacked together. Burned cans in assorted sizes were stashed under the cardboards and there were remains of old fires. Rags were tied to the brush, snapping in the hard wind.

Sister said, "Maybe they're all in the box cars now. It's starting to get cold."

She was right. The November wind had a bite to it and the cold stung our hands and froze our breaths as we spoke.

"You want to go over to them box cars?" she asked. We looked at the Railroad Crossing sign where the box cars stood.

I was prepared to answer when a voice roared from somewhere behind us.

"Now, you young ones, you git on home! Go on! Git!"

A man crawled out of the weeds and looked angrily at us. His eyes were red and his face was unshaven. He wore a red plaid shirt with striped gray and black pants too large for him. His face was swollen and bruised. An old woolen pink scarf hid some of the bruise marks around his neck and his top coat was splattered with mud.

Sister looked at him. She stood close to me and told him defiantly, "You can't tell us what to do! You don't know us!"

He didn't answer Sister but tried to stand. He couldn't. Sister ran to him and took his arm and pulled on it. "You need help?" she questioned.

He frowned at her but let us help him. He was tall. He seemed to be embarrassed by our help.

"You Indian, ain't you?" I dared to ask him.

He didn't answer me but looked at his feet as if they could talk so he wouldn't have to. His feet were in big brown overshoes.

"Who's your people?" Sister asked. He looked to be about Uncle Ralph's age when he finally lifted his face and met mine. He didn't respond for a minute. Then he sighed. "I ain't got no people," he told us as he tenderly stroked his swollen jaw.

"Sure you got people. Our folks says a man's always got people," I said softly. The wind blew our clothes and covered the words.

But he heard. He exploded like a firecracker. "Well, I don't! I ain't got no people! I ain't got nobody!"

"What you doing out here anyway?" Sister asked. "You hurt? You want to come over to our house?"

"Naw," he said. "Now you little ones, go on home. Don't be walking round out here. Didn't nobody tell you little girls ain't supposed to be going round by themselves. You might git hurt."

"We just wanted to talk to hobos," Sister said.

"Naw, you don't. Just go one home. Your folks is probably looking for you and worrying bout you."

I took Sister's arm and told her we were going home. Then we said "Bye" to the man. But Sister couldn't resist a few last words, "You Indian, ain't you?"

He nodded his head like it was a painful thing to do. "Yeah, I'm Indian."

"You ought to go on home yourself," Sister said. "Your folks probably looking for you and worrying bout you."

His voice rose again as Sister and I walked away from him. "I told you kids, I don't have any people!" There was exasperation in his voice.

Sister would not be outdone. She turned and yelled, "Oh yeah? You Indian, ain't you? Ain't you?" she screamed, "We your people!"

His top-coat and pink scarf flapped in the wind as we turned away from him.

We went home to Momma and Dad and Uncle Ralph then. Uncle Ralph met us at the front door. "Where you all been?" he asked and looked toward the railroad tracks. Momma and Dad were talking in the kitchen.

"Just playing, Uncle," Sister and I said simultaneously.

Uncle Ralph grabbed both Sister and I by our hands and yanked us out the door. "Awkuh!" he said, using the Pawnee expression to show his dissatisfaction.

Outside, we sat on the cement porch. Uncle Ralph was quiet for a long time and neither Sister or I knew what to expect.

"I want to tell you all a story," he finally said. "Once, there were these two rats who ran around everywhere and got into everything all the time. Everything they were told not to do, well, they went right out and did. They'd get into one mess and then another. It seems that they never could learn."

At that point Uncle Ralph cleared his throat. He looked at me and said, "Sister do you understand this story? Is it too hard for you? You're older."

I nodded my head up and down and said, "I understand."

Then Uncle Ralph looked at Sister. He said to her, "Sister, do I need to go on with this story?"

Sister shook her head from side to side. "Naw, Uncle Ralph," she said.

"So you both know how this story ends?" he said gruffly. Sister and I bobbed our heads up and down again.

We followed at his heels the rest of the day. When he tightened the loose hide on top of his drum, we watched him and held it in place as he laced the wet hide down. He got his drumsticks down from the top shelf of the closet and began to pound the drum slowly.

"Where you going, Uncle Ralph?" I asked. Sister and I knew that when he took his drum out, he was always gone shortly after.

"I have to be a drummer at some doings tomorrow," he said.

"You a good singer, Uncle Ralph," Sister said. "You know all them old songs."

"The young people nowadays, it seems they don't care bout nothing that's old. They just want to go to the Moon." He was drumming low as he spoke.

"We care, Uncle Ralph," Sister said.

"Why?" Uncle Ralph asked in a hard challenging tone that he seldom used on us.

Sister thought for a minute and then said, "I guess because you care so much, Uncle Ralph."

His eyes softened and he said, "I'll sing you an *Eruska* song, a song for the warriors."

The song he sang was a war dance song. At first Sister and I listened attentively but then Sister began to dance the man's dance. She had never danced before and she tried to imitate what she had seen. Her chubby body whirled and jumped the way she'd seen the men dance. Her head tilted from side to side the way the men moved theirs. I laughed aloud at her clumsy effort and Uncle Ralph laughed heartily too.

Uncle Ralph went in and out of our lives after that. We heard that he sang at one place and then another, and people came to Momma to find him. They said that he was only one of a few who knew the old ways and the songs.

When he came to visit us, he always brought something to eat. The Pawnee custom was that the man, the warrior, should bring food, preferably meat. Then whatever food was brought to the host was prepared and served to the man, the warrior, along with the host's family. Many times Momma and I, or Sister and I, came home to an empty house to find a sack of food on the table. I or Momma cooked it for the next meal and Uncle Ralph showed up to eat.

As Sister and I grew older, our fascination with the hobos decreased. Other things took our time, and Uncle Ralph did not appear as frequently as he did before.

Once while I was home alone, I picked up Momma's old photo album. Inside was a gray photo of Uncle Ralph in an army uniform. Behind him were tents on a flat terrain. Other photos showed other poses but in only one picture did he smile. All the photos were written over in black ink in Momma's handwriting. "Ralphie in Korea," the writing said.

Other photos in the album showed our Pawnee relatives. Dad was from another tribe. Momma's momma was in the album, a tiny gray-haired woman who no longer lived. And Momma's momma's Dad was in the album; he wore old Pawnee leggings and the long feathers of a dark bird sat upon his head. I closed the album when Momma, Dad, and Sister came home.

Momma went into the kitchen to cook. She called me and Sister to help. As she put on a bibbed apron, she said, "We just came from town, and we saw someone from home there." She meant someone from her tribal community.

"This man told me that Ralphie's been drinking hard," she said sadly. "He used to do that quite a bit a long time ago but we thought that it had stopped. He seemed to be alright for a few years." We cooked and then ate in silence.

Washing the dishes, I asked Momma, "How come Uncle Ralph never did marry?"

Momma looked up at me but was not surprised by my question. She answered, "I don't know, Sister. It would have been better if he had. There was one woman who I thought he really loved. I think he still does. I think it had something to do with Mom. She wanted him to wait."

"Wait for what?" I asked.

"I don't know," Momma said and sank into a chair.

After that we heard unsettling rumors of Uncle Ralph drinking here and there.

He finally came to the house once when only I happened to be home. He was haggard and tired. His appearance was much like that of the whiteman that Sister and I met on the railroad tracks years before.

I opened the door when he tapped on it. Uncle Ralph looked years older than his age. He brought food in his arms. "*Nowa,* Sister," he said in greeting. "Where's the other one?" He meant Sister.

"She's gone now, Uncle Ralph. School in Kansas," I answered. "Where you been, Uncle Ralph? We been worrying about you."

He ignored my question and said, "I bring food. The warrior brings home food. To his family, to his people." His face was lined and had not been cleaned for days. He smelled of cheap wine.

I asked again, "Where you been, Uncle Ralph?"

He forced himself to smile. "Pumpkin Flower," he said, using the Pawnee name, "I've been out with my warriors all this time."

He put one arm around me as we went to the kitchen table with the food. "That's what your Pawnee name is. Now don't forget it."

"Did somebody bring you here, Uncle Ralph, or are you on foot?" I asked him.

"I'm on foot," he answered. "Where's your Momma?"

I told him that she and Dad would be back soon, I started to prepare the food he brought.

Then I heard Uncle Ralph say, "Life is sure hard sometimes. Sometimes it seems I just can't go on."

"What's wrong, Uncle Ralph?" I asked.

Uncle Ralph let out a bitter little laugh. "What's wrong?" he repeated. "What's wrong? All my life, I've tried to live what I've been taught but, Pumpkin Flower, some things are all wrong!"

He took a folded pack of Camel cigarettes from his coat pocket. His hand shook as he pulled one from the pack and lit the end. "Too much drink," he said sadly. "That stuff is bad for us."

"What are you trying to do, Uncle Ralph?" I then asked.

"Live," he said.

He puffed on the shaking cigarette awhile and said, "The old people said to live beautifully with prayers and song. Some died for beauty too."

"How do we do that, Uncle Ralph, live for beauty?" I asked.

"It's simple, Pumpkin Flower," he said. "Believe!"

"Believe what?" I asked.

He looked at me hard. "*Aw-kuh!*" he said, "that's one of the things that is wrong. Everyone questions. Everyone doubts. No one believes in the old ways anymore. They want to believe when it's convenient, when it doesn't cost them anything and when they get something in return. There are no more believers. There are no more warriors. They are all gone. Those who are left only want to go to the Moon."

A car drove up outside. It was Momma and Dad. Uncle Ralph heard it too. He slumped in the chair, resigned to whatever Momma would say to him.

Momma came in first. Dad then greeted Uncle Ralph and disappeared into the back of the house. Custom and etiquette required that Dad, who was not a member of Momma's tribe, allow Momma to handle her brother's problems.

She hugged Uncle Ralph. Her eyes filled with tears when she saw how thin he was and how his hands shook.

"Ralphie," she said, "you look awful but I am glad to see you."

She then spoke to him of everyday things, how the car failed to start and the latest gossip. He was silent, tolerant of the passing of time in this way. His eyes sent me a pleading look while his hands shook and he tried to hold them still.

When supper was ready, Uncle Ralph went to wash himself for the meal. When he returned to the table, he was calm. His hands didn't shake so much.

At first he ate without many words, but in the course of the meal he left the table twice. Each time he came back, he was more talkative than before, answering Momma's questions in Pawnee. He left the table a third time and Dad rose.

Dad said to Momma, "He's drinking again. Can't you tell?" Dad left the table and went outside.

Momma frowned. A determined look grew on her face.

When Uncle Ralph sat down to the table once more, Momma told him, "Ralphie, you're my brother but I want you to leave now. Come back when you are sober."

He held a tarnished spoon in mid-air and he put it down slowly. He hadn't finished eating but he didn't seem to mind leaving. He stood, looked at me with his red eyes and went to the door. Momma followed him. In a low voice, she said, "Ralphie, you've got to stop drinking and wandering-or don't come to see us again."

He pulled himself to his full height then. His frame filled the doorway. He leaned over Momma and yelled, "Who are you? Are you God that you will say what will be or will not be?"

Momma met his angry eyes. She stood firm and did not back down.

His eyes finally dropped from her face to the linoleum floor. A cough came from deep in his throat.

"I'll leave here," he said. "But I'll get all my warriors and come back! I have thousands of warriors and they'll ride with me. We'll get our bows and arrows. Then we'll come back!" He staggered out the door.

In the years that followed, Uncle Ralph saw us only when he was sober. He visited less and less. When he did show up, he did a tapping ritual on our front door. We welcomed the rare visits. Occasionally he stayed at our house for a few days at a time when he was not drinking. He slept on the floor.

He did odd jobs for minimum pay but never complained about the work or money. He'd acquired a vacant look in his eyes. It was the same look that Sister and I had seen in the hobos when we were children. He wore a similar careless array of clothing and carried no property with him at all.

The last time he came to the house, he called me by my English name and asked if I remembered anything of all that he'd taught me. His hair had turned pure white. He looked older than anyone I knew. I marvelled at his appearance and said, "I remember everything." That night I pointed out his stars for him and told him how *Pahukatawa* lived and died and lived again through another's dreams. I'd grown and Uncle Ralph could not hold me on his knee anymore. His arm circled my waist while we sat on the grass.

He was moved by my recitation and clutched my hand tightly. He said, "It's more than this. It's more than just repeating words. You know that, don't you?"

I nodded my head. "Yes, I know. The recitation is the easiest part but it's more than this, Uncle Ralph."

He was quiet but after a few minutes his hand touched my shoulder. He said, "I couldn't make it work. I tried to fit the pieces."

"I know," I said.

"Now before I go," he said, "do you know who you are?"

The question took me by surprise. I thought very hard. I cleared my throat and told him, "I know that I am fourteen. I know that it's too young."

"Do you know that you are a Pawnee?" he asked in a choked whisper.

"Yes, Uncle," I said.

"Good," he said with a long sigh that was swallowed by the night.

Then he stood and said, "Well, Sister, I have to go. Have to move on."

"Where are you going?" I asked. "Where all the warriors go?" I teased.

He managed a smile and a soft laugh. "Yeah, wherever the warriors are, I'll find them."

"Before you go," I asked, "Uncle Ralph, can women be warriors too?"

He laughed again and hugged me merrily. "Don't tell me you want to be one of the warriors too?"

"No, Uncle," I said, "Just one of yours." I hated to let him go because I knew that I would not see him again.

He pulled away. His last words were, "Don't forget what I've told you all these years. It's the only chance not to become what everyone else is. Do you understand?"

I nodded and he left. I never saw him again.

The years passed quickly. I moved away from Momma and Dad and married. Sister left them before I did.

Years later in another town, hundreds of miles away, I awoke in a terrible gloom, a sense that something was gone from the world the Pawnees knew. The despair filled days though the reason for the sense of loss went unexplained. Finally, the telephone rang. Momma was on the line. She said, "Sister came home for a few days not too long ago. While she was here and alone, someone came and tapped on the door, like Ralphie always does. Sister yelled, 'Is that you, Uncle Ralph? Come on in.' But no one entered."

Then I understood, Uncle Ralph was dead. Momma probably knew too. She wept softly into the phone.

Later Momma received an official call that confirmed Uncle Ralph's death. He had died from exposure in a hobo shanty, near the railroad tracks outside a tiny Oklahoma town. He'd been dead for several days and nobody knew but Momma, Sister and me.

The funeral was well attended by the Pawnee people, Momma reported to me as I did not attend. Uncle Ralph and I had said our farewells years earlier. Momma told me that someone there had spoken well of Uncle Ralph before they put him in the ground. It was said that "Ralph came from a fine family, an old line of warriors."

Ten years later, Sister and I visited briefly at Momma's and Dad's home. We had been separated by hundreds of miles for all that time. As we sat under Momma's flowering mimosa trees, I made a confession to Sister. I said, "Sometimes I wish that Uncle Ralph were here. I'm a grown woman but I still miss him after all these years."

Sister nodded her head in agreement. I continued. "He knew so many things. He knew why the sun pours its liquid all over us and why it must do just that. He knew why babes and insects crawl. He knew that we must live beautifully or not live at all."

Sister's eyes were thoughtful but she waited to speak while I went on. "To live beautifully from day to day is a battle that warriors have to plot for as long as they can. It's a battle all the way. The things that he knew are so beautiful. And to feel and know that kind of beauty is the reason that we should live at all. Uncle Ralph said so. But now, there is no one who knows what that beauty is or any of the other things that he knew."

Sister pushed back smoky gray wisps of her dark hair. "You do," she pronounced. "And I do too."

"Why do you suppose he left us like that?" I asked.

"It couldn't be helped," Sister said. "There was a battle on."

"I wanted to be one of his warriors," I said with an embarrassed half-smile.

She leaned over and patted my hand. "You are," she said. Then she stood and placed one hand on her bosom and one hand on my arm. "We'll carry on," she said.

I touched her hand resting on my arm. I said, "Sister, tell me again. What is the battle for?"

She looked down toward the fence where a hobo was coming through. We waved at him.

"Beauty," she said to me. "Our battle is for beauty. It's what Uncle Ralph fought for too. He often said that everyone else just wanted to go to the Moon. But remember, Sister, you and I done been there. Don't forget that, after all, we're children of the stars."

Turtle Meat

Joseph Bruchac III

O LD MAN, come in. I need you!"
The old woman's cracked voice carried out to the woodshed near the overgrown field. Once it had been planted with corn and beans, the whole two acres. But now mustard rolled heads in the wind and wild carrot bobbed among nettles and the blue flowers of thistles. *A goat would like to eat those thistles*, Homer LaWare thought. *Too bad I'm too old to keep a goat.* He put down the ax handle he had been carving, cast one quick look at the old bamboo fishing pole hanging over the door and then stood up.

"Coming over," he called out. With slow careful steps he crossed the fifty yards between his shed and the single-story house with the picture window and the gold-painted steps. He swung open the screen door and stepped over the dishes full of dog food. *Always in front of the door,* he thought.

"Where?" he called from the front room.

"Back here, I'm in the bathroom. I can't get up."

He walked as quickly as he could through the cluttered kitchen. The breakfast dishes were still on the table. He pushed open the bathroom door. Mollie was sitting on the toilet.

"Amalia Wind, what's wrong?" he said.

"My legs seem to of locked, Homer. Please just help me to get up. I've been hearing the dogs yapping for me outside the door and the poor dears couldn't even get to me. Just help me up."

He slipped his hand under her elbow and lifted her gently. He could see that the pressure of his fingers on the white wrinkled flesh of her arm was going to leave marks. She'd always been like that.

51

She always bruised easy. But it hadn't stopped her from coming for
him...and getting him, all those years ago. It hadn't stopped her
from throwing Jake Wind out of her house and bringing Homer
LaWare to her farm to be the hired man.

Her legs were unsteady for a few seconds but then she seemed to
be all right. He removed his arms from her.

"Just don't know how it happened, Homer. I ain't so old as that,
am I, Old Man?"

"No, Amalia. That must of was just a cramp. Nothing more than
that."

They were still standing in the bathroom. Her long grey dress had
fallen down to cover her legs but her underpants were still around
her ankles. He felt awkward. Even after all these years, he felt
awkward.

"Old Man, you just get out and do what you were doing. A woman
has to have her privacy. Get now."

"You sure?"

"Sure? My Lord! If I wasn't sure you think I'd have any truck with
men like you?" She poked him in the ribs. "You know what you
should do, Old Man? You should go down to the pond and do that
fishing you said you were going to."

He didn't want to leave her alone, but he didn't want to tell her
that. And there was something in him that urged him towards that
pond, the pond where the yellow perch had been biting for the last
few days according to Jack Crandall. Jack had told him that when he
brought his ax by to have Homer fit a new handle.

"I still got Jack's ax to fix, Amalia."

"And when did it ever take you more than a minute to fit a handle
into anything, *Old Man?*" There was a wicked gleam in her eye. For
a few seconds she looked forty years younger in the old man's eyes.

He shook his head.

"Miss Wind, I swear those ladies were right when they said you
was going to hell." She made a playful threatening motion with her
hand and he backed out the door. "But I'm going."

It took him another hour to finish carving the handle to the right size. It slid into the head like a hand going into a velvet glove. His hands shook when he started the steel wedge that would hold it tight, but it took only three strokes with the maul to put the wedge in. He looked at his hands, remembering the things they'd done. Holding the reins of the last horse they'd had on the farm-twenty years ago. Or was it thirty? Lifting the sheets back from Mollie's white body that first night. Swinging in tight fists at the face of Jake Wind the night he came back, drunk and with a loaded .45 in his hand. He'd gone down hard and Homer had emptied the shells out of the gun and broken its barrel with his maul on his anvil. Though Jake had babbled of the law that night, neither the law nor Jake ever came back to the Wind farm. It had been Amalia's all along. Her father'd owned it and Jake had married her for it. She'd never put the property in any man's name, never would. That was what she always said.

"I'm not asking, Amalia," that was what Homer had said to her after the first night they'd spent in the brass bed, just before he'd dressed and gone back to sleep the night away in his cot in the shed. He always slept there. All the years. "I'm not asking for any property, Amalia. It's the Indian in me that don't want to own no land."

That was Homer's favorite saying. Whenever there was something about him that seemed maybe different from what others expected he would say simply, "It's the Indian in me." Sometimes he thought of it not just as a part of him but as another man, a man with a name he didn't know but would recognize if he heard it.

His father had said that same phrase often. His father had come down from Quebec and spoke French and, sometimes, to his first wife who had died when Homer was six, another language that Homer never heard again after her death. His father had been a quiet man who made baskets from the ash trees that grew on their farm. "But he never carried them into town," Homer said with pride. "He just stayed on the farm and let people come to him if they wanted to buy them."

The farm had gone to a younger brother who sold out and moved

West. There had been two other children. None of them got a thing, except Homer who got his father's best horse. In those years Homer was working for Seneca Smith at his mill. Woods work, two-man saws and sledding the logs out in the snow. He had done it until his thirtieth year when Amalia had asked him to come and work her farm. Though people had talked, he had done it. When anyone asked why he let himself be run by a woman that way he said, in the same quiet voice his father had used, "It's the Indian in me."

The pond was looking glass smooth. Homer stood beside the boat. Jack Crandall had given him the key to it. He looked in the water. He saw his face, the skin lined and brown as an old map. Wattles of flesh hung below his chin like the comb of a rooster.

"Shit, you're a good-looking man, Homer LaWare," he said to his reflection. "Easy to see what a woman sees in you." He thought again of Mollie sitting in the rocker and looking out the picture window. As he left he heard her old voice calling the names of the small dogs she loved so much. *Those dogs were the only ones ever give back her love,* he thought, *not that no-good daughter. Last time she come was Christmas in '68 to give her that pissy green shawl and try to run me off again.*

Homer stepped into the boat. Ripples wiped his face from the surface of the pond. He put his pole and the can of worms in front of him and slipped the oars into the oarlocks, one at a time, breathing hard as he did so. He pulled the anchor rope into the boat and looked out across the water. A brown stick projected above the water in the middle of the pond. *Least it looks like a stick, but if it moves it . . .* The stick moved . . . slid across the surface of the water for a few feet and then disappeared. He watched with narrowed eyes until it reappeared a hundred feet further out. It was a turtle, a snapping turtle. Probably a big one.

"I see you out there, Turtle," Homer said. "Maybe you and me are going to see more of each other."

He felt in his pocket for the familiar feel of his bone-handled knife. He pushed the red handkerchief that held it deep in his pocket more firmly into place. Then he began to row. He stopped in the middle of the pond and began to fish. Within a few minutes he began to pull in the fish, yellow-stomached perch with bulging dark eyes. Most of them were a foot long. He stopped when he had a dozen and began to clean them, leaving the baited line in the water. He pulled out the bone-handled knife and opened it. The blade was thin as the handle of a spoon from thirty years of sharpening. It was like a razor. Homer always carried a sharp knife. He made a careful slit from the ventral opening of the fish up to its gills and spilled out the guts into the water, leaning over the side of the boat as he did so. He talked as he cleaned the fish.

"Old Knife, you cut good," he said. He had cleaned nearly every fish, hardly wasting a moment. Almost as fast as when he was a boy. *Some things didn't go from you so . . .*

The jerking of his pole brought him back from his thoughts. It was being dragged overboard. He dropped the knife on the seat and grabbed the pole as it went over. He pulled up on it and it bent almost double. *No fish pulls like that.* It was the turtle. He began reeling the line in, slow and steady so it wouldn't break. Soon he saw it, wagging its head back and forth, coming up from the green depths of the pond where it had been gorging on the perch guts and grabbed his worm.

"Come up and talk, Turtle," Homer said.

The turtle opened its mouth as if to say something and the hook slipped out, the pole jerking back in Homer's hands. Its jaws were too tough for the hook to stick in. But the turtle stayed there, just under the water. It was big, thirty pounds at least. It was looking for more food. Homer put another worm on the hook with trembling hands and dropped it in front of the turtle's mouth.

"Turtle, take this one too."

He could see the wrinkled skin under its throat as it turned its head. A leech of some kind was on the back of its head, another hanging onto its right leg. It was an old turtle. Its skin was rough, its shell green with algae. It grabbed the hook with a sideways turn of its head. As Homer pulled up to snag the hook it reached forward with its paws and grabbed the line like a man grabbing a rope. Its front claws were as long as the teeth of a bear.

Homer pulled. The turtle kept the hook in its mouth and rose to the surface. It was strong and the old man wondered if he could hold it up. Did he want turtle meat that much? But he didn't cut the line. The mouth was big enough to take off a finger, but he kept pulling in line. It was next to the boat and the hook was only holding because of the pressure on the line. A little slack and it would be gone. Homer slipped the pole under his leg and grabbed with his other hand for the anchor rope, began to fasten a noose in it as the turtle shook its head, moving the twelve-foot boat as it struggled. He could smell it now. The heavy musk of the turtle was everywhere. It wasn't a good smell or a bad smell. It was only the smell of the turtle.

Now the noose was done. He hung it over the side. It was time for the hard part now, the part that was easy for him when his arms were young and his chest wasn't caved in like a broken box. He reached down fast and grabbed the tail, pulling it so that the turtle came half out of the water. The boat almost tipped but Homer kept his balance. The turtle swung its head, mouth open and wide enough to swallow a softball. It hissed like a snake, ready to grab at anything within reach. With his other hand, gasping as he did it, feeling the turtle's rough tail tear the skin of his palm as it slipped from his other hand, Homer swung the noose around the turtle's head. Its own weight pulled the slip knot tight. The turtle's jaws clamped tight with a snap on Homer's sleeve.

"Turtle, I believe I got you and you got me," Homer said. He slipped a turn of rope around his left foot with his free arm. He kept pulling back as hard as he could to free his sleeve but the turtle had it. "I understand you, Turtle," he said, "you don't like to let go." He breathed hard, closed his eyes for a moment. Then he took the knife in his left hand. He leaned over and slid it across the turtle's neck. Dark fluid blossomed out into the water. A hissing noise came from between the clenched jaws, but the turtle held onto the old man's sleeve. For a long time the blood came out but the turtle still held on. Finally Homer took the knife and cut the end of his sleeve off, leaving it in the turtle's mouth.

He sat up straight for the first time since he had hooked the turtle and looked around. It was dark. He could hardly see the shore. He had been fighting the turtle for longer than he thought.

By the time he had reached the shore and docked the boat the sounds of the turtle banging itself against the side of the boat had stopped. He couldn't tell if blood was still flowing from its cut throat because night had turned all of the water that same color. He couldn't find the fish in the bottom of the boat. It didn't matter. The raccoons could have them. He had his knife and his pole and the turtle. He dragged it back up to the old Ford truck. It was too heavy to carry.

There were cars parked in the driveway when he pulled in. He had to park near the small mounds beside his shed that were marked with wooden plaques and neatly lettered names. He could hear voices as he walked through the darkness.

"Old fool's finally come back," he heard a voice saying. The voice was rough as a rusted hinge. It was the voice of Amalia's daughter.

He pushed through the door. "Where's Amalia?" he said. Someone screamed. The room was full of faces and they were all looking at him.

"Old bastard looks like he scalped someone," a pock-faced man with grey crew-cut hair muttered.

Homer looked at himself. His arms and hands were covered with blood of the turtle. His tattered right sleeve barely reached his elbow. His trousers were muddy. His fly was half-way open. "Where's Amalia?" he demanded again.

"What the hell have you been up to, you old fart?" said the raspy voice of the daughter. He turned to stare into her loose-featured face. She was sitting in Amalia's rocker.

"I been fishin'."

The daughter stood up and walked toward him. She looked like her father. Jake Wind was written all over her face, carved into her bones.

"You want to know where Moms is, huh? Wanta know where your old sweetheart's gone to? Well, I'll tell you. She's been sent off to a home that'll take care of her, even if she is cracked. Come in and find her sittin' talking to dogs been dead for years. Dishes full of dog food for ghosts. Maybe you better eat some of it because your meal ticket's been cancelled, you old bastard. This man is a doctor and he's decided my dear mother was mentally incompetent. The ambulance took her outta here half an hour ago."

She kept talking, saying things she had longed to say for years. Homer LaWare wasn't listening. His eyes took in the details of the room he had walked through every day for the last forty years, the furniture he had mended when it was broken, the picture window he had installed, the steps he had painted, the neatly stacked dishes he had eaten his food from three times each day for almost half a century. The daughter was still talking, talking as if this were a scene she had rehearsed for many years. But he wasn't listening. Her voice was getting louder. She was screaming. Homer hardly heard her. He closed his eyes, remembering how the turtle held onto his sleeve even after its throat was cut and its life was leaking out into the pond.

The screaming stopped. He opened his eyes and saw that the man with the grey crew-cut hair was holding the daughter's arms. She was holding a plate in her hands. Maybe she had been about to hit him with it. It didn't matter. He looked at her. He looked at the other people in the room. They seemed to be waiting for him to say something.

"I got a turtle to clean out," he said, knowing what it was in him that spoke. Then he turned and walked into the darkness.

American Horse

Louise Erdrich

THE WOMAN SLEEPING on the cot in the woodshed was
Albertine American Horse. The name was left over from her
mother's short marriage. The boy was the son of the man she had
loved and let go. Buddy was on the cot too, sitting on the edge
because he'd been awake three hours watching out for his mother
and besides, she took up the whole cot. Her feet hung over the edge,
limp and brown as two trout. Her long arms reached out and slapped
at things she saw in her dreams.

Buddy had been knocked awake out of hiding in a washing
machine while herds of policemen with dogs searched through a
large building with many tiny rooms. When the arm came down,
Buddy screamed because it had a blue cuff and sharp silver buttons.
"Tss," his mother mumbled, half awake, "wasn't nothing." But
Buddy sat up after her breathing went deep again, and he watched.

There was something coming and he knew it.

It was coming from very far off but he had a picture of it in his
mind. It was a large thing made of metal with many barbed hooks,
points, and drag chains on it, something like a giant potato peeler
that rolled out of the sky, scraping clouds down with it and jabbing
or crushing everything that lay in its path on the ground.

Buddy watched his mother. If he woke her up, she would know
what to do about the thing, but he thought he'd wait until he saw it
for sure before he shook her. She was pretty, sleeping, and he liked
knowing he could look at her as long and close up as he wanted. He
took a strand of her hair and held it in his hands as if it was the rein to

a delicate beast. She was strong enough and could pull him along like the horse their name was.

Buddy had his mother's and his grandmother's name because his father had been a big mistake.

"They're all mistakes, even your father. But *you* are the best thing that ever happened to me."

That was what she said when he asked.

Even Kadie, the boyfriend crippled from being in a car wreck, was not as good a thing that had happened to his mother as Buddy was. "He was a medium-size mistake," she said. "He's hurt and I shouldn't even say that, but it's the truth." At the moment, Buddy knew that being the best thing in his mother's life, he was also the reason they were hiding from the cops.

He wanted to touch the satin roses sewed on her pink tee-shirt, but he knew he shouldn't do that even in her sleep. If she woke up and found him touching the roses, she would say, "Quit that, Buddy." Sometimes she told him to stop hugging her like a gorilla. She never said that in the mean voice she used when he oppressed her, but when she said that he loosened up anyway.

There were times he felt like hugging her so hard and in such a special way that she would say to him, "Let's get married." There were also times he closed his eyes and wished that she would die, only a few times, but still it haunted him that his wish might come true. He and Uncle Lawrence would be left alone. Buddy wasn't worried, though, about his mother getting married to somebody else. She had said to her friend, Madonna, "All men suck," when she thought Buddy wasn't listening. He had made an uncertain sound, and when they heard him they took him in their arms.

"Except for you, Buddy," his mother said. "All except for you and maybe Uncle Lawrence, although he's pushing it."

"The cops suck the worst though," Buddy whispered to his mother's sleeping face, "because they're after us." He felt tired again, slumped down, and put his legs beneath the blanket. He closed his eyes and got the feeling that the cot was lifting up beneath him, that it was arching its canvas back and then traveling, traveling very fast and in the wrong direction for when he looked up he saw the three of them were advancing to meet the great metal thing with hooks and barbs and all sorts of sharp equipment to catch their bodies and draw their blood. He heard its insides as it rushed toward them, purring softly like a powerful motor and then they were right in its shadow. He pulled the reins as hard as he could and the beast reared, lifting him. His mother clapped her hand across his mouth.

"Okay," she said. "Lay low. They're outside and they're gonna hunt."

She touched his shoulder and Buddy leaned over with her to look through a crack in the boards.

They were out there all right, Albertine saw them. Two officers and that social worker woman. Vicki Koob. There had been no whistle, no dream, no voice to warn her that they were coming. There was only the crunching sound of cinders in the yard, the engine purring, the dust sifting off their car in a fine light brownish cloud and settling around them.

The three people came to a halt in their husk of metal—the car emblazoned with the North Dakota State Highway Patrol emblem which is the glowing profile of the Sioux policeman, Red Tomahawk, the one who killed Sitting Bull. Albertine gave Buddy the blanket and told him that he might have to wrap it around him and hide underneath the cot.

"We're gonna wait and see what they do." She took him in her lap and hunched her arms around him. "Don't you worry," she whispered against his ear. "Lawrence knows how to fool them."

Buddy didn't want to look at the car and the people. He felt his mother's heart beating beneath his ear so fast it seemed to push the satin roses in and out. He put his face to them carefully and breathed the deep, soft powdery woman smell of her. That smell was also in her little face cream bottles, in her brushes, and around the washbowl after she used it. The satin felt so unbearably smooth against his cheek that he had to press closer. She didn't push him away, like he expected, but hugged him still tighter until he felt as close as he had ever been to back inside her again where she said he came from. Within the smells of her things, her soft skin and the satin of her roses, he closed his eyes then, and took his breaths softly and quickly with her heart.

They were out there, but they didn't dare get out of the car yet because of Lawrence's big, ragged dogs. Three of these dogs had loped up the dirt driveway with the car. They were rangy, alert, and bounced up and down on their cushioned paws like wolves. They didn't waste their energy barking, but positioned themselves quietly, one at either car door and the third in front of the bellied-out screen door to Uncle Lawrence's house. It was six in the morning but the wind was up already, blowing dust, ruffling their short moth-eaten coats. The big brown one on Vicki Koob's side had unusual black and white markings, stripes almost, like a hyena and he grinned at her, tongue out and teeth showing.

"Shoo!" Miss Koob opened her door with a quick jerk.

The brown dog sidestepped the door and jumped before her, tiptoeing. Its dirty white muzzle curled and its eyes crossed suddenly as if it was zeroing its cross-hair sights in on the exact place it would bite her. She ducked back and slammed the door.

"It's mean," she told Officer Brackett. He was printing out some type of form. The other officer, Harmony, a slow man, had not yet reacted to the car's halt. He had been sitting quietly in the back seat, but now he rolled down his window and with no change in expression unsnapped his holster and drew his pistol out and pointed it at the dog on his side. The dog smacked down on its belly, wiggled under the car and was out and around the back of the house before Harmony drew his gun back. The other dogs vanished with him. From wherever they had disappeared to they began to yap and howl, and the door to the low shoebox style house fell open.

"Heya, what's going on?"

Uncle Lawrence put his head out the door and opened wide the one eye he had in working order. The eye bulged impossibly wider in outrage when he saw the police car. But the eyes of the two officers and Miss Vicki Koob were wide open too because they had never seen Uncle Lawrence in his sleeping get up or, indeed, witnessed anything like it. For his ribs, which were cracked from a bad fall and still mending, Uncle Lawrence wore a thick white corset laced up the front with a striped sneakers lace. His glass eye and his set of dentures were still out for the night so his face puckered here and there, around its absences and scars, like a damaged but fierce little cake. Although he had a few gray streaks now, Uncle Lawrence's hair was still thick, and because he wore a special contraption of elastic straps around his head every night, two oiled waves always crested on either side of his middle part. All of this would have been sufficient to astonish, even without the most striking part of his outfit — the smoking jacket. It was made of black satin and hung open around his corset, dragging a tasseled belt. Gold thread dragons struggled up the lapels and blasted their furry red breath around his neck. As Lawrence walked down the steps, he put his arms up in surrender and the gold tassels in the inner seams of his sleeves dropped into view.

"My heavens, what a sight." Vicki Koob was impressed.

"A character," apologized Officer Harmony.

As a tribal police officer who could be counted on to help out the State Patrol, Harmony thought he always had to explain about Indians or get twice as tough to show he did not favor them. He was slow-moving and shy but two jumps ahead of other people all the same, and now, as he watched Uncle Lawrence's splendid approach, he gazed speculatively at the torn and bulging pocket of the smoking jacket. Harmony had been inside Uncle Lawrence's house before and knew that above his draped orange-crate shelf of war medals a blue-black German luger was hung carefully in a net of flat-headed nails and fishing line. Thinking of this deadly exhibition, he got out of the car and shambled toward Lawrence with a dreamy little smile of welcome on his face. But when he searched Lawrence, he found that the bulging pocket held only the lonesome looking dentures from Lawrence's empty jaw. They were still dripping denture polish.

"I had been cleaning them when you arrived," Uncle Lawrence explained with acid dignity.

He took the toothbrush from his other pocket and aimed it like a rifle.

"Quit that, you old idiot." Harmony tossed the toothbrush away. "For once you ain't done nothing. We came for your nephew."

Lawrence looked at Harmony with a faint air of puzzlement.

"Ma Frere, listen," threatened Harmony amiably, "those two white people in the car came to get him for the welfare. They got papers on your nephew that give them the right to take him."

"Papers?" Uncle Lawrence puffed out his deeply pitted cheeks. "Let me see them papers."

The two of them walked over to Vicki's side of the car and she pulled a copy of the court order from her purse. Lawrence put his teeth back in and adjusted them with busy workings of his jaw.

"Just a minute," he reached into his breast pocket as he bent close to Miss Vicki Koob. "I can't read these without I have in my eye."

He took the eye from his breast pocket delicately, and as he popped it into his face the social worker's mouth fell open in a consternated O.

"What is this," she cried in a little voice.

Uncle Lawrence looked at her mildly. The white glass of the eye was cold as lard. The black iris was strangely charged and menacing.

"He's nuts," Brackett huffed along the side of Vicki's neck. "Never mind him."

Vicki's hair had sweated down her nape in tiny corkscrews and some of the hairs were so long and dangly now that they disappeared into the zippered back of her dress. Brackett noticed this as he spoke into her ear. His face grew red and the backs of his hands prickled. He slid under the steering wheel and got out of the car. He walked around the hood to stand with Leo Harmony.

"We could take you in too," said Brackett roughly. Lawrence eyed the officers in what was taken as defiance. "If you don't cooperate, we'll get out the handcuffs," they warned.

One of Lawrence's arms was stiff and would not move until he'd rubbed it with witch hazel in the morning. His other arm worked fine though, and he stuck it out in front of Brackett.

"Get them handcuffs," he urged them. "Put me in a welfare home."

Brackett snapped one side of the handcuffs on Lawrence's good arm and the other to the handle of the police car.

"That's to hold you," he said. "We're wasting our time. Harmony, you search that little shed over by the tall grass and Miss Koob and myself will search the house."

"My rights is violated!" Lawrence shrieked suddenly. They ignored him. He tugged at the handcuff and thought of the good heavy file he kept in his tool box and the German luger oiled and ready but never loaded, because of Buddy, over his shelf. He should have used it on these bad ones, even Harmony in his big-time white man job. He wouldn't last long in that job anyway before somebody gave him what for.

"It's a damn scheme," said Uncle Lawrence, rattling his chains against the car. He looked over at the shed and thought maybe Albertine and Buddy had sneaked away before the car pulled into the yard. But he sagged, seeing Albertine move like a shadow within the boards. "Oh, it's all a damn scheme," he muttered again.

"I want to find that boy and salvage him," Vicki Koob explained to Officer Brackett as they walked into the house. "Look at his family life-the old man crazy as a bedbug, the mother intoxicated somewhere."

Brackett nodded, energetic, eager. He was a short hopeful red-head who failed consistently to win the hearts of women. Vicki Koob intrigued him. Now, as he watched, she pulled a tiny pen out of an ornamental clip on her blouse. It was attached to a retractable line that would suck the pen back, like a child eating one strand of spaghetti. Something about the pen on its line excited Brackett to the point of discomfort. His hand shook as he opened the screendoor and stepped in, beckoning Miss Koob to follow.

They could see the house was empty at first glance. It was only one rectangular room with whitewashed walls and a little gas stove in the middle. They had already come through the cooking lean-to with the other stove and washstand and rusty old refrigerator. That refrigerator had nothing in it but some wrinkled potatos and a package of turkey necks. Vicki Koob noted that in her perfect-bound notebook. The beds along the walls of the big room were covered with quilts that Albertine's mother, Sophie, had made from bits of old wool coats and pants that the Sisters sold in bundles at the mission. There was no one hiding beneath the beds. No one was under the little aluminum dinette table covered with a green oilcloth, or the soft brown wood chairs tucked up to it. One wall of the big room was filled with neatly stacked crates of things—old tools and springs and small half-dismantled appliances. Five or six television sets were stacked against the wall. Their control panels spewed colored wires and at least one was cracked all the way across. Only the topmost set, with coathanger antenna angled sensitively to catch the bounding signals around Little Shell, looked like it could possibly work.

Not one thing escaped Vicki Koob's trained and cataloguing gaze. She made note of the cupboard that held only commodity flour and coffee. The unsanitary tin oil drum beneath the kitchen window, full of empty surplus pork cans and beer bottles, caught her eye as did Uncle Lawrence's physical and mental deteriorations. She quickly described these "benchmarks of alcoholic dependency within the extended family of Woodrow (Buddy) American Horse" as she walked around the room with the little notebook open, pushed against her belly to steady it. Although Vicki had been there before, Albertine's presence had always made it difficult for her to take notes.

"Twice the maximum allowable space between door and threshold," she wrote now. "Probably no insulation. 2-3 inch cracks in walls inadequately sealed with whitewashed mud." She made a mental note but could see no point in describing Lawrence's stuffed reclining chair that only reclined, the shadeless lamp with its plastic orchid in the bubble glass base, or the three dimensional picture of

Jesus that Lawrence had once demonstrated to her. When plugged in, lights rolled behind the water the Lord stood on so that he seemed to be strolling although he never actually went forward, of course, but only pushed the glowing waves behind him forever like a poor tame rat in a treadmill.

Brackett cleared his throat with a nervous rasp and touched Vicki's shoulder.

"What are you writing?"

She moved away and continued to scribble as if thoroughly absorbed in her work. "Officer Brackett displays an undue amount of interest in my person," she wrote. "Perhaps?"

He snatched playfully at the book, but she hugged it to her chest and moved off smiling. More curls had fallen, wetted to the base of her neck. Looking out the window, she sighed long and loud.

"All night on brush rollers for this. What a joke."

Brackett shoved his hands in his pockets. His mouth opened slightly, then shut with a small throttled cluck.

When Albertine saw Harmony ambling across the yard with his big brown thumbs in his belt, his placid smile, and his tiny black eyes moving back and forth, she put Buddy under the cot. Harmony stopped at the shed and stood quietly. He spread his arms wide to show her he hadn't drawn his big police gun.

"Ma Cousin," he said in the Michif dialect that people used if they were relatives or sometimes if they needed gas or a couple of dollars, "why don't you come out here and stop this foolishness?"

"I ain't your cousin," Albertine said. Anger boiled up in her suddenly. "I ain't related to no pigs."

She bit her lip and watched him through the cracks, circling, a big tan punching dummy with his boots full of sand so he never stayed down once he fell. He was empty inside, all stale air. But he knew how to get to her so much better than a white cop could. And now he was circling because he wasn't sure she didn't have a weapon, maybe a knife or the German luger that was the only thing that her father, Albert American Horse, had left his wife and daughter besides his name. Harmony knew that Albertine was a tall strong woman who took two big men to subdue when she didn't want to go in the drunk tank. She had hard hips, broad shoulders, and stood tall like her Sioux father, the American Horse who was killed threshing in Belle Prairie.

"I feel bad to have to do this," Harmony said to Albertine. "But for godsakes, let's nobody get hurt. Come on out with the boy why don't you. I know you got him in there."

Albertine did not give herself away this time. She let him wonder. Slowly and quietly she pulled her belt through its loops and wrapped it around and around her hand until only the big oval buckle with turquoise chunks shaped into a butterfly stuck out over her knuckles. Harmony was talking but she wasn't listening to what he said. She was listening to the pitch of his voice, the tone of it that would tighten or tremble at a certain moment when he decided to rush the shed. He kept talking slowly and reasonably, flexing the dialect from time to time, even mentioning her father.

"He was a damn good man. I don't care what they say, Albertine, I knew him."

Albertine looked at the stone butterfly that spread its wings across her fist. The wings looked light and cool, not heavy. It almost looked like it was ready to fly. Harmony wanted to get to Albertine through her father but she would not think about American Horse. She concentrated on the sky-blue stone.

Yet the shape of the stone, the color, betrayed her.

She saw her father suddenly, bending at the grill of their old grey car. She was small then. The memory came from so long ago it seemed like a dream—narrowly focused, snapshot clear. He was bending by the grill in the sun. It was hot summer. Wings of sweat, dark blue, spread across the back of his work shirt. He always wore soft blue shirts, the color of shade cloudier than this stone. His stiff hair had grown out of its short haircut and flopped over his forehead. When he stood up and turned away from the car, Albertine saw that he had a butterfly.

"It's dead," he told her, "Broke its wings and died on the grill."

She must have been five, maybe six, wearing one of the boy's tee-shirts Mama bleached in hilex-water. American Horse took the butterfly, a black and yellow one, and rubbed it on Albertine's collarbone and chest and arms until the color and the powder of it were blended into her skin.

"For grace," he said.

And Albertine had felt a strange lightening in her arms, in her chest, when he did this and said, "For grace." The way he said it, grace meant everything the butterfly was. The sharp delicate wings. The way it floated over grass. The way its wings seemed to breathe fanning in the sun. The wisdom of the way it blended into flowers or changed into a leaf. In herself she felt the same kind of possibilities and closed her eyes almost in shock or pain she felt so light and powerful at that moment.

Then her father had caught her and thrown her high into the air. She could not remember landing in his arms or landing at all. She only remembered the sun filling her eyes and the world tipping crazily behind her, out of sight.

"He was a damn good man," Harmony said again.

Albertine heard his starched uniform gathering before his boots hit the ground. Once, twice, three times. It took him four solid jumps to get right where she wanted him. She kicked the plank door open when he reached for the handle and the corner caught him on the jaw. He faltered, and Albertine hit him flat on the chin with the butterfly. She hit him so hard the shock of it went up her arm like a string pulled taut. Her fist opened, numb, and she let the belt unloop before she closed her hand on the tip end of it and sent the stone butterfly swooping out in a wide circle around her as if it was on the end of a leash. Harmony reeled backward as she walked toward him swinging the belt. She expected him to fall but he just stumbled. And then he took the gun from his hip.

Albertine let the belt go limp. She and Harmony stood within feet of each other, breathing. Each heard the human sound of air going in and out of the other person's lungs. Each read the face of the other as if deciphering letters carved into softly eroding veins of stone. Albertine saw the pattern of tiny arteries that age, drink, and hard living had blown to the surface of the man's face. She saw the spoked wheels of his iris and the arteries like tangled threads that sewed him up. She saw the living net of springs and tissue that held him together, and trapped him. She saw the random, intimate plan of his person.

She took a quick shallow breath and her face went strange and tight. She saw the black veins in the wings of the butterfly, roads burnt into a map, and then she was located somewhere in the net of veins and sinew that was the tragic complexity of the world so she did not see Officer Brackett and Vicki Koob rushing toward her, but felt them instead like flies caught in the same web, rocking it.

"Albertine!" Vicki Koob had stopped in the grass. Her voice was shrill and tight. "It's better this way, Albertine. We're going to help you."

Albertine straightened, threw her shoulders back. Her father's hand was on her chest and shoulders lightening her wonderfully. Then on wings of her father's hands, on dead butterfly wings, Albertine lifted into the air and flew toward the others. The light powerful feeling swept her up the way she had floated higher, seeing the grass below. It was her father throwing her up into the air and out of danger. Her arms opened for bullets but no bullets came. Harmony did not shoot. Instead, he raised his fist and brought it down hard on her head.

Albertine did not fall immediately, but stood in his arms a moment. Perhaps she gazed still farther back behind the covering of his face. Perhaps she was completely stunned and did not think as she sagged and fell. Her face rolled forward and hair covered her features, so it was impossible for Harmony to see with just what particular expression she gazed into the headsplitting wheel of light, or blackness, that overcame her.

Harmony turned the vehicle onto the gravel road that led back to town. He had convinced the other two that Albertine was more trouble than she was worth, and so they left her behind, and Lawrence too. He stood swearing in his cinder driveway as the car rolled out of sight. Buddy sat between the social worker and Officer Brackett. Vicki tried to hold Buddy fast and keep her arm down at the same time, for the words she'd screamed at Albertine had broken the seal of antiperspirant beneath her arms. She was sweating now as though she'd stored an ocean up inside of her. Sweat rolled down her back in a shallow river and pooled at her waist and between her breasts. A thin sheen of water came out on her forearms, her face. Vicki gave an irritated moan but Brackett seemed not to take notice, or take offense at least. Air-conditioned breezes were sweeping over the seat anyway, and very soon they would be comfortable. She smiled at Brackett over Buddy's head. The man grinned back. Buddy stirred. Vicki remembered the emergency chocolate bar she kept in her purse, fished it out, and offered it to Buddy. He did not react, so she closed his fingers over the package and peeled the paper off one end.

The car accelerated. Buddy felt the road and wheels pummeling each other and the rush of the heavy motor purring in high gear. Buddy knew that what he'd seen in his mind that morning, the thing coming out of the sky with barbs and chains, had hooked him. Somehow he was caught and held in the sour tin smell of the pale woman's armpit. Somehow he was pinned between their pounds of breathless flesh. He looked at the chocolate in his hand. He was squeezing the bar so hard that a thin brown trickle had melted down his arm. Automatically, he put the bar in his mouth.

As he bit down he saw his mother very clearly, just as she had been when she carried him from the shed. She was stretched flat on the ground, on her stomach, and her arms were curled around her head as if in sleep. One leg was drawn up and it looked for all the world like she was running full tilt into the ground, as though she had been trying to pass into the earth, to bury herself, but at the last moment something had stopped her.

There was no blood on Albertine, but Buddy tasted blood now at the sight of her, for he bit down hard and cut his own lip. He ate the chocolate, every bit of it, tasting his mother's blood. And when he had the chocolate down inside him and all licked off his hands, he opened his mouth to say thank you to the woman, as his mother had taught him. But instead of a thank you coming out he was astonished to hear a great rattling scream, and then another, rip out of him like pieces of his own body and whirl onto the sharp things all around him.

Tahotahontanekent-seratkerontakwenhakie

Salli Benedict

DEEP IN THE WOODS, there lived a man and his wife, and their newborn baby boy. The baby was so young that his parents had not yet given him a name. Hunting was very bad that winter and they had very little to eat. They were very poor.

One day around suppertime, a little old man came to their door. He was selling rabbits.

"Do you wish to buy a rabbit for your supper?" he asked.

The woman who met him at the door replied that they were very poor and had no money to buy anything.

It was growing dark and the man looked very tired. The woman knew that he had travelled very far just to see if they would buy a rabbit from him. She invited him to stay for supper and share what little they had to eat.

"What is your name?" the husband asked as he got up to meet the old man.

"I have no name," the little man replied. "My parents were lost before they could name me. People just call me Tahotahontanekent-seratkerontakwenhakie which means, 'He came and sold rabbits.'"

The husband laughed. "My son has not been named yet either. We just call him The Baby."

The old man said, "You should name him so that he will know who he is. There is great importance in a name." The old man continued, "I will give you this last rabbit of mine for a good supper, so that we may feast in honor of the birth of your new son."

In the morning, the old man left. The parents of the baby still pondered over a name for the baby.

"We shall name the baby after the generous old man who gave him a feast in honor of his birth. But he has no name," the mother said.

"Still, we must honor his gift to our son," the husband replied. "We will name our son after what people call the old man, Tahotahontanekentseratkerontakwenhakie which means, 'He came and sold rabbits.'"

"What a long name that is," the mother said. "Still, we must honor the old man's wish for a name for our son and his feast for our son."

So the baby's name became Tahotahontanekentseratkerontakwenhakie which means, "He came and sold rabbits," in honor of the old man.

The baby boy grew older and became very smart. He had to be, to be able to remember his own name. Like all other children he was always trying to avoid work. He discovered that by the time his mother had finished calling his name for chores, he could be far, far away.

Sometimes his mother would begin telling him something to do, "Tahotahontanekentseratkerontakwenhakie...hmmmm..." She would forget what she wanted to have him do, so she would smile and tell him to go and play.

Having such a long important name had its disadvantages too. When his family travelled to other settlements to visit friends and other children, the other children would leave him out of games. They would not call him to play or catch ball. They said that it took more energy to say his name than it did to play the games.

News of this long, strange name travelled to the ears of the old man, Tahotahontanekentseratkerontakwenhakie. "What a burden this name must be for a child," the old man thought. "This name came in gratitude for my feast for the birth of the boy. I must return to visit them."

The old man travelled far to the family of his namesake, Tahotahontanekentseratkerontakwenhakie. The parents met the old man at the door and invited him in. He brought with him food for another fine meal.

"You are very gracious to honor me with this namesake," he said. "But we should not have two people wandering this world, at the same time, with the same name. People will get us confused, and it may spoil my business. Let us call your son Oiasosonaion which means, 'He has another name.' If people wish to know his other name, then he can tell them."

Oiasosonaion smiled and said, "I will now have to call you Taho-tahontanekentseratkerontakwenhakie tanon Oiasahosonnon which means, 'He came and sold rabbits and gave the boy another name.'"

Everyone laughed.

The Gleams

Ralph Salisbury

LATELY WHEN I am ordered into the mountains, I think it is a mountain itself I am meant to destroy.

I tell Maria this. I would tell no one else, but she trusts me, she knows I have saved her life many times, she knows I may have to do so again, she knows—the almost obsidian black shine of her eyes patiently looking at me, sizing me up, measuring how much of me is left, how much is merely action, that she could command from the most inexperienced recruit, anyone.

"I do not think Headquarters would order you to blow away a mountain," she says. "Red Wolf, I do not think that they would ask you to injure a God. Even if you could."

She says very little this mission.

I remember when I became silent. I remember when speech became my own stalker, when each word was an ordinary rifle bullet, its air-tunneling teakettle sound really silence compared to the volcanic blast of its birth, only its speed impressive, but each bullet each word more than enough to shut me up forever—sentences enfilade—fire across a sector where an enemy might attack—important not to be there.

Maria only points at a cloud, black and shaggy like a bear gnawing snow off a peak. But the same wind driving thin oxygen into our gasping lungs drives the bear off, and the mountain is there still, the mottled white bone of an animal more ancient than Brontosaurus, grazing the blue swamp of the sky.

So it is humans, of course, like ourselves, we must fear, their shiny machinery that must dance to the music our rocketlaunchers make.

With Maria so silent, I see myself, no longer forty and tiring sooner each year, each mission, no longer a man just five and a half feet tall, and of The Yunwiya, race nearly extinct like the dinosaurs — see myself as a woman of the same size, same race, and young, her mouth my mouth closed on the words that might expose herself to further, deeper words inside her, words that might destroy whatever of herself combat has, so far, spared.

A glorious meadow we are naked without a word our camouflage uniforms drab big-petalled flowers our weapons gleaming remainders of ice beside the little lake in which our bodies are quickly the glory of sunrise clouds reflected amid the reflections of pines no taller than ourselves.

Such pleasures may get us killed sometimes, but as long as we are lucky this beauty will keep us from merely one day stopping mid-stride, already dead though no enemy knows we are anywhere near.

Our love-making, too; how can we cease being man and woman, our lives to fulfill before the soldier each of us is is killed.

We leave — inside us, still, the meadow, its little lake and two hours of our mission lost to sedge fine as blanket weave.

Of course it's a dam. I hurt. But what did I expect — this high and crossing the divide, then following a pencil line of stream down a map of increasingly lush ferns, flowers, pines increasingly large, ourselves smaller and smaller amid the shadows of boughs and more and more drab, only the unavoidable shine of the rocket-launchers' barrels insides a kind of glory.

Of course it's in daylight, no way of hitting the flood gates at night with random firing.

Six rockets apiece. Twelve flood gates to hit. And how many thousands to drown?

We are running, with only our shadows to encumber us.

Expensive equipment abandoned, we are standing by the box of a post office the hour before tax deadline, taking checks from the mouths of small children and burning their food, their toys, in another country, whose lights will not go on tonight.

We are Yunwiya-Cherokee-Cave Dwellers, enemies renamed us in contempt. We are Yunwiya, the children of a defeated nation now fighting for the conqueror.

We run past the lake, pausing only for a drink that will let us run further.

The sun goes out like a searchlight hit by a bullet.

The stars take our hands, tug us onward.

Only the coyotes are talking.

We reach the border, the line where cloud and moon fight their eternal war.

We are over. We are safe. For a time. Our intentions now fact: disaster, death.

I love you, I say, am again in the lake she is naked beside me and, weaponless, we kiss, though our uniforms, from amid the lilies, are stalking us, nearing, the gleams of their weapons aimed.

Aniwaya, Anikawa, and the Killer Teen-agers

Ralph Salisbury

IN THEIR OWN logical way, High Command values time as much as I do; four wonderful, restful hours of beautiful dreams-after my last night of steak, beaujolais, dancing and the companionship of a beautiful patriot-I am rushed to an airstrip, flown over enemy mountains and parachuted into a meadow covered with small, fragrant blooms.

Before dawn, I have followed a river's glistening snake's subtle natal-cord curvings down to tracks which form a game of tic-tac-toe and have climbed onto a sawdust-piled gondola-car in a long, slow freight-train headed toward collision with the rising sun.

For awhile, then, I am on what my espionage instructors called "Native Time," watching the same range of mountains I grew up in across the border taper down to disappear under farms patterned as precisely as designs on a ceremonial-blanket, watching the sun's burning fist drive itself into the blue ice belly of the west-where a country that designates me "Native" not "Citizen" exists-watching the stars move beautifully along their invisible tracks.

The next dawn, I step down from the train slowing to a bone-jolting stop beside mountainous sawdust piles, one of which I climb, burrowing in to make myself a hiding place, a soft, resin-fragrant nest.

My orders are: to "infiltrate the Native work-crews immediately."

Im
med
i
ate
ly
is a wonderful long, slow word.

She is with me, my beautiful beaujolais-haired companion but rejecting me, contemptuous of the little Native in patched blue jeans and too-big sweatshirt faded the color of a street. Where is her warrior resplendent in blue tunic, chest a rainbow signalling mysterious deeds, some so secret, so important, they will only be acknowledged by a crimson rectangle flecked with gold, until final victory.

Naked, we were young and equals in splendor.

The only splendor I awake to is the final suicide lunge of sun against factory-smoke.

It is noon. My companion of two nights ago will be awakening about now, in the big crimson bed where I last saw her, naked, tanned gold like the leaf on my medal.

There is no immediately visible work-crew to infiltrate, but there soon will be, I know because of pile after pile of sawdust and the big concrete building whose cannonshape smoke-stack has just obliterated the sun.

I look for a heavy stick to tie my blanket-bundle to, a heavy stick, a weapon that does not look like a weapon. No luck. Two nights ago I could have chosen among strong branches up in the mountains, but then I was hurrying to catch a train down to these mountains of sawdust—enough wood in them to make an army of clubs, but all that wood will only go to fuel the factory in making whatever war-weapons it supplies.

The first human I see is a tall, skinny native, the second a cop.

"Come here, you." The cop sees two natives.

For the rest of the day, I am dancing with a long-handled shovel, unloading the train which brought me.

Slowly, slowly the dozens of golden rectangles of sawdust shaped by gondola cars is translated into one more sawdust mountain, at first gleaming gold in daylight, then rising gray as ash in smoke-subdued moonlight, the only illumination in a city blacked-out to prevent bombing planes from locating it.

My side's bombing planes, I have to remind myself.

Here it is the same as when I left the reservation-caught, put to work, hard work-insults, cuffs on the head.

Caught for war, first draft-dog soldier. Volunteered for Commando, endured things worse so they'd get, finally, better. Enduring hard duty now in hope of another successful mission, reward, another great dinner, lovely companion, big bed crimson as the ribbon of a Distinguished Service Medal.

Here no steak and beaujolais, for sure, no dinner of any sort, only a cop-stick poked into my gut.

Then he demands, "What's your age?"

I say, "Fifty-two," which is my age, twenty-five, turned backwards. Remembering is a behind the lines agent's most important weapon, especially if he has not even a club.

"Get back to work."

It's dark, the cop can barely see that my hair is gray, its dye as dingy as the factory-smoke. The cop's memory of this afternoon tells him my body looks younger than the gray-dyed hair suggests and that I am a likely military recruit, but his memory is jostled aside by his need to keep watch over ten gondola cars and on two natives unloading each car. He has to keep moving, keep us moving, get the job done, or his high command may decide he'd be of more use dancing with a shovel himself.

No dinner and no pay, but when the cars are all unloaded, about midnight, we are marched to the factory cafeteria to eat leftovers off plastic trays waiting to be washed. After eating, we are ordered to wash the trays, hundreds of them. Then we are marched out under the smoke-paled stars and told to report for more unloading tomorrow.

"Where do we sleep?" I ask the tall, skinny native I'd worked with.

"On your back."

To keep him from being suspicious, I have had to tell him I'm newly arrived off the reservation most distant from his and am Anikawa, Deer Clan. He's Aniwaya, Wolf Clan; we will not be friends.

Another Native tells me to sweep my tracks behind me and climb a sawdust pile, where I can sleep dug in out of sight, because White gangs come hunting us on Saturdays after the guards have gone home to bed.

"It's too late tonight," the Wold Clan man says. "They probably were here but left when they saw us still unloading, with a cop still on duty."

He might be saying this to get me killed. I sweep my tracks, climb high and dig deep into sawdust.

Thus it is that I wake from dreams of tree ghosts searching for their lost shapes in the sad smoke, and the screams are those of the tall, skinny Wolf Clan Native, not mine.

A gang of eight have him staked to the ground between sawdust piles, and, as flames flare up from his clothing, I see that his captors are big early-teenagers, not quite old enough yet for their army.

The Wolf Clan man is so skinny his arms look like burning sticks—and, from a head burned bare and blackened like the burl of a tree, the screams could be those of the tree ghosts I have dreamed, the Wolf Clan man's body slowly going up in smoke to be lost in the sawdust smoke.

Now his lips are burned off, but his glistening jaw muscles still move the white teeth, the glistening tongue, and I know what sounds are stirring the smoke from his burning flesh. Shock, that blessing the Creator gives us, numbing him to pain at last, he is chanting his death song, asking that his spirit be taken into the shadow land of the sunset, and, at the same time, invoking revenge. He is Wolf Clan, and throughout Creation spirit after spirit is joining him in the force of hatred and pride.

Deer Clan, I join my prayer to his.

His torturers are now uttering a graceless, drunken chant of their own, threatening all of the Natives hidden among the sawdust piles.

I immediately heed their threats, burying myself up to the nose in the flesh of a thousand trees.

For a long time I lie and breathe the sweet powerful scent of resin, my second skin, my armor. Lodgepole Pines, the trees where I parachuted down — Lodgepole because they are tall and straight and we'd used them for building our lodges, where all of the people came together. In the old days, the Wolf Clan people and my own had shared such a lodge.

With many pine-scented breaths, I pray while the stars move in their stately dance through the smoke of a factory functioning all night for war. I pray for revenge and for a life of dignity and beauty beyond victory day.

"We'll be back," the killer teen-agers are shouting.

They keep their word. The next night, Sunday, all eight of them come, drinking, threatening, their knives gleaming in the occasional victories of the moon.

I slip from shadow to shadow while they run from sawdust pile to sawdust pile, seeking a victim.

They find no one. Just as the cop had found no one to unload his sawdust in exchange for leftovers off plastic trays. All of the people swarmed onto the first empty train to leave after the death of the Wolf Clan man. The people have a little revenge; a factory crew has to take time off from their skilled work inside and labor, unloading the gondola cars, the enemy teen-agers unintentionally as effective as our own saboteurs. I witness this from a sawdust pile already too high for any more unloading but still safely far from the piles where bulldozers load trucks, that will deliver sawdust to the plant-furnaces.

The Wolf Clan man has shown me our revenge. The crucifix shape of his burning flesh charred an outline four times his size with the spread of gasoline in earth more sawdust than clay. All day, I have seen this sign amid the labors of my enemies preparing for war. The shape so huge, so vividly black amid the golden sawdust, I can see it even after I have slipped up to the little hill where supply cars are sidetracked, waiting until they are needed — on a hill so they can roll down without an engine.

When the eight dark shapes appear in moonlight atop a sawdust mound, I release the brakes of the first huge, gasoline-filled tank-car, letting it roll down toward the small campfire I left amid the sawdust. I have opened all the hose valves. I have waited to do this just as an empty train has begun slowly moving out into the night.

"It's lucky we were scheduled to move out just before the whole damned place blew up," I hear the train crew telling each other, stopped, up in the mountains now, switching rails.

Their "luck" has already left the train, his dark-clothed shape become one with that of a small pine.

Their "luck" has been some time now with his tall, skinny brother's people.

No gold-leafed crimson medal-ribbons here, no gold-leaf-skinned ladies in huge crimson beds. But I have a wife.

No steak and beaujolais. Food is hard to get here. But, well warned, no more of our people go down to eat garbage — become overcooked meat.

The High Command will have aerial photos.

"The Native agent lost no time getting started. What will he accomplish next?" I hear them saying — as I harvest my crops, drag wood up close to my log hut for winter, dreaming of the flower that will still be blooming between my wife's graceful legs, even in snow-living on Native Time.

The Power of Horses

Elizabeth Cook-Lynn

THE MOTHER and daughter steadied themselves, feet planted squarely, foreheads glistening with perspiration; each grasped a handle of the large steaming kettle.

"Ready?"

"Un-huh."

"Take it then," the mother said. "Careful." Together they lifted the tub of boiled beets from the flame of the burners on the gas stove and set it heavily on the table across the room. The girl let the towel which had served as a makeshift pot holder drop to the floor as the heat penetrated to the skin, and she slapped her hand against the coolness of the smooth painted wall and then against her thigh, feeling the roughness of the heavy jeans with tingling fingers. To stop the tingling, she cupped her fingers to her mouth and blew on them, then raised her apologetic eyes and looked at her mother. Without speaking, as if that was the end of it, she sank into the chrome chair and picked up the towel and began wiping the sweat from her face. The sun came relentlessly through the thin gauze curtains and the hot wind blew across the stove, almost extinguishing the gas flames of the burner, making the blue edges turn yellow and then orange and then white. The towel was damp now and stained purple from the beets and the girl leaned back in the chair and laid the towel across her face, feeling her own hot breath around her nose and mouth.

"Your hands get used to it, Marleen," the mother said, not even glancing at the girl nor at her own rough, brown hands, "just have to

keep at it," saying this not so much from believing it as from the
need to stop the feeling of futility in the girl and the silence between
them. The mother gingerly grasped the bleached stems of several
beets and dropped them into a pan of cold water, rolling one and
then another of the beets like balls in her hands, pushing the purple-
black skins this way and that, quickly, deftly, removing the peel and
stem and tossing the shiny vegetable into another container.
Finishing one, she hurriedly picked up another, as if by hurrying she
could forestall the girl's rebellion.

The woman's arms, like her hands, were large, powerful. But,
despite the years of heavy work, her sloping shoulders and smooth,
long neck were part of a tender femininity only recently showing
small signs of decline and age. The dark stains on her dark face might
have seemed like age spots or a disfigurement on someone else but on
the woman they spread delicately across her cheeks, forehead and
neck like a sweep of darkened cloud, making her somehow
vulnerable and defenseless.

"Your hands'll get used to it, Marleen," she repeated, again
attempting to keep the girl's unwillingness in check and an avenue to
reasonable tolerance and cooperation open.

The brief rest with the towel on her face seemed to diminish the
girl's weariness and for an instant more she sat silently, breathing
peacefully into the damp towel. As the girl drew the towel across
her face and away from her eyes, something like fear began to rise in
her and she peered out the window where she saw her father
standing with a white man she had never seen before. Her father was
looking straight ahead down the draw where the horses stood near
the corral. They always want something from him, she thought, and
as she watched the white man put a cigarette in his mouth and turn
sideways out of the wind, the flame of his lighter licking toward his
bony profile, she wondered what it was this time. She watched the
man's quick mannerisms and she saw that he began to talk earnestly
and gesture toward his green pick-up truck which was parked close
to the barbed wire fence encircling the house and yard.

The girl was startled out of her musings at the sound of her mother's, "Yu-u-u-u," softly uttered indication of disapproval, insistent and always compelling a change in the girl's behavior. And she turned quickly to get started with her share of the hot beets, handling them inexpertly but peeling their hot skins away as best she could.

After a few minutes, during which the women worked in silence, only the monotonous hiss of the burning gas flame between them, the girl, surprised, thought: Her sounds of disapproval aren't because I'm wasting time; instead, they are made because she is afraid my father and the white man will see me watching them. Spontaneously, defensively, she said, "They didn't see me." She looked into the brown stained face but saw only her mother's careful pretense of being preoccupied with the beets as she picked up a small knife to begin slicing them. All last winter, everytime I came home, I spied on him for you, thought the girl, even riding my horse over to Chekpa's through the snow to see if he was there. And when I came back and told you that he was, you acted as if you hadn't heard anything, like now. So this is not the beginning of the story nor is it the part of the story that matters, thought the girl, and she started to recognize a long, long history of acrimony between her parents, thinking, in hindsight, that it would have been better if she had stayed at Stephen Mission. But then, she remembered her last talk with Brother Otto at the Mission as he sat before her, one leg languidly draped over the other, his collar open, showing his sparse red chest hairs, his watery pale eyes looking at her searchingly, and she knew that it wasn't better to have stayed there.

He had sat quivering with sympathy as she had tried to tell him that to go home was to be used by her mother against her father. I rode over to Chekpa's, she told him, hating herself for letting out the symptoms of her childish grief, despising him for his delicate white skin, his rapt gaze, the vicariousness of his measly existence. Até was there cutting wood for the eldest of the Tatiopa women, Rosalie, the one he was supposed to marry, you know, but instead, he married my mother. My mother had sent me there and when I rode into the yard and saw him, he stood in uncertainty, humiliated in the eyes of

Chekpa, his old friend, as well as all of those in the Tatiopa family. Worse yet, she knew, humiliated in the eyes of his nine-year-old daughter.

In her memory of that awful moment, she didn't speak nor did her father, and so she had ridden out of the yard as abruptly as she had come, standing easily in the stirrups, her face turned toward her right shoulder out of the wind, watching the slush fly behind the horse's hooves. She didn't cut across Archie's field as she usually did but took the long way, riding as hard as she could alongside the road. When she got to the gate, she reined in, dismounted and led her horse through the gate and then, slowly, down the sloping hill to the tack shed. She stood for a long time with her head against the wide, smooth leather of the stirrup shaft, her eyes closed tightly, the smell of wet horse hair in her nostrils. Much later she had recited the event as fully as she could bear it to the Mission school priest much like she had been taught to recite the events of her sinful life. I have taken the Lord's name in vain, I have taken the Lord's name in vain, I have taken...

Damn beets, damn all these damn beets, the girl thought, and she turned away from the table back to the stove where she stirred the second, smaller pot of sliced beets and she looked out through the gauze curtains to see if her father and the white man were still there. They had just run the horses into the corral from the small fenced pasture where they usually grazed when they were brought down to the place.

"He must be getting ready to sell them, is he?" she asked her mother.

Her mother said nothing.

"How come? I didn't know he was going to sell," the girl said slowly, noticing that her horse, two quarterhorse brood mares and a half-Shetland black and white gelding she had always called "shota" had been cut out of the herd and were standing at the far corner of the pasture, grazing. The heat shimmered above the long buffalo grass and the girl's thoughts drifted and, vaguely, she heard her mother say, "You'd better spoon those sliced ones into these hot jars, Marleen." And then, almost to herself, her mother started talking as if in recognition of what the girl did not know about the factual and philosophical sources from which present life emerges. "I used to have land myself, daughter," she began. "On it, my grandfather had many horses. What happened to it was that some white men from Washington came and took it away from me when my grandfather died because they said they were going to breed game birds there — geese, I think.

"There was no one to do anything about it," she continued. "There was only this old woman who was a mother to me and she really didn't know what to do, who to see, or how to prevent this happening.

"Among the horses there on my land was a pair of brood mares just like those two out there," she pointed with her chin to the two bays at the end of the pasture. And looking at the black and white horse called "shota," she said, "And there was also another strange, mysterious horse, Su'ka wak a', i-e-e-e." She used the word for "mysterious dog" in the Dakota language. And the mother and daughter stood looking out the window at the "shota" horse beside the bays, watching them pick their way through the shimmering heat and through the tall grass slowly, unhurried. The beets were forgotten, momentarily, and the aging woman remembered the magic of those horses and especially the one that resembled the "shota" horse, thinking about that time, that primordial time when an old couple of the tribe received a gift horse from a little bird and the horse produced many offspring for the old man and woman, and the people were never poor after that. Her grandfather, old Bowed Head, the man with many horses, had told her that story often during her childhood when he wished to speak of those days when all creatures knew one another. And it was a reassuring thing: I wish this tribe to be strong and good, the mysterious horse had told the old man, and so I keep giving my offspring every year and the tribe will have many horses and this good thing will be among you always.

"They were really fast horses," said the mother, musing still, filling in the texture of her imagination and memory. "They were known throughout our country for their speed, and the old man allowed worthy men in the tribe to use them in war or to go on a hunt with them. It is an old story," the woman concluded as though the story were finished, as though commenting upon its history made everything comprehensible.

As the girl watched her mother's extraordinary vitality which rose during the telling of these events, she also noted the abruptness with which the story seemed to end and the kind of formidable reserve and closure which fell upon the dark stained features of the older woman as she turned again to the stove.

"What happened to the horses?" the girl wanted to know. "Did someone steal them? Did they die?"

After a long silence, her mother said, "Yes, I suppose so," and the silence again deepened between them as they fell to filling hot jars with sliced beets and sealing hot lids upon them, wiping and stroking them meticulously and setting them one by one on a dim pantry shelf.

The girl's frustration was gone now and she seemed mindless of the heat, her own physical discomfort and the miserableness of the small squalid kitchen where she and her mother moved quietly about, informed now with the wonder of the past, the awesomeness of the imagination.

The sun moved west and the kitchen fell into shadow. The wind died down. The mother and daughter finished their tedious task and carried the large tub of hot water out through the entryway a few feet past the door and emptied its contents upon the ground. The girl watched the red beet juice stain the dry, parched earth in which there was no resistance, and she stepped away from the redness of the water which gushed like strokes of a painter's brush, suddenly black and ominous as it sank into the ground. She looked up to see the white man's green pick-up truck disappearing over the rise, the dust billowing behind the heavy wheels, settling gently in the heat.

The nameless fear struck at her again and she felt a knot being drawn tightly inside her and she looked anxiously toward the corral. Nothing around her seemed to be moving, the air suddenly still, the sweat standing out in beads on her face and her hands, oddly moist and cold.

As she ran toward the corral, she saw her mother out of the corner of her eye still grasping one handle of the boiler tub, strangely composed, her head and shoulders radiant in the sun.

At the corral a moment later, she saw her father's nearly lifeless form lying face down in the dirt, his long grey hair spread out like a fan above him, pitifully untidy for a man who ordinarily took meticulous care with his appearance. He had his blue cotton scarf which he used as a handkerchief clutched tightly in his right hand and he was moaning softly.

The odor of whiskey on his breath was strong as she helped him turn over and sit up, and in that instant the silent presence of the past lay monumentally between them so that he did not look at her nor did he speak. In that instant, she dimly perceived her own innocence and was filled with regret that she would never know those times to which Até would return if he could, again and again. She watched as he walked unsteadily toward the house, rumpled and drunk, a man of grave dignity made comic and sad and helpless by circumstances which his daughter could only regard with wonderment.

"Keyapi: Late one night when the old man had tied the horses near his lodge, someone crept through the draw and made ready to steal them; it was even said that they wanted to kill the wonderful horses. The mysterious gift horse called to the sleeping old man and told him that an evil lurked nearby. And he told the old man that since such a threat as this had come upon them and all the people of the tribe, the power of the horses would be diminished and no more colts would be born and the people would have to go back to their miserable ways."

As her father made his way to the house, walking stiffly past her mother who pretended to be scrubbing the black residue from the boiler, the girl turned and walked quickly away from the corral in the opposite direction.

I must look: she thought, into the distance, and as she lifted her eyes and squinted into the evening light she saw the Ft. George road across the river, beyond the bend in the river so far away that it would take most of the day for anyone to get there. I must look: at the ground in front of me where my grandmothers made paths to the ti (n) psina beds and carried home with them long braided strands over their shoulders. I must look: she thought, into the past for the horse that speaks to humans.

She took long strides and walked into the deepening dusk. She walked for a long time before returning to the darkened house where she crept into her bed and lay listening to the summer's night insect sounds, thinking apocalyptic thoughts in regard to what her mother's horse story might have to do with the day's events.

She awoke with a start, her father shaking her shoulder. "You must ride with me today, daughter, before the horse buyer comes back," he said. "I wish to take the horses away out to the far side of the north pasture. I am ready to go, so please hurry."

The girl dressed quickly, and just as dawn was breaking she and her father, each leading two horses with the others following, set out over the prairie hills. These were the hills, she knew, to which the people had come when the Uprising was finished and the U.S. Cavalry fell to arguing with missionaries and settlers about "the Indian problem." These were the hills, dark blue in this morning light, which she knew as repositories of sacred worlds unknown to all but its most ancient tenants.

When they reached the ridge above Dry Creek, the girl and her father stopped and let the horses go their way wildly. The "shota" horse led them down the steep prairie hills and into the dry creek bed and, one by one, the horses disappeared into the stand of tall cottonwood trees which lined the ravine.

She stood beside her father and watched them go. "Why were you going to sell them?" she asked abruptly.

"There are too many," he replied, "and the grass is short this summer."

"It's been too hot," he said, wiping his face with the blue handkerchief and he repeated, "The grass is short this summer."

With that, they mounted their horses and rode home together.

Sleeping In Rain

Gordon Henry

I

WAKE CHANTS circle, overhead, like black crows watching her will stumble through weak moments. Like when she heard the carriage outside and went to the window with his name on her lips. Or when she looked over in the corner and saw him sleeping, with his mouth open, in the blue chair, next to the woodstove. She saw them, dissembled reflections, on the insides of her black glasses. Moments passed, etched, like the lines of age in the deep brown skin of her face. She's somewhere past ninety now; bent over, hollow boned, eyes almost filled. She lives in a room. A taken care of world. Clean sheets, clean blankets, wall-to-wall carpeting, a nightstand, and a roommate who, between good morning and good night, wanders away to card games in other rooms. Most of her day is spent in the chair, at the foot of the bed. Every now and then, she leaves and takes a walk down one of the many hallways of the complex. Every now and then, she goes to the window and looks out, as if something will be there.

II

Motion falls apart in silence, tumbling, as wind turns choreographed snow through tangents of streetlights. I am alone; to be picked up at the Saint Paul bus terminal. I fucked up. Dropped out. Good, it's not what I wanted. What is a quasar? The tissue of dreams. Fuck no, there are no secrets. There is nothing hard about astronomy, sociology, calculus, or Minnesota winters. Those are

just reasons I used to leave. To go where? To go watch my hands
become shadows over assembly lines?

   A voice clicks on in the darkness. "We are now in Saint Paul and
will be arriving at the Saint Paul terminal." Let me guess. In five
minutes. "In ten minutes," the driver says. It figures.

III

My uncle's eyes have long since fallen from the grasp of stars. Now,
they are like the backends of factories; vague indications of what
goes on beneath the tracks of comb in his thick black hair. He was
waiting when I arrived. Waiting, entranced in existence. A series of
hypnotic silences, between words, that had to be spoken. Silences
leading me to a beat-up car in a dark parking lot. I am too far away
from him; too far away to be leaving for something further. I don't
believe he doesn't like me. No, that's not quite what I'm getting at.
It's something I saw when his shadow exploded into a face as he bent
down, over the steering wheel, to light his cigarette.

IV

The cold white moon over houses too close together. Front
windows, where shadows pass in front of blue lights of televisions. I
am one of them now; a sound on wood stairs. There is a sanctuary of
dreams waiting for my footsteps to fade.

V

The old woman dreams she is up north, on the reservation. It is
autumn. Pine smoke hanging over the tops of houses, leaves
sleepwalking in gray wind, skeletal trees scratching ghost gray sky.
She is in the old black shack. At home. Stirring stew in the kitchen.
The woodstove snaps in the next room. Out the window, he lifts the
axe. He is young. She watches as it splits a log on the tree stump. He
turns away and starts toward the house. He is old. He takes out his
pipe and presses down tobacco. She goes to the door to meet him.

She opens the door. She tries to touch him. He passes through her, like a cold shiver, and walks into a photograph on the wall.

VI

The mind bends over, in the light through a window, down and across the body of Jesus Christ as he stumbles through the sixth station of the cross. It comes to me sometimes, when I close my eyes. September sun in the old church. Smoke of sweet grass in stained glass light. Red, blue and yellow light. Prisms of thought behind every eye. Chippewa prayers stumbling through my ears. Old Ojibwa chants fading away in the walk to the cemetery. I look at the hole in the ground. I look at the casket beside it. I look at the hole, I look at the casket. At the hole, at the casket, at the hole, at the casket, at the hole.

The clock glows red across the room; a digital 2:37. My cousin lies in darkness. Another figure covered up in sleep.

VII

Dust swims in sunlight of an open door as dreams evaporate in the face of a clock.

VIII

"Get up, I said. It's raining. It's raining and you, lying there. Get up, old man, I said." It is my uncle talking. He found the old man where he lay in the rain. He had fallen asleep and fallen down from his seat on an old bench I tried to set on fire when I was ten or eleven. The next week they buried him in the coolness of Autumn coming. Weeks after, the old woman thought she heard his carriage outside the window of her new room in the city.

IX

Cities of snow melt, blurred in liquid between wiper blades. We are waiting for the light to change. My uncle is driving. The old woman is waiting. Not really for us. Not for us, but waiting. I will see her this morning. This afternoon I will be gone. Another bus. Home. The light changes in the corner of my eye turning away.

X

The room never moves for her. It is not like snow falling, like leaves falling, like stones through water. It is a window, a bed, and a chair.

XI

As the old woman touches me it is like air holding smoke. I am something else. Vestiges of prayer, gathered in a hollow church. Another kind of reflection. A reflection on the outsides of her black glasses. A reflection that cries when eyes leave it.

As the old woman touches me it is like air holding smoke. I am something else. Fleet anguish, like flying shadows. A moment vanishing. A moment taken, as I am being.

As the old woman touches me it is like air holding smoke. It spins it. It grasps it. It shapes it in a wish. After that there is a mist too fine to see.

Telephone Poles

Audrey La Forme

REVA WAS STANDING at the window and staring out into the garden when she heard Gary get up and go into the bathroom. The sun had climbed above the treeline and its reflection was making the surface of the lake seem alive with tiny, shimmering creatures. The dew had been heavy the night before and the moisture pulled on the plants, making them look small and helpless. Streams of light flowed into the room, filling it with a warm, pulsing brightness. She opened the window wide, closed her eyes and let the cool air caress her face. The scraping of a chair being dragged from beneath the table turned her around.

Automatically, she reached for the coffee pot on the stove. By the time she turned to face her husband, her expression had become smooth. She looked up at him but he avoided her gaze and continued to roll the sleeves of his shirt.

Without looking in her direction, Gary swung his large frame into the chair "I'll phone Jake at noon and let him know," he said, still avoiding her eyes.

"What's the rush?" She was startled by his words and her own voice sounded strained and unfamiliar. "I mean, it's Saturday. Won't he need a little time to set things up?"

"Things are ready to move now, Rev. He can't hold the job any longer than Monday. And if I'm not there..." He let his words hang.

"It's just so fast. I wish we could slow it down. Don't you?"

Gary didn't answer. He leaned back in his chair and ran his hands through his dark hair.

Reva turned to start breakfast. Her hands moved smoothly and surely, secure in the routine of their morning. But she wanted to scream as her mind raced, forward, backward. She was amazed to see her hands endure. She felt so detached from them.

When she turned again, Gary was sitting, gazing at the lake. He stared beyond her garden, his large hands cupped around his coffee. Reva set his breakfast down, sat across from him and followed his eyes across the lake. She felt him glance in her direction, then he ate in silence.

"It's perfect," she breathed. "The trees look so tall and straight. They could be instant telephone poles," she laughed.

"They probably will be," he said, sipping his coffee.

"With the plant closed, everyone will be leaving." Then she leaned forward as if to compel the answer she wanted. "There's no need, is there?"

"They can be shipped out easy enough," he answered.

She looked down into her garden and then at the lake. "And all this?"

"They can take anything they want," he said in a tired voice.

"Even if we stayed, then it could only be for so long."

"Seems like it," he said, lighting a cigarette.

"Yes," she said as if she didn't hear him, "everything is only for so long."

"Okay, don't start."

"I'm not trying to start anything. I was only asking what will happen here."

"Let's not argue, okay?"

"I'm not trying to. I said the trees could be telephone poles. Isn't that the truth?"

"It's true," he said, crossing his arms and looking directly at her.

She knew she was irritating him but she waved away her impulse to be silent and she pressed on. "And I made the breakfast the same as before. But it isn't the same anymore, is it?"

Again his eyes met hers, and this time they held. He shook his head, "No, it's not the same anymore."

Reva turned her head away and looked back out the window. "But they are so beautiful. Just the way they are now."

"More coffee?" he asked, rising.

She resented the shift but pushed her empty cup toward him. "Please."

The cool breeze off the lake flipped the curtains away from the window and streamed into the room, mingling with the heat of the morning sun.

"Coffee's still hot," he said, warning her.

"It's still early."

She watched him finish pouring them both another cup and then as he turned back to the stove. He looked awkward as he replaced the pot. When the plant closed permanently, he didn't believe it. They should have given us some notice, he said. She was relieved when he finally exploded. He had been working on a wooden chest, refinishing it and it was almost done. He must have gouged himself with one of the tools he was using. Suddenly, he was pounding on the top of it and when it jumped open he pulled the lid off. He kept hitting it for a long time as she watched from the kitchen window. Later he came in and she dressed his hand. Neither of them mentioned the incident. But she had expected that. It was the nothingness, right now, that made her afraid.

When Gary sat back in his chair she could feel him watching her. She looked down at the faded floor.

"It's not all that bad, Rev," he said. "We can come back after a while."

She couldn't look up.

"We'll find a good place. It'll have a big backyard. Room for the kids and a garden."

"What about here?"

"We'll be back."

"And when we come back, everything will be the same?" she asked.

"It'll still be here."

"Do you really think so?"

"It won't be any different. Johnson's just down the road. He'll keep an eye on the place."

Reva reached out and caught a corner of the curtain that had been lifted by the breeze. She fingered the ruffled seam and let it fall.

"And we'll all be happy there, in the city?"

"Look at all the ones who have already left. They're still there," he said, referring to family, friends, those who had left a long time ago.

They left to look for work, Reva thought, the plant quit hiring long ago. Finally, it shut down and Reva read that the company had moved out of the county. The rest of the article mentioned the cost of labor and decreased profits.

"Good for them," she said out loud.

"There's nothing here, dammit," he swore, his voice rising, but his eyes looked tired, his shoulders sagged.

She wanted to reach out and touch his arm. She wanted to tell him, to reassure him. But of what, she thought, I don't know myself.

The ringing of the telephone startled them both. Reva didn't move to answer it. Gary strode across the room and picked it up before the third ring. He mouthed the name "Johnson" at her and turned away.

Rob and Paula chose that moment to race out from the hallway. They crashed and rolled into the living room and Reva felt grateful for their noisy entrance. She shook her head, marvelling at their endless energy. They never seemed to tire. It was Paula, their youngest, who broke away from the ruckus and jumped into Reva's lap.

"Mom, Rob says we're gonna move to the city," she said, her lip curling into a pout. Her wide, brown eyes and avid expression reminded Reva of the bear cub they had stumbled across the summer before. When he caught their scent, he raised his face in their direction and Reva was taken back by the mortality of the expression. For a moment the cub seemed torn between a desire to come closer and to run. She had felt so dejected when it turned to run, lifting its head and bawling out. Reva pulled Paula closer, not wanting her to ask her question again.

"Uncle Jake called last night," Rob called from the floor. "Dad's gonna go work for him," he said, taking a few precious moments to tie his shoe. "Paula says I'm making it up but Dad told me."

Reva felt the smile that had formed on her face grow stiff and tight. "Well, we'll have to see," she said. She felt her face grow warm as they waited for more. Rob sat and continued to watch her from the floor. Paula drew her head back and looked into her face. She couldn't stand it.

"Why don't you two get something to eat and head outside? I'll bet the water's pretty warm," she added, nodding towards the lake.

For a moment she felt their silent accusation. Then it broke and they went, at once a tangle of arms, legs and shrieks. Reva didn't stop them when they raced off to change into their swimming suits, forgetting about breakfast, and by the time they pounded back down the hall she was back in the kitchen. Gary was still on the phone in the next room, his deep voice was an occasional rumble. Like thunder before the storm, Reva thought and she shivered.

The kitchen brightened and Reva turned and looked around, her eyes widening as she took in the whole room. Everything appeared sharp and clear. It lasted for a few moments and then dimmed. She was aware that she had taken a few steps, then she stopped and leaned against the table. It was an odd sensation that started like a lump in her chest and spread until she felt like a helpless, quivering mass of flesh. She wanted to cry, scream and laugh all at once. She felt as though she were trembling, yet her hands were still. But when she squeezed the edge of the table her arms felt weak and drained. She clutched with what little strength remained and she felt the inner trembling subside. Her sigh was like an explosion in the silence of the room.

The banging of the screen door made Reva look up in time to watch the kids leap from the back porch and tear off towards the lake. Then she realized the queer feelings were gone. She wondered if she had really felt anything at all. And within seconds she had changed into her swimsuit. Retracing her steps in the hall, she thought of how often she had been working in her garden or in the house. She needed a break. She noticed the house was silent. Gary was no longer on the phone. She eased the screen door shut and looked out on the lake. Rob and Paula were taking turns diving from a raft Gary had anchored for them offshore. She walked along the worn path to the dock. She had it all to herself. Now all she wanted was a very small part of the lake.

Reva closed her eyes, and as she lifted her arms for the dive, her final glimpse took in the treeline across the lake. The water closed in and over her. She pushed herself toward the bottom of the lake, feeling the sand and coarse pebbles along the bottom with her hands. Then she rose for the surface. As she broke through the top, she turned to face the shore. Their home was a blurred outline a short distance away. She began wiping the water from her eyes and felt the warmth of her own tears in her hands. Not here, she thought, not here. Her tears fell and mixed with the lake. She was helpless until they stopped.

When Reva opened her eyes again, she pushed her way toward the shore, not taking her eyes from the house. The sun was high overhead but she felt a chill go through her as she rose from the water. Gary had come out and was on the porch. She watched him in the distance as he lit another cigarette. She wondered if he had telephoned Jake yet.

Yaikni

Maurice Kenny

I

LENA HEARD their laughter as she watched the other women picking berries in a distant patch. She lazed in the morning sun, content to watch the women and stare at the sky busy with birds cutting clouds and decorating trees. Overhead, a crow flew south, cawing shrillingly to the workers in the field.

"*Agaya, agaya!*" she whispered to herself. "*Agaya!* Dog! Ol' crow, you're like a dog, wandering from back porch to porch sniffin' for dry bones." She waved the crow away with a stiff hand.

The meadow, covered in chicory blue and hawk weed orange, sloped from a wooden knoll down to a rushing creek bordered by iris and skunk cabbage. A short walk from the village, the meadow had been picked clean every spring for as many years as the oldest villager could remember. Late June, directly after summer solstice, the berries were always there, usually in profusion. And the women always came to pick even though they cultivated hybrid berries in gardens behind the barns. No larger than a thumb-nail, they were always delicious, sweet as rich honey, red as the setting sun. Spring's first gift. Children, of course, usually ate more than they dropped into the berry cans slung on their little arms.

Lena now recalled the many times she had walked to this patch with her own mother. How much she actually disliked bending, stooping, kneeling under the broiling sun to pick hour after hour. Once she had a nose-bleed, and her mother led her into the shade of a beech tree, dressed the injured nose and allowed her to play the rest of the day with a doll. She learned fast-to pinch her nose. When it bled, her mother would invariably take her out of the field. Since the first bleeding she could not eat berries. The very thought made her blood run. But there she was now, after all those many, many years picking berries with her daughter and her own great-grand-daughter. After many years away from her home village, kin, the patch. She wondered if her nose would bleed now, again. Well, she wouldn't pick too many. Wouldn't bleed. She'd just sit quietly, pluck one or two for her own tongue, perhaps tease little Annie with one, and ignore the empty bucket beside her in the grasses.

"*Agaya.*" She called again after the crow now only a fly-speck on the sky.

The sun slowly moved south in no hurry, rising higher and higher. The near-cloudless sky shimmered in heat vapors. The trees on the woody knoll sent long fingery shadows down across the meadow. Lena's glance followed their trail up the knoll. She knew the cool, the shade of the maple and the birch, the elm and sumac, the scotch pine. She ached to find a tall sycamore and sit under it, her back leaning against its comforting bark. Scanning the woods on the rim of the knoll, she spotted an old man leaning on a cane. His back bent in age. His hat brim covered his face. She thought it shrouded his face. Of course, it was Mr. Peters. *Onkiakenro.* An old childhood friend. Still breathing, alive, like herself, wandering like the crow, a dog, from house to house, sometimes offering cheer, sometimes a salve for a burnt finger, a remedy for a cold or common-sense advice. He'd visited her twice recently. Came to her daughter's house right to the supper table, sat down, drank tea, and hardly with a "thank you, mam" strolled out into the night's darkness. He'd barely said a word. She remembered how he'd been such a quiet boy. Now he was a silent man. Mr. Peters vanished into the woods.

"Gramma, I wanna go home. I wanna go home, Gramma. I'm tired."

Annie was fretting.

Children had no real appreciation of work, of berries, of being in an open meadow, of the warmth of the sun. Wait until their bones are old and dry, the hollow sockets whistling with wind, break at the touch of a breeze. No appreciation at all. Why do they bring the little ones anyway? Always tired, always thirsty, never want to relieve themselves in the bushes. Always hungry. And they ate more berries than they put in the bucket. If the men want jam and shortcake, then they should keep the children with them. That wouldn't do, surely. The women'd go home and find their little arms broken, eyes put out, little bodies burnt. Men were not good baby-sitters for sure. Useless to argue. Foolish.

Again she heard the women laughing. A good story probably or some rare gossip.

Sluggishly, lethargically she plucked one little berry not much larger than the end-knob of her thumb. Very red, very juicy, and she dropped it into her bucket with six others. She just didn't feel much like picking today. She was tired too. Like Annie, and thirsty. Could eat a cookie if she'd thought to have brought one. "Oh! Boy!" she exclaimed aloud, "good thing I went before we left the house. I'd be in a fine fix."

A mosquito flitted around her wrinkled face, and she shot out a hand to grasp it but failed the mark. It landed on her ear-lobe and stabbed. "Monster." She drew away her palm and a spot of blood glowed on the sweaty flesh.

"You alright, Ma," her daughter, Lulu, called out.

She nodded. "Yes," she called back. "Mosquitoes." She forced a big smile so Lulu could see she was doing fine, but under her breath she whispered, "*Agaya.*"

She rolled seven little berries around in the bucket with her stiff fingers. One-two, three-four, five-six, seven. Seven little berries. Seven little dwarfs. Seven little gifts from the Little-People. She felt good, real good, thinking of the stories of the Little-People her own mother had told in the berry meadows. Of how they gave the strawberries to the ragged boy who had in turn given them his hunt, squirrels, to eat when they were starving. How they protected still to this moment the people from the forest witches. She chuckled. They were good stories. Good stories. The Little-People are good people. She plucked a berry which was slightly larger than the usual. It still had a white bottom, like a baby's bottom. She shrugged and patted the whitened bottom tenderly and dropped it pell mell into the bucket. It was hard. It rolled around like a boy's marble.

Again wisps of laughter came from the other women squatting in the blue meadow. Gossip, the source of all stories, she thought. Oh! if it were only winter and they could sit in the parlor and tell stories, forget this heat, this back-breaking work. Have coffee and Lulu's shortbread cookies. And gossip of the old days, times. But there weren't many left from the old days. Not many. A few. And she'd forgotten most of them, the stories and the old friends and relatives. Been away tooooo long. Too long.

She held up her hands. "Dog bones," she whispered. "Bones. I'm all bones."

True, she was thin, not an extra ounce anywhere on her body. Lulu said she'd fatten her up. Corn soup would do it. Mush. But all she really ever wanted to eat was pop corn. Lulu laughed at this at first. And then a frown replaced the laughter. Then a scowl, finally a brief scolding. She didn't gain the weight. And she was glad about that. She was just naturally skinny though her six sisters had been heavy to just plain fat, obese. She knew that had killed them all, one by one. Fat. She abhorred fatness. Just like those gossiping women over there in the field. They were all fat. Great rolls of it hung from their arms and thighs. They'd live to regret their greed, their fat.

Not far off she heard Annie squeal. "Gramma, a mouse. A mouse, Gramma."

"It won't hurt you."

Above flew a hawk, but she knew it would not descend for its lunch, not with those laughing women making so much noise. She felt a little sorry for Annie who'd been surprised and she felt sorry for the eventually doomed mouse. And she, indeed, felt sorry for the hawk who would do without food. Well, it was probably too fat anyway. No, not really, hawks and other creatures knew better. They knew how to survive. People had gone silly gobbling down all the food they could push into their mouths and stomachs. Downright silly.

As she predicted, the hawk flew off to a branch of a dying tamarack at the eastern edge of the meadow. It took a stance as though ready to defend the territory of its hunt, waiting for the women to abandon the field to make its kill. Lena could feel its eyes burn into her back.

One more berry plopped into her bucket. Child's play, she thought. This is child's play. And as though competing with her great-grand-daughter, she commenced to furiously pluck handfulls of berries and tossed them into the bucket. The fruit was overripe, squashy, so glutted with juice the sticky waters ran between her knobby fingers curled with arthritic curves. She flung the mashed berries to the others and reached down for more, her gnarled hands touching down into the sun-warm vines, the crisp leaves turning red like the fruit itself, like paint, like phlox, hibicus...wild flowers, like blood, menstrual blood, hospital blood, scarlet like the morning star, crimson like clouds afire at sunset, red like the spanked bottom of a naughty child, like anger on the cheek. Chagrined with herself, her own present laziness, apathy, her sense of competition with little Annie finally took hold and for moments she busied herself with work, bending under the noon sun and plucking berry after berry, refusing to taste even one, to slip undetected one sweet berry between her teeth. Shortly, the bucket bottom was covered. She took a breather, languishing from work in the heat.

A soft breeze brought a bug into her bucket, a lady-bug fell into her fruit.

"Lady-bug, Lady-bug, fly away home. Your house is on fire and your children are alone. Lady-bug. Lady-bug, fly away home. Lady-bug, Lady-bug, your house is on fire, your children alone. Lady, Lady. Lady, Lady-bug..."

She couldn't remember the entire rhyme. She chanted over and over, "Lady-bug, Lady-bug," hoping the rest of the words would follow. She worked herself into an anger so vicious she began pounding the air with her fists. Clenched hammers, the rolled hands struck the air, and the vines, the ground, her own chest.

"Ma! Ma, you alright?"

The women picking further away now in the wide meadow looked up from work.

"Ma, answer me. You alright?"

Her eyes looked up from the vines. They were seared with anger. Her glance turned toward the knoll. There he was again lurking about the woods. Mr. Peters. He stood in silence like a tree framed in a windless mirage.

"Ma, answer me! You alright?"

Lulu's voice grew, concerned, louder as it came closer.

"Lady-bug, Lady-bug. Fly, fly, damn you, fly away home. Or I'll burn down your house. I'll cut off your children's heads. Damn you."

She picked up the bucket and flung out the berries.

Lulu stood by her mother and motioned to the other women to hurry. She looked at the old woman among the berries, her faded blue house dress soiled with scarlet juice, her hands and face running red, her bunned white hair framing the startled face was flecked with berry stain. She pulled out the comb that kept her hair in place and it cascaded down like the rapids of a swift river.

"She's a *witch!*" Annie screamed.

"Get out, get out," the old woman cried.

"Gramma, she's a *witch,* a witch!" little Annie screamed and screamed again as she stomped her feet.

"Get out of my bucket and go care for your children! Out of my woods. Out of my way. My house is burning and my children are alone."

Annie began to dance in a circle around her great-grandmother crying and, terrified, tearing at her own dark hair. She screamed and pushed her hands against her face and eyes to hide. She thrashed about, breaking from Lulu's inept grasp, and ran off to the women hurrying towards Lulu.

"Get out of my bucket. Out! *Agaya, agaya.* You filthy dog! Leave my bones alone. My bones are mine. Scat, I say, scat. You fell in my berries. Get home to your children, get home!"

The sounds, the words came from the very center of her total being, her long years of hurt and disappointment, frustration and her loneness in a world she then could not possibly comprehend. Her madness, these insane actions bubbled from her blood, the sinews of her flesh and spirit, a spirit half broken by life itself.

"It won't go home, Lulu. It won't go home, Lu. Its house is burning." She wept. Hot tears streamed from her eyes red now with pain.

"Mama, Mama, it will go home. It will, Mama. It'll go home and protect its children."

Soothing, but Lulu's words could not possibly penetrate.

She threw her hands to her tear-stained face and hid behind the bones. When she pulled them off her brow, her cheeks, her chin were smeared with red juice. It trickled in jagged rivulets down the withering flesh of her throat.

"It won't go *home*, Lulu."

"Yes, it will, Ma. Everything goes home, Mama. Everything."

"That damn lazy Lady-bug won't."

"Ma, quiet down."

"I'll put her house on fire."

Lulu hugged her mother close. They weaved like a mullein stalk wobbling in the faint breeze brushing the meadow.

"What's wrong? What happened? Lena, you alright?" the women questioned.

"I don't know," Lulu responded. "I just don't know what happened. She's screaming about a lady-bug and pointing to the hill."

The older woman cried wretched tears. She slobbered like a child.

"The sun's gotten to her, Lu. Better take her home. Let her rest."

Lena simply stood, her reddened hands immobile at her side, her dress stained with sprinkles of berry juice, her face smeared and contorted, her frizzled white hair lifting gently in the breeze. She stood like an admonished child, guilty and shamed. Her back stooped, she was broken before the women, before her grand-child.

"Annie, come now. We're going to take Gramma home."

The child had run off to a thicket of crabapple and knelt behind the sapling bushes crying for Lulu to come fetch her away from the witch. The witch who would chop off her head, burn down her house, and suck out her breath–just like in the stories Lulu has told her winter nights ago.

II

A bat darted in and out of maple shadows above Mina Mount's head. She walked quickly down the twilight highway. Her back was killing her from stooping most of the day at berry picking, and the sun had caused a brute pain to pound at her temples. At that moment, she'd prefer sitting on the couch watching "The Joker's Wild" on TV, but she was out of bread. None for supper and none for her husband's breakfast. The road was brightly lit by a flashing red and blue neon sign and one gas pump light. A car was parked by the pump, but as she approached the driveway it roared its motor and pulled away into the darkness of the night.

Mina opened the door. A bell tinkled overhead.

"Just a loaf of bread, Hattie. That's all I need."

"You been berry pickin', huh?"

She heaved a sigh and replied a low, "Yes."

"I see the sun on your nose. Fiery red."

"We picked 'til about three. Ol' Lena Bottoms gave out."

"Gave out?"

"Had some kind of fit. Said she couldn't get lady-bugs out of her bucket. Started hollerin' blue blazes. Poor Lulu. Couldn't do a thing with her mother. Just held on to her close. Little Annie ran away. Screaming her grandma was a witch. She did look it with juice all over her face. We took her home to bed. I don't envy Lu. She's got her hands full with that ol' lady, I'll tell you."

"Lu should never have brought her back up here."

"It's her home, Hattie. She was born here."

"Yes, she was born here, I don't care. She didn't ever much live around though."

The shopkeeper took the dollar bill offered.

"She lived down there in Brooklyn all those years with that Irish guy. You know, I can't remember her living here, can you?"

"Not really." Hattie handed out the change from the bill. "Well no, I can't remember her, only the stories, and they were wild and thick."

"Gossip."

"Maybe. I don't know. Lu's about my age, 'bout fifty. Lena left when Lu was five, six years old. I know Lena's sister, Mary, brought her up."

"Right, she sure did."

"Lena drove down with some Caugnawaga men from Montreal who were going to work in steel. Never heard from her again." She slammed the cash register shut.

"Not directly, Hattie. Heard *about* her."

"Yeah. Those men came back with some high tales. She was fast. Hittin' all the bars. Kept a lot of boys happy, they said."

"Right. *They* said. Probably gossip. I recall my mother saying Lena had a rough time when her Tom died. Guess there was a lotta love between those two."

"Maybe. Why you suppose Lu went to Brooklyn for her?"

"She was bad. No money, no man. Was in some kind of house getting sick." She pointed to her head and twirled her finger in the air. "Batty. Lu isn't the kind who'd let her own mother die in a place like that. Even that Lena had abandoned her. Lu's a good woman. Hasn't been easy on her all these years either. All those boys she had to raise after her own man died."

"Funny how he went hunting and never came back from the woods."

"Some hunter probably shot him for deer and left him to rot. Well, she's just got the one boy and Annie left. He'll never go now his own wife ran off. Suppose Lu thought her mother'd make good company."

"Suppose. Get a lotta berries?"

"Plenty. Gonna jam some, freeze some, and eat some tonight. Okay. Gotta get back for supper."

"Night!"

"Night," Mina called out and shut the screen door behind her.

III

Though it was late they were still at the table eating supper. Lulu cut a pork chop into little pieces for Annie who sulked in her chair, straining to avoid contact with her great-grandmother who stirred tea in a pot.

"Eat it up now." Lulu pushed the plate before the young girl. "Ma? More potatoes?"

Before Lena could reply, a knock was heard at the door which opened by itself. Mr. Peters stood within the threshold. He walked into the kitchen without bidding a good evening or an apology for obviously disturbing the meal. That was not like him at all. Mr. Peters never entered a house without invitation. Lulu was perplexed by his actions.

"Have a chair, Mr. Peters."

He commanded a chair next to Lena. "*Onkiakenro*," he said, glancing at his old childhood friend. "*Etsagnon!*" Lena didn't understand. She'd been forgetting her language.

"Feast?" Lulu asked the guest.

"*Etsagnon*," he repeated. "*Akoserakeh*-winter."

Lulu was perplexed. She didn't know what to say, how to respond.

Lena avoided his face, the lines which had crept into the brown skin now darker from the new sun. She poured tea into her cup, blew against the liquid, and then poured some into her saucer and sipped.

"*Akoserakeh*," he said again in a low voice.

"Been a hot day. We've been berry picking most of it." Lulu made some attempt at sociability even though she knew he wasn't listening to her. Instead, he took a pipe from his pocket, a pouch, filled with tobacco, lit it, drew a gulp of hot smoke and exhaled. Lulu urged Annie to eat her chop.

"Ma had a touch of sun. She's doing fine now."

Lena spilled tea on the tablecloth.

"Look what Gramma did."

"Hush. Gramma isn't feeling good."

Mr. Peters drew more smoke and blew a small puff to the right, another to the left, one puff was blown up and another was blown down.

"*Etsagnon,*" he said quietly.

"I don't understand." Lulu was not only perplexed but now nervous. Why a feast. And then, that moment, right now? When then?

His voice was dark as his flesh, deep and rich though gentle, soft as down. Though spoken quietly, the sounds filled the kitchen. His eyes danced and his black hair fell across his brow, making him appear a much younger man though he was certainly Lena's age. There was a black prominent mole to the side of his right eye and it drew Lulu's attention.

"Sure you won't..." She stopped from asking if he wouldn't take some tea. It wasn't the time. He hadn't come to socialize.

Lena grew fluttery, jittery. She rose from the table, excused herself, and wandered into the parlor.

"Ma's not been well since she came home."

The man nodded agreement.

"The move, the trip north, settling in, well, it's been hard on her."

"*Akoserakeh*-winter. It won't be long before snow will cover the fields."

He spoke to the air of the room, the corners of the poorly lighted kitchen, the dark windows glazed from the single light bulb hanging above the table.

"It'll stay long, this time."

Lulu was not only startled but now thoroughly upset. Had he gone batty too, like her mother.

"Dandelions are withering. The pretty weeds."

He pinched tobacco from his pouch and blew a sprinkle onto Lena's vacant chair. "Already the seeds fly on the morning breeze."

"Yes. Spring came fast, and summer goes fast. Corn is knee high in July. Got squash on the vines." She almost gurgled out words. "My beans aren't doing well." She rattled a forced conversation but received no appropriate response from Mr. Peters.

He took from his shirt pocket a small feather and placed it on the table.

"Blue-bird, blue-jay."

Lulu's nerves were decidedly on edge.

From another pocket-he seemed full of pockets-he drew out a pinch of soil, earth dark and rich, so rich it appeared a melon could sprout from its womb, the tiny mound that it was.

"Sweetgrass on the air."

"We've got to start cutting for baskets soon."

"Sweetgrass on the air," he repeated as though to remind himself, his remark not necessarily meant for Lulu. "I'll go." He stood, went to the parlor door, touched the wood frame and returned to the table. Glancing down at little Annie who sat frozen in fear, he again reached into a pocket and withdrew a small Kraft jam jar, unscrewed the lid, stuck his finger into the contents, sucked his finger dry, screwed the lid once more into place, and set it down upon the white tablecloth.

Lulu was quiet. She knew. In her own ageing bones she knew. Yes, she knew. *Etsagnon.* Outside, off in the distance she could hear men singing. Their voices raised on the early summer night, dark and heavy, solemn and penetrating, constant.

Mr. Peters stepped to the door, rattled the knob and walked into the night.

She stared at the jam jar. Just stared, hardly breathing. She stood and circled the table. Annie had stayed absolutely quiet. Now she broke into tears. "I'm tired. I wanna go to bed, Gramma,"

The singing stopped. The sound of a drum crossed the night, but only momentarily. Then the drum stopped too. Was silent.

"Can I go to bed?" That was strange coming from Annie who fought every night the eventual need to go to her bed.

"Yes, your father will be home soon. Yes, go to bed."

Annie commenced beating the cut up chop she hadn't eaten with her fork.

Lulu knew. Yes, she knew. Everyone knew but Lena, her mother. Maybe Lena did know. Maybe. She got Annie washed up for the night, into pajamas, and tucked under cool sheets. She strolled listlessly back into the kitchen where she cleared the table and washed the dishes at the sink. When that was finished and the dishes put up into the cupboard, she went to the parlor.

Her mother slept. Short staccato snores thumped the darkness. Lulu turned on a light, went to her mother's rocker, bent and kissed her on the cheek. "Oh," she exclaimed benignly, startled by her rash action. "I haven't kissed my mother's cheek since I was five years old. Not since she went away. Not since she . . . left me." She stared down on the sleeping old woman withering away into age, withering into greyness, whiteness. Her cheek and brow were as white as the tablecloth. She'd been out in the sun all morning and not a drop of color. This paleness wasn't natural. She spotted a blotch of red berry juice stuck hard in the old woman's white hair. "We missed some, Mama, when we washed you up." She smiled and left the parlor.

In the kitchen again she remembered the Kraft jam jar and picked it up. Slowly, hesitantly she unscrewed the lid. "*Yaikni.*" She raised the jar to her dry lips. "*Yaikni.*" She swallowed the strawberry juice.

Lena's snores ceased. She was deep into dreams.

"*Yaikni,*" Lulu repeated, and screwed the lid in place.

The night was quiet except for a fire-bug beating against the kitchen window. "*Yaikni,*" she breathed the word again, and again, "*Yaikni.*"

She slid into a chair and buried her face in the apron still bound around her waist.

The Hunter

Larry Littlebird

MAYBE IT WAS because I was a child and saw it that way, or maybe it really is the way I remember it, growing up in my mother's village.

It is fall. There is a special clarity in the way light appears at this time of year. And it gives my memory a sense of another time, a time when my young eyes can see beyond the haze and the world stands out, still, brilliant, and defined. In the fall, all talk and thoughts turn to hunting. As the stories of the deer and the hunter unfold detail by detail, in my child's mind, images of the deer appear and take shape.

They say the deer is a spirit. A creature of God's creation, it needs supplication, understanding, and reverence. It is a blessing, a gift bestowed upon humankind as a remembrance of our own life's interconnected course, an interwoven thread from the beginning of all living time. It is meat for the body and soul.

Endowed with a keen sense of sight, smell, and hearing plus additional uncanny abilities beyond human dimension, this creature cannot be simply slaughtered and used. The deer's realm is the pristine spaces of mountain and plain, its very domain is a sanctuary. Its essence is life; to kill it is to waste it.

This new and wondrous creature begins to occupy me, looming magnificently magnified and imagined in my thoughts as I roam mesas and arroyos playing, as I eat and sleep.

I want to be a hunter, one of the men afield in the fall, gun in hand, bandolier of shiny bullets around my waist, a bright red kerchief about my head. Can I be a man who will endure the rigors of the hunt? The all-night prayer and singing? A man who from daylight till sunset, without food, without drink, will evidence the stamina of a strong people? I wonder.

With a child's anticipation and delight, the fall evenings are spent around the little outdoor fires on the village edge waiting into the night for the signal that will tell everyone a hunter returns. For seeming nights on end, we wait until at last the bright orange spark that lights the shadow of the far southern hill sends me scurrying with the other boys and girls toward the only road by which the hunters will enter. Gathering excitedly at the road's edge, laughing and whispering, speculating about which party of men are returning, our noisy exuberance is suddenly cut silent. A low murmuring sounds from the far deep night. The joyous rise of men's voices singing their songs of the deer coming home to our village reaches us through the darkness.

Someday I will arrive home like these men, my face painted to signify my sacred purpose, greeted reverently by the people, blessed and made welcome. I dream of that day, but how?

One day my grandmother simply tells me, "Day by day, little by little, you will learn. Keep your eyes open, your mouth shut and become obedient to those in authority around you. Life is sacred to us, and you are sacred. You carry it in your heart the best you can. Treat all things as you want to be treated, then some day you will be ready." It is simple and I believe her. But I still want to kill a deer.

With a little boy's forgetfulness, these questions I ponder so seriously easily give way to other equally important concerns as the season passes. Will there be enough snow this year for my home-made sled I've worked so hard to find enough scrap boards to make? Will I ever learn to spin my brightly painted wooden top, whipping it off the tight string as accurately as my older cousin? Will my small frail hand ever grasp the correct grip on the beautiful glass marble that would allow me to win a few? The seasons come and go, invisibly blending one into another, and even though I still leave more marbles in the ring than fill my pockets, visions of the deer never quite leave me.

During this time I learn to use a home-made inner tube band slingshot until cans, bottles, even objects tossed into the air are accurately and consistently knocked down. After that, proficiency with a rifle comes easily. Even then, something tells me hunting is more than expertise with a weapon. Gradually, I am obsessed by one recurrent thought, "to kill a deer without wasting it."

The year of my first deer hunt, my uncles carefully instruct me on what a man does when he wants to hunt. I do as I am taught; I do it all correctly but I don't kill a deer.

"Killing a deer isn't everything to hunting," my uncles say. "Fasting and praying, a man works hard giving his self to the spirit the deer belongs to. We are only human, we cannot say what our giving should bring. Yes, we want badly to bring home that big buck; we can only work truthfully at doing that. The Creator will see our honesty; we must believe our reward will come about. There should be no disappointment."

Trying not to feel disappointed, I think all this over. I prepared so carefully-my rifle, my bullets, my actions, my thoughts, my prayers. Where am I at fault? Then I remember.

I remember that little boy sitting by the outdoor fires watching for the returning hunters. I remember what he felt in his heart when he saw the stripe-painted faces of the men arriving home from the deer's mountain sanctuary, their beings permeated with invisible blessings, strength, well-being.

I remember water that is made holy as the paint is washed from their faces by the women. I remember the little boy who is told to drink that sacred water. I remember eagerly drinking that murky brown liquid, the taste of sweet sediment in my mouth. The grown-ups laugh and make joking remarks but I drink it anyway because I believe them when they tell me it will make me a strong hunter. I feel my body shudder as the essence touches my young heart that wants only to be a hunter.

It is the desire to be a hunter who will not waste a deer's life that I remember. My feet have touched the mountains where deer live; I have breathed in the same air and drunk of their water. I've gotten close, yet no deer has come to my hungry gun. There is no fault. Had I killed a deer that first year, would I have recalled the little boy who wanted to be a hunter? Or remembered the child who believed the stories old men and old women tell in that other long ago time?

Surely, the deer is a spirit, and I must die if I am to be one. Day by day, little by little, as I embrace and struggle with this gift, my worldly desires must die, my physical needs must die. I must die to the selfish lusts that would entice my body and entrap my soul, until at last, unthinking and clear-eyes, innocent like a child, I am free to believe and know the secret pulsing in the hot flowing blood the hunter hunts. And, somewhere, the red living waters of the pure-eyed deer wait for me.

Coyote Meets Raven

Peter Blue Cloud

COYOTE WAS VISITING in British Columbia. "Hey," he asked, "do you people have guys like me around? Who's your local joker and doctor anyway?"

A Raven flew down and perched on Coyote's shoulder to croak out, "I am the greatest doctor there is or ever was! I am my own beginning and my own ending. Mine was the first voice ever!"

Coyote looked at the big black bird and said, "You sound just like the missionaries down to the south, but I'll take you at your word, and you can get off my shoulder now. You're kind of heavy, you know?"

"Too late! Too late! I've got your power in my belly now. You'll never again be what you used to be!"

"As long as you don't start yelling, 'Nevermore! Nevermore!' it's all okay with me," Coyote responded, studying the Raven and making plans. "Well," he said, "you're in your own country and have an advantage, but let's anyway have a power contest, okay? But let's do it friendly and play a handgame since I see that you people up here play the same gambling games we do down south."

And so they gambled for two days and a night. On the second night Coyote began growing bored and decided to leave his body and travel around. He left his gambling concentration in a hollow hallucination of empty skin and took off.

He walked down to the beach to be with the ocean. There at the beach's edge stood a huge totem pole. Atop the pole was a great bird like none other Coyote had ever seen. There was something about

120

the bird which drew him and he climbed up there for a closer look.

The Thunderbird was a sleeping power, a force awaiting its own time. It was transfixed in dreaming. Coyote sat way up there on a wing thinking of Raven and studying Thunderbird.

Well, he thought, as long as I am Coyote I might as well leave a trick behind me. Yes, I think I will sing Raven into this bird and leave him captured here. He's a good gambler, I'll have to admit, but I get the feeling that he thinks he's better than I am.

Coyote closed his eyes and began humming. His humming became words:

> Ho, ho, guts and blood,
> heh, heh, dreaming power.
> Raven, I call you.
> Raven, I sing you.
> Fly here to this place.
> Be captured here forever.
> Ho, ho, heh, heh, ho!

He was just beginning the third round of the four-round song when he heard a croaking laugh. He opened his eyes to the interruption. He no longer sat atop the Thunderbird; the Thunderbird sat upon him, its claws dug into his skull.

Only the beak of the Thunderbird moved when it spoke, still made of cedar and clattering. "Hah, you guessed it, I see. Yes, it is me, Raven. You have captured nothing but yourself for I am not to be captured." Then Raven continued his own song to lock Coyote into the totem.

And Coyote finished his power-capture song.

"Look down to the beach, Coyote. Don't you see a dozen of me down there feasting and talking?"

"Eating rotten fish and squawking, yes! But you are also captured in this pole. And look over there at that spruce tree up the hill. See that grey movement? That's Coyote!"

There was a roar from Thunderbird for that great creature had come to life. Its voice was that of howling winds and crashing waves.

"You miserable wretches! You pitiful, puny self-lovers! You punk lice living in the armpits of yourselves! How dare you disturb my meditation! Don't you know that I can end time by waking? No, of course you don't! And you probably don't even know that I helped create you! A mistake, I now see.

"I am going to make two lesser totems and put you side by side on them. I'm going to put each of you atop one, looking at the ocean and unable to see the other. Then you can argue into eternity.

"Perhaps you'll even learn to meditate and begin to know the beauty of Creation. And further, I'm going to make each of you a little bit like you might be someone else, maybe Eagle or Wolf.

"I will let you taste real beauty and power while keeping your puny egos intact.

"Coyote, when a part of you returns to the desert country, you'll find Raven and his nation waiting for you. And every time you hunt you will leave part of the feast for Raven. And Raven will thank you with the croaks and graws you find so discordant. Perhaps each of you will learn to live with and respect the other. Now go!"

And Thunderbird once again became a cedar meditation. And Raven and Coyote studied the ocean for many seasons, each sitting atop his own totem pole.

Coyote woke up in a dry wash north of Gallup. The cries of ravens had awoken him. "Coyote, Coyote, wake up, we are hungry! Wake up, Coyote!"

"I'm lean and I'm mean," said Coyote to no one in particular. He drank at a spring, then washed his face. He sat on a small hill to watch the sun rise. A raven perched close by and let out a tentative croak. Coyote opened his backpack and took out a can of pork and beans and a couple rounds of somewhat dried-out frybread. As he ate he threw some of the food to the raven.

They didn't speak to one another but grimaced each time their eyes met, giving looks which just might pass for smiles.

And we might add that to this very day...etc. But, we won't.

Stinkbug

Peter Blue Cloud

T HERE ARE MANY different kinds of bugs in this world,"
Coyote was telling his grandchildren. "Creation must be
partial to bugs because it made so many more than other creatures.

"Of course, bugs do have a lot in common with us: some are very
good-looking, some sort of good-looking, and there's even some
that smell kind of bad."

Coyote was so busy talking that he didn't notice a stinkbug right
close to his foot. "Just a minute," said the stinkbug. "Just because
you don't think you smell bad doesn't mean that other creatures
agree. Matter of fact, you, Coyote, smell kind of rank to me!

"And for another matter of fact, we stinkbugs kind of enjoy our
own smell."

Coyote couldn't argue with that and felt bad for what he'd said.
He wanted to get out of this story quickly.

Just then he heard the circular whisperings of Coyote Old
Woman stirring a basket of acorn mush. "Hear that?" he asked.
"Now there's something everyone understands. Why don't we all
go have some mush?"

Stinkbug liked the idea. He loved mush and gladly set aside
Coyote's recent insult. "Yes," he said, "I'd really liked to do that.
We stinkbugs love acorn mush, but it's very hard for us to grind the
meal, you know. We have to tie pebbles to our feet and stomp those
acorns for a long time."

Just then an acorn lying close by said bitterly and a bit acidly,
"And I suppose you creatures think us acorns enjoy being ground up

123

and stomped on? All we really want to do is to grow into saplings, you know."

Coyote thought that this story had gone on long enough and was even getting a bit confusing.

So he ended it, right here!

She Keeps The Dance Turning Like The Earth

Duane Niatum

I

REACHING A TELEPHONE booth that smells of urine and cigarette butts, he drops a dime into the slot, enjoys the sound of its fall, what it does to place and time. He draws a bird above a sea wave on the glass as he waits for an answer. He hears her say hello, wonders what she will be thinking as he tells her about the letter from his mother. He can see the men of his village throw their salmon net across the river as he speaks. Not far beyond the men is the willow clearing, the seven fires surrounding Thunderbird's totem-the presence that draws him closer to the one clear ceremony of his mind. He knows that he will have to visit his sister's grave. And he tells Rachel as the thought grows more persistent. He tells her that he will need to go alone; take a sweat-bath to clean himself of sorrow.

As if from the sky above the camas meadow, he hears from the other side of the valley, "I want to go with you..." But he says, not this time, and that he will call her in a day or two. At last, he seems to hear her say something about driving carefully on the freeway; how she has been a friend of Claire, but he is already far into the interior, into the forests of his ancestors, nearing the Klallam ground where his sister is buried. Slowly he becomes a mountain bird drifting beyond the Hoko River, in circles of sunlight and rain, growing as amber as the bones of his people. She says, "Don't forget that you're at war on the freeway." He thinks he answered, "Rachel, when are you not at war?" And then the wire is voiceless? He feels there will be many opportunities to reassure love when he returns. He steps back into the street, and to his car.

II

He had come to ask her why. *Sis, I'm slightly potted, and I'm sorry about it,* he whispers quietly, but he had to talk with her. *You know, you could've come to me, talked about whatever drove you here,* he told her. *Sis, I'm going mad trying to figure out why you didn't call or write. I'd have listened, held you close.* Stepping nearer to the stone, he stares into the mist. It is almost as if they are talking...

"Crow, help me! Moma says she doesn't love me. Wishes I'd hurry and run away! Can't stand the sight of me!"

"Claire, I told you she won't change. It's her way-forever."

"She's my mother, Crow. And yours!"

"Does that make her a saint? She's always been cruel and will wound you again. Call me a liar, but wait and see..."

"I can't turn away from her. I love her, and she loves me! She's my mother and I won't leave her."

"You can. Why not live with grandfather near the white fir village? You'll never hear her say, 'I love you...'"

He fights to be more calm He wants to console her some way. *Christ, you were my family! Together we outran the nightmare. You were quite critical of me once... remember? You said I hated life. Was too bitter, proud. Then one day you asked:* Why don't we take a vision quest into the mountains of First People? *We did. We followed the sun, moon, earth, river, heard tales of deer, bear, elk, and blue jay. So why did you leave the path of the old ways more depressed than when we entered? And I've good news. Rachel is helping me from falling into that cold trap of hate. Yes, she is showing me how to leave that childhood behind: get off that train that's going no where but back to the family ruins where I got on. Damn, I'm sorry. You know this. Sis, my mind's a wreck lately. Will I ever know why you stopped in mid-air?*

The shy bolt of a rabbit perhaps, from the underbrush, startles him. He has lived in the city where the senses are alien. He grows solemn, seeming to be lost to the wind among the madronas, over the river: the swallows chattering, the hawk echoing his longing in the blackening sky; movement everywhere. His family sits around the last fire, celebrating salmon's return. They sing for the long trek they must dream into the river bed at the beginning of the winter snows. Drumming for the moon's blessing, his wife and grandchildren, sitting under his cedar shield, Old Man of the forest beats the ceremony into the mossy earth. Crow sighs. He wishes his grandfather were still alive. He would tell him how to step in darkness. Yet these are the remains of Old Man's gifts; the bits and pieces that mark the zig-zag path to his solitude, the pulse of his grandfather's songs. And like the fern-shadowed creatures around him, he steps back into the evening's deep-orange twilight.

Sis, that was what you told me when I wouldn't admit you were right. When I wouldn't listen. And somehow, I broke the chaos wheel . . . and you went and killed yourself. That's all. Sure, I feel myself slipping over the edge. I can feel the earth shocks that never end. But don't tell me that's all there is. I can't deal with that. It's not enough. Hell, I'm your brother, and more than that-your friend, your gypsy-I was your life-long friend. I never ran out on you. You can believe that, Sis. Never, and if I see a way out a little longer, then you're going to be there too . . . for we did time in the same pit together, and that's a life chain. I promise. I'll never break it . . . because didn't you tell me this was the redskin's spring?

III

Crow stands looking at Rachel. He feels the gods have been kind. But he can see she is unhappy with him because of his brooding over Claire's death. He knows she has felt excluded from his world these past few weeks. Yet he is surprised, slightly disappointed at her impatience, especially since she has been living with him for several autumns and often shares in the way he works things out. He comes closer to her, looks beyond those shadows that are her doubts, into the field of her eyes, green as the full leaf moon, flaming with question, and speaks softly. "Please—come here and sit with me. Forgive. I think I'm really exhausted for the first time. Here, by the window, we'll watch the sun fall, hear the swallow dart in and out of the evening."

"No, Crow. You're avoiding me. It hurts."

"True, but not maliciously, and for a good reason."

"What's that?"

"Hey, that's a weird frown. You know as well as I."

"Two months. No, nearly three months, Crow."

Gathering energy from the silence, the moon in the alder branches outside, he searches for her hands, to hold them in the moment. Since she doesn't try to pull them away, he is confident. As long as the magic flows through their fingers, time will leave them the art in themselves.

Feeling awkward, he thinks. Will she share with him this secret? If he offers her a song? And replies.

"Rachel, why should we compete with the sparrow? 'The sun is the nomad of the moon,' it seems to say, 'and cherry blossoms will soon be on their way to meet the river and the stones.'"

Rachel looks away from him; speaks almost to herself. "I feel you're not living with me, Crow. You're like a ghost in our house. We've stopped doing things together, seeing friends, going places. Worse, we've stopped holding one another. I may leave you...."

She looks to see what his reaction will be and is about to continue when he answers.

"Okay. But I need a drink for this. Is there any wine left, sad eyes? In a few days. Just a little longer, Rachel. We'll find the center again."

"All right! Crow, you're impossible!"

"Sometimes I wish I were. Thanks. Want a sip? It feels good pressed to the lips."

"Have you heard anything I've said?"

He can see she is still apprehensive. He had hoped she could see his love for her passes through many colors, has as fine a grain as cedar, and is far from cold, and that Claire was not merely a sister, but a friend. He is sure she understands his absolute loyalty to the old chanters, the longhouse roots, is sympathetic, but her eyes suggest she is thinking: "But aren't you carrying this on a little too much like a redskinned Hamlet?" When it fades, he says, "Rachel, I see her face struggling to rise from the dirt. I see her peering up at me, panicked, as if to say, 'Did I stop the dance too soon?'"

Retreating from his gaze, she stands by the window where she picks up one of his clown figures that is part of a series of miniatures cast in bronze that are arranged on top of a nearby bookcase. This, he recalls, was his last work. She moves her hand over the torso; he can feel her hands touch him; his body quivers. They are her favorites and had inspired a recent essay. Her voice sounds tired, melancholic, yet, it is neither abstract, nor caustic.

"Crow, I too am sad. But she wouldn't want you to fall apart, throw *your* life into the river. She idolized you. You were big brother, the one who carved the scars into totems, rose from the street with both fists swinging, while never forgetting the beauty in the legends of your elders. She adored you for that. You can't allow the fatalism of some of your people to destroy this. You've your work. You're doing what you set out to do. You've had a well-received show. That's covering a lot of ground. And what about me? Our dream of sharing everything? Crow, I've feelings too. And I haven't done any research on the artbook for months."

Lost, he swims in her despair, sees the tears begin to fall, and is ashamed. She must be going over in her mind the things he has neglected lately, the unfinished pieces, the art fellowship. How his teacher's recommendation would almost guarantee the grant to travel abroad. How Paris, Rome, London would feed their new dreams and journals and many surprising things. And she might also be thinking of the way he runs, her favorite metaphor being like the elk who runs forever in the brush.

Searching for the dark oval of her face, he hopes to catch her eye. He asks her to roam with confidence down the road of his spirit, but her face is concealed behind the long blond curls of her hair. He tries to draw her back with his calling, as he passes with awe into her solitude, into the tall grass of herself.

"Beautiful woman, for you I'm going to find a butterfly in the woods that are my soul's first drawings. I swear it will form itself from the ash of my ancestors—very soon, very soon. I'm not sure about the rest...not sure at all. Meanwhile, can I have a cup of coffee to rattle the nerves?"

Playfully, but not hiding her irritation, she mimes his clownish gestures as he leaves for the kitchen.

"Funny, funny. Get me one too, Woody Allen of the Bella Bella!"

"Here. Quick, before it spills. I poured too much."

"Oops, hot, hot. Thanks. Crow?"

"Yes?"

"I miss her. I thought we were close friends."

"I know. In fact, was grateful. Happy. But, do you know what chases me down the night? Her death's brought me to my knees. I can't seem to hold things together. And I thought that kinetic spirit had everything for her. I don't understand. And I think I need to. Everytime I'm convinced I've buried the past—I mean the violent and ugly past that terrified us both as children—I see her dancing with those eyes that radiated love for the rhythms of the seasons, the moons, the body, the rainbow of her pleasures. Rachel, it's irony gone berserk! She danced before she walked! And it isn't right...twenty years old."

"No, it isn't. But your abandonment of me and your work won't bring her back and could push us apart, permanently. You must stop. I'm ready to scream, Crow."

He puts his arms around her shoulders and answers resignedly. "You look as beat as I feel. Why not go to bed and we'll talk tomorrow? After breakfast. Promise. We'll get it together, one way or another."

She runs to bed. He hears her crying before falling off to sleep. He sits by the window, not moving, thinking about what she said. What has happened since the letter arrived. Rubbing the sweat from his brow, he senses his anxiety about the promise. It sounds so definite; final. He hasn't thought in this manner for many years; and probably never will again. Whatever, he can no longer stand the suffering he has made her go through since he received the news. It is advancing near the quiet end; nearly one. He goes to the bed, covers her, kisses the side of her face, turns off the lamp, and returns to his chair by the window. He might have sat there for nearly an hour or two before deciding to take a walk along the river, drift into dawn like a reed.

He wanders the riverbank, stepping lightly over the broken grass and pebbles and bits of wood. The pieces are falling into place? At least, the planes are faintly recognizable for what they are? The lines have an end? And what are we to do with the drifts of form? And what about the colors in a maple leaf? He wonders if it is necessary to understand any of this. And why has his sister's death clipped his wings, broken his spirit, left him feeling like a hollow shell? And where did he first meet this new demon that turns his hands and heart to clay? This creature that tosses him around these nights like a scarecrow, he swore he had tricked years ago.

The fog that had settled in the valley begins to lift as he continues along the empty morning street. Standing on a small bridge, he seems to be drawing in deep breaths of the cold air. He looks into the oil-filmed water; notices his reflection rise toward him like a ghost. He shudders but does not turn away, or run. His childhood paddles across the thin mirror of the water like a procession of his years, wearing the masks that have haunted him in nightmares. It is now he knows an exorcism must be made. He owes it to Rachel, he believes, and himself. Maybe more importantly, to Claire's spirit dancing somewhere out there over the water, still turning like the earth. And this is what Rachel will hear in the morning.

As if settled by the wind, roaming through the ancient poplars, their undulant rhythms might be considered to accent his brisk steps, his return to the apartment. Within, at the center of his being, a strange creature starts to spiral its way out of him, somehow making his walk happy with anticipation. The change quickens the flight of his soul on its long journey home. Tomorrow, he tells the river, its trees and waterbirds, he will talk with Rachel and begin work on a series of new pieces. The first is to be called "Heron Growing Still With Winter." He will gamble on this impulse closing the moon on his past, when the bird from a darker marsh finds its home among the agate beaches of his life.

He met one other person on his walk. An old man who looked past and through him with a glance. He realized the old man, pillaging through the garbage, had discarded him with an arrogant shrug that was, without a doubt, grotesquely dignified; like the fight to live in one's skin, to be allowed to stay there. When he had greeted the elder with a wave of his arm, he almost forgot his sister's suicide, the raw image of her face floating in the water of his mind, her black eyes frozen with bewilderment, her hand reaching for his.

It was then something told him he would have to swim in the icy water. As he had neared the edge, he found himself chanting to the black feathers of his spirit. He wanted to be naked as it in the fog, and, as if the towering creature behind him was his father, he had leaped into the river to find the courage to carve crow's moon from the shield of his remaining life.

IV

Upon reaching the studio, he closes the door to the apartment and tiptoes to where Rachel lies sleeping. He sits down on a cushion beside the mattress. As he is taking off his clothes, his keys slip from his pocket to the floor. Rachel rolls over and lifts her sleepy-green eyes to his.

"Hello, darling, have you been up long? What's the time?"

"All night. Would you believe, it's about ten."

"Crow, when will it end?" He senses a reproach.

"Right now! And incredible Rachel, I ask that you please close your eyes, because the Muse and I have a surprise for you. We both believe you deserve it." He gets the cedar carving that is hidden beneath his coat on the chair. "Okay." When she notices the bird, she appears truly startled, as her eyes seem to dance in its form.

"Why, Crow, it's beautiful. When did you..."

"It's yours, Rachel. For staying up yourself last night, and all

those other nights! It's the beginning of a series. I start playing with
the clay tomorrow. It'll probably include six pieces in the suite. Oh,
do I want to carve. I feel it in my gut. It's a welcome old pain! An
elder I saw early this morning reminded me of what my grandfather
said when I was expelled from school one time for fighting and my
mother applauded the school. Do you remember?"

She shakes her head and smiles.

"Anyway, my grandfather said I should listen carefully to the
cedar spirit that guards the four directions out of the daily storms.
That I should bend in the wind as the heron bends. That because he
was very old, I was very young, and our village but a song—I should
give myself to the old myths; the animals and people waiting
beneath the bark. This did it. I can't believe it's so simple; macabre.
But there it is, so basic I could cry. Better yet—laugh. And laugh.
And laugh again! But let's quit talking because I'm anxious to raid
your nest, you sexy wench. Grr. Grr."

She winks, pulls the covers from her body. He laughs. "Nice,"
then pauses, more serious. "Rachel, this morning I watched the
ground beneath my feet give like water. The only order I know is
you. It's where I am. And I must live with it, since it's permanent.
Can you?"

For the first moment, in what he considers to be a lost season, she
searches for the small lodge of his soul, passes into the inner regions
of his eyes, and he is overjoyed to feel her hand run up and down
his spine.

"Crow, I couldn't wish for anything more."

He stands next to the bed, naked, and raises her arms to his
shoulders, drawing her to him. Speaking in whispers, he kisses her
hair, her eyes, her nose, finds her soft-moist mouth. He runs his lips
across her breasts, down the lean curves of her stomach, down into
her secret folds, as they begin to fall to the mattress. He desires more
than anything now to give her happiness, a fire in her head and loins
equal to his. He wants to feel her break into blossom.

The Sinh Of Niguudzagha

Mary Tall Mountain

NIGUUDZAGHA had been abroad since first light. He emerged silently from the stand of spruce and trudged along a small bridge of planks thrown down across the slough. The dark side of Graveyard Hill rose in front of him. Unhurriedly he climbed the long slanting path. His steps paused at intervals that he might rest and draw the sharp clean air deeply into his lungs. Strength flowed through his slender body and into the crevices of his brain. Here and there he stopped at a grave sunken beneath the grass, only its tilted wooden cross marking its presence. Names and images slipped through his mind, locking him so intensely into the past that it startled him when he found he had reached the crest of the Hill. The oldest gravehouses had fallen into scatters of boards and glass. Only the sturdiest remained. One of these stood at the point of the Hill, its corrugated iron walls leaning out to the river. At the roofpeak was nailed the large oval mirror of a bureau, the once ornate walnut frame buffeted and bleached white by storms. The glass was still intact. It flashed above the village like a watchful eye.

Wild rosebushes grew here, and the dry blossoms clung to bare stems. Niguudzagha stood motionless. With a stubby thumb he rubbed a rose into his palm and scattered its dust out on the wind. Parting the grasses, he came down upon the brow of the dome to the place where no graves were. He waited against the stillness of the Hill, his eyes lifted to the eastern rim of earth along which the mountains crouched like dark sleeping animals.

No-oy thrust his burning face out of the dark descent beyond the mountains.

A column of mist poured down the river, whitely muffling its broad curve. Far out in the Kaiyuh, little creeks swarmed in the meadows like coiled snakes. A moose stood haunch-deep in a lake, his immense antlered bulk a still, black speck. The waterways were filled with the distantly shrill commotion of feeding birds. A flurry of pale wings shaped itself roughly into a ladder, drifted south, and faded into enormous stretches of sky.

No-oy slipped higher with the imperceptible wheel of earth. His first blaze struck across the mist and lighted Niguudzagha's thick white hair. Niguudzagha lowered himself stiffly into a bowl of tamped-down grass curtained by weeds that rattled sparse and faint in small gusts of wind. *No-oy* pressed heat through the heavy red plaid of his mackinaw and he held out his hands. His lips moved. Heat crept steadily into his flesh.

Dew lay on the bark and plants he had gathered and heaped loosely in the sack at his belt. The sack was worn and stained with juices from the plants. He had knotted it of string in squares to let the green creatures breathe. Gently he touched a leaf of dock, sensing through the paper-thin skin of his fingertips the rushing life under its hairy surface. He sniffed the sharp scent and murmured a few words. Leaning forward in the dry nest, he tucked the sack under the weeds. Then he lay back and let the earth clasp his narrow bones.

He was the last medicine man.

Closing his eyes, he summoned *sinh*. After a time, *sinh* floated down to him. His vision subtly altered. Against the screen of his eyelids he saw the people coming out of their cabins to the river, tiny shapes in barest motion upon the fastnesses of the land. Their voices floated up, no louder than the piping of insects. He sent *sinh* wandering through Nulato village, and the faces passed before him with their secrets. Niguudzagha was the oldest among the people. There was nothing he did not know about them. In this was power, but he demanded nothing of it. All he desired had been given. He felt regret only that a portion was now lost to them of the ancient and harmonious balance between the worlds in which they moved.

Andrew's face came before him. His clear questioning gaze fixed

itself upon Niguudzagha's. Andrew, first son of Big Mike. His death
had come in the time of leaves falling. He had gone out to set net for
dog salmon. His canoe overturned. His faint shouts were heard from
the shore, and then was heard only the voice of the river. When his
friends reached the strong middle current, he was gone.

The people grieved because Niguudzagha could not peform the
ceremonies for Andrew as in old times. The priests had warned them
that to summon and speak with the *yeega'* of the dead in that manner
was an evil thing. But there was a yet more serious matter. Andrew
had gone into strange places and his wife and children could not lay
him in the family plot. They were terrified. His spirit was surely
lost. They implored Niguudzagha to find it. Having forseen, he
acquiesced. He performed the rite in the silence and secrecy of night
beneath the cold dark river.

He imparted these matters to Andrew in reassuring soft mutters
of Athabaskan. Andrew's face withdrew. Niguudzagha knew with a
rush of certainty that he had gone safely to his right place. His *yeega'*
roamed tranquil in the other world, much like this one except that
there, it was the time of big snow. About him, speaking familiarly,
the animals and birds attended him. He was set free of the other
spirits who prowled fearsomely upon the earth. A shadow curtain
had lifted from his senses, and he was one with the world above.

Creases of pleasure curved Niguudzagha's cheeks and he settled
deep into the nest. His old clawlike hands clasped and loosened. He
drifted slowly back to himself and was immediately seized by the
warmth of *No-oy*. Looking up, he spoke into the great blazing eye:
"Now it is made good."

Since his youth he had talked to *No-oy*. He was even then given
over to the things of earth. In the days of *esnaih,* when the band
followed the call of animals and birds and of the fish of the river, he
left the other children playing and wandered in lone places. As his
years increased, he passed hours considering the ways of the earth
and creatures. When he tired, his mind emptied of all but the great
land breathing about him. A day came when he realized he had been
lying on the ground engaged in speech with an alder tree.

At this Niguudzagha smiled, remembering that he had not feared that first messenger who would be one of his familiars. After his first speech with the alder, he ate and drank nothing for three days and kept silence as men did before the hunt. In the woods, fasting and faint, he sometimes fell down and lay unconscious. He awakened with a sense of having wandered timelessly in vast bright spaces beyond the world. He staggered when he stood. Incomprehensible words came from his lips. He began to fly out far above his mind, and crawling on his belly cried once to an unknown being: "Give me wisdom to counsel others!" When he emerged from the trance he did not know how he could have spoken so. It was the way elder persons talked.

Niguudzagha's mind flickered again to the people. Today they were in vital balance. Daily he assured himself of their well-being, for they were surrounded by the *yeega'* of unseen creatures. The mysteries, he thought, were beyond the small comprehension of any man. At certain seasons the spirits were honored in ceremonies by all the people gathered as one. He performed, alone with *sinh* and the lesser guides, other rites too potent for the telling. He never spoke of them, and never uttered the names of *yeega'*.

The people were loath to speak of these matters of the spirit world to the *Gisakk* priests. It was bad luck. *Yeega'* would be angered. But they confided, a little at a time and under subtle questioning. "Over us all is the Master of the world. Everything in the world is by him," they said. "He care about our game and fish. A man has to be careful. If he step on his catch or dirty it, it don't look right. It's like we don't care."

"One should never offend the giver of food, the avenger of waste?" one of the Fathers had asked Niguudzagha long ago.

Niguudzagha told him, "If we mistreat *yeega'*, then when the people are hard up, all this would come back and we would know we are being punished."

"You believe in God, then," the Father said.

With reluctance, Niguudzagha replied, "There is some Being who look down on us and see what we do. He is every place, but he has no name."

Now he scratched his head with a feeling of helplessness. He was sorry he had revealed this knowledge belonging to the people. But in a way, the Father seemed like another medicine man. Except for one thing. Niguudzagha had a persistent sense that he and the Father were not considered equals. Father wore a certain manner of authority. This went with the giving of orders, Niguudzagha thought. And only the Being of no name gave orders to the people until *Gisakk* came among them. As to himself, he knew he had always lived in the presence of the Being. This mysterious perception had been infused into him by the incessant dreams.

Gaagateeya', his grandfather, had understood. Grandfather was full of years and well accustomed to dreaming. One day he looked into the boy's face with eyes curtained by a white film. "Ah, Kuskaga!" he exclaimed.

That was Niguudzagha's name then, a name that meant harpoon for his parents had wished him to be keen and straight. The name had been worn by an ancestor deep in the past when the people lived by the sea. Kuskaga held himself utterly still for long periods, in the manner of the harpoon, waiting for that creature which he saw coming toward him in the watery, shifting shapes of the dreams.

The filmed eyes of Gaagateeya' wavered and Kuskaga thought they could see his face only as a blur. "You visit with the trees," Gaagateeya' said.

"Yes, my grandfather."

"You talk to trees?"

Kuskaga shuffled his feet restlessly. "They talk too," he said.

"Ahhh, my youngest son." Grandfather's white look glided out and fixed upon the gleam of *No-oy* dancing on the river. "You talk to any other?" The eyes shone purely, like dentalium shell.

"Many other." Kuskaga bent his head and studied the stones of the ground.

"Who?"

Hesitantly, "*Doyon . . . Nokinbaa . . . Ggaał . . . Dotson'* "*

"Oho!" Grandfather said. "These you dream?"

*Wolverine . . . Snowy Owl . . . King Salmon . . . Raven

"I don't know..." Kuskaga hesitated. "One time I talk to real *Dotson'* on a tree!"

"Oh, that fellow! What did he say?"

"He tell me I have to wait, that's all."

With a smile, Grandfather said, "You get scared and nervous, yah?"

"All the time," Kuskaga admitted.

Grandfather's eyes closed. After a while he said, "That's good." He pulled Kuskaga to his knee. "You have fourteen years now, isn't it? Always you wait for something and you wonder what is that thing. Now I tell you. You will be medicine man, I think."

Kuskaga's breath caught, and his mind circled among all he had seen and heard. At last he had received an answer to the endless puzzle of his mysterious actions. His chest tightened. "How can this be?"

"All these creatures are your helpers," Grandfather said. "They bring big message. First you will learn all about our people and the land we walk upon here. You will know animals and their *yeega'*. At a time when it is right, your *sinh* will come. When that happens, you will go far out of yourself. And you will be medicine man. But you will learn more. You will know the secret language of *sinh*. You will make *yeega'* songs and sing to game and fish. Then you will pass under the river."

At this, Kuskaga shivered. He gasped, thinking: I dream too much. I have no strength. How can I do medicine man's work?

Grandfather smiled. His broad front teeth protruded, a wide space at each side like Beaver's. Kuskaga remembered with a shock that Grandfather was a medicine man of the old time. He had been named Gaagateeya' for Beaver, the builder. He passed under the river like Beaver.

Now Grandfather became animated. His voice came forth powerfully. "You will get strong and well, and you will lose fear. You will cure and counsel. All will come, if it is to be. It is a gift of the Being." His small bright face glowed toward his grandson.

Instantly Kuskaga knew Grandfather had heard his thought.

"I see you remember I make medicine before," Grandfather

continued. "I just wait for you to get ready. I perceive much, youngest son."

Kuskaga stared at him. "Oh! You see with blind eyes?"

Gaagateeya' nodded. "Not just this place I see, but others. Where I may wish to be, I'm there." He raised his hand.

An exquisite pain flashed through Kuskaga's being. A breath of sudden wind stirred his hair. All about was a fluttering of wings and the raucous warning cries of *Dotson'*. A cloud drew across *No-oy's* face. Two feral eyes glowed in the darkened air, and Kuskaga hid his face behind his arm.

He felt himself return from an infinite distance.

"You see?" Grandfather said.

Kuskaga entered another condition. His dreams began to shift and change. Sometimes he took the shape of *Doyon*, and grunting, clawed the earth in rage. Once he went into the body of *Nokinbaa* and saw tiny scurrying moles and lemmings with such clarity that he felt an intense blood hunger.

He perceived ever more deeply into the meanings of his calling. Constantly he was accompanied by the cries of birds and the shuffling whirr of their wings. He prowled for miles back into the empty tundra, acquiring knowledge of the spirit of night and discerning the ways of its living things.

Gaagateeya' endlessly instructed his youngest son.

Kuskaga's face grew a solemnity that was transformed in rare moments by a great belly laugh that shook the length of his frame. He loomed skyward and his ebony eyes gazed down at Grandfather from his new height. The hollows between his ribs filled and he became lean and solid with muscle. The child's nervousness was replaced by a deepening serenity. He was nineteen when one day Gaagateeya' called him. Grandfather wore a look of pride that he quickly hid. His head came painfully erect between his crooked shoulders. "I call you youngest son no more," he said in the soft tones of Athabaskan.

Kuskaga squatted before him, his slim bronzed face intent. He fixed each detail of Grandfather's person solidly into his memory.

"Now I can teach you nothing."

"Ahhh," Kuskaga breathed.

"You must learn the rest of your part alone."

Kuskaga's *yeega'* was heavy. He stared at Grandfather's hands lying idle on his thighs, and he laid his own big hand over them. He felt the small knobs grown upon the ends of the fingers with a thrill of regret mingled with tenderness. Standing, he opened his *yeega'* to the powerful current that passed from Grandfather's *yeega'* into him. In silence he turned and strode away on the boardwalk. He felt the eyes of pearl gleaming behind him.

Only a few days later, in the early dusk of the month of freeze-up, Kuskaga sat on a log among dark spruce trees. Snow sifted lightly from their branches. The forest grew still, and the silence tensed all around. His nerves and muscles gathered and he quivered with anticipation.

There was a swift breath of wings upon his face.

And he passed profoundly into another place. He was almost dreaming, yet not wholly; it was more than dream: it was an endless thought in an absence of time, a slow flood carrying him to the center of existence. He flowed upon it, weightless.

The brown head appeared. An ivory disc of minute feathers lay flat around the immense yellow-moon eye with its fixed black pupil, staring past him. Now he glimpsed the beak, an ebony hook resting in the bronze breast overlaid with delicate creamy stripes blending into a body of dappled rust. Below, he saw the pale ruffled boots, and at last the merciless shining black talons, curled around a dead willow branch.

Suddenly feathers rippled and stood out. The talons shifted. The intricate tail feathers quivered. The brown head turned full to him. The ear tufts lifted high over the eyes, the eyes that dilated to unbearable intensity.

Great Horned Owl was asking a question.

Will you choose? came the words into Kuskaga's mind.

His larynx bobbed wildly in his throat. His fingers groped forward and dabbed at the exquisite feathers of the breast. Owl sidled away on the branch.

Tell Sinh. What do you want? Again the deep voice filled Kuskaga's mind. His mouth was full of dryness and he swallowed again. He was made dumb by the hammering of his heart.

Ho-hohoo ho ho - ho-hohoo ho ho. Often before, he had listened to the low call of Owl, but now his hearing had become painfully acute. The beak opened, and the hoots, pitched more loudly, hummed through him like the singing of a fine wire. Fierce yellow eyes flashed shut and open, and he saw their clean surfaces, flat as glass.

I call you Niguudzagha now. The voice was as sad as a mourning chant.

He perceived he had been in this place with Owl many times, grieving for the past, for the future of the people. With a flash of foreknowledge he envisioned all the smothered griefs of living. He endured upon his *yeega'* the weight of years falling with the force of a blow. It was too great. His tears fell, and he saw the wind spirit rising, the blowing snow.

Owl blinked rapidly. *Take my name, Niguudzagha.*

Ahhh. He had known these words by some means, unearthly it might be, in dreams or in another time. They were so familiar he had not recognized them for the words he had awaited all his life. There was an instant clamor of roaring, grunting and squawking from unseen presences all around. He shivered with the chill of their malice.

"Yes! It is my name. I claim it!"

As soon as he said the words, the din faded.

His head came up and he looked directly into the yellow eyes and he went closer, and closer, until he lay small and flat against Owl's enormous eye. He was plunged instantly into a vast and fiery brilliance. There came a rush more swift than wind. He entered the immense round darkness behind the eye of Owl.

He was naked in the place of no light, falling past the jagged walls of an abyss. Lightning streaked around him. Talons lifted him high and laid him belly down on the wings of Owl. They spiralled up toward a far splash of light. It grew larger and there appeared two towering dark cliffs whose feet stood in a river beside the colossal bones of ancient animals. The cliffs moved rumbling toward each other. Owl swooped through the narrowing gap, and it crashed shut. A bellow of fury echoed from the river as they emerged into a grove of alders.

Owl turned his head with a steady stare. There is the Woman, he muttered. She paced forward in a robe of feathers, gazing with a single eye of many flashing facets. In them was mirrored the dancing universe. Silently she offered him a basket glittering with gold and another, heaped with bitter bark. He grasped the basket of bark.

Smiling, the Woman thrust a harpoon straight through his heart, impaling him upon the back of Owl. The harpoon flew to his hand and he hurled it into the sky. Chanting in a new tongue, he flattened himself again upon Owl's mighty feathers, and everything fell away as they flew out over the cliffs of darkness.

His mind hummed: *Niguudzagha.* He was lying in a drift of snow. The dawn gaze of *No-oy* slanted through the spruces and found his eyes. He sat straight up. Sweat wadded his parka. "Medicine man." Now he uttered the words, savoring their sound. Bending his knees he stared meditatively at his boots. A set of deep scratches lay in the short dense reindeer hair of the calf of each boot.

And he remembered the flight.

He sat bemused. Gradually he was aware of an object lying beside him. Taking it up in delicate fingers, he blew away the dust of snow. It was only a small bundle. He held it, feeling for its *yeega'.* It was gentle, reassuring, and there was in it a true goodness. He opened the packet of pearly sealgut. It loosed familiar creatures' fur smells. Now that one was the fine curled feather of *Nikinbaa,* and here were two glossy feather of *Dotson'.* These tufts were the stiff hairs of *Midziy,* the reindeer, plucked from his beard. And this was a piece of the white backbone of Ggaał! Ahhh! This was the amulet of the creatures of his dreams!

"I am Niguudzagha," he shouted, jumping to his feet. He started to dance. He was surely going to burst right out of his body! Then he thought of Owl. There was the clear sense of his voice, coming again as it had in his dream. Or was it a dream?

This is your amulet. Great Horned Owl is your Sinh. You have taken his name. The splendid words rolled around him as a shower of snow fell on his hair and he saw the whipping shadows of rising wings.

Now Niguudzagha returned slowly from his reflections. His body lay flat and quiescent in the nest. His slitted eyes idly watched the play of *No-oy* who, halfway up the sky, flicked fingers of light through the clouds. The shadow of a reed fell across Niguudzagha's face. After these many years he had acquired a resemblance to Owl. It was chiefly in the fierce gaze of his black eyes. The dense white brows protruded like ear tufts, although they grew long and he had to cut them with his knife. His head with its full shock of hair was shaped like the round feathered skull of Owl. His bones were fine and almost as fragile as Owl's, and his loose garments had the layered appearance of plumage.

Unsteadily he got to his feet and swayed until his balance returned. He yawned gustily and stretched his arms to the sky like curved wings. He inched down the crooked trail that clung to the face of the Hill, hooking his powerful toes like talons.

He could have made the descent in the dark.

Hawk's Flight:
An American Fable

Gerald Haslam

AWAKE EARLY, he had crept sleepily up the gully to relieve himself. He was not yet old enough to stand guard, and on mornings like this he was grateful to be sleeping inside beneath warm robes. There had been no one visible when he started up the gully, so he hadn't walked as far from home as usual. Still he walked too far. Savages leapt upon him before he could shout a warning and, in the instant before he was beaten unconscious, he realized fully it was the attack they had for so long dreaded.

He vaguely perceived that morning, yet through haze he heard shouts and screams from his village, frenzied yips of savages, pops and cracks of rifles. A child flashed up the gully past him with a mounted savage behind her. In a moment there was a scream, then the horseman rode back down the gully breathing hard. Painfully turning his head, he saw where the girl lay, her crushed head in a pool of blood, her tiny features stunned and askew.

Struggling to rise, he glimpsed, before collapsing, men trying to defend their families—his own father perhaps—and he caught the hot leer of one savage's eye. He knew he was done, that everyone was done, as he slipped back into the void.

How many hours or days or weeks they dragged him, leather thong round his neck, he could not say. He had stumbled and staggered barefoot over rocky ground for endless miles. When he fell, they jerked him until he was unconscious from choking, but

145

always stopped to revive him just in time to deny him merciful
death. Yet he was dead; he had died with his family back at the
village. Only his body lived.

They dragged him finally into their compound where villagers beat
and spat upon him. Children threw rocks at him, shouting in their
incomprehensible tongue. He did not have to know their words to
understand what they said. He was taken before their chief, a small,
decorated man. There was a good deal of loud talk, again
incomprehensible, then he was forced into a small wooden hut.

He needed water; he needed food; he needed rest. Lying painfully
on a grass-covered corner of the hut, sleep came to him finally in the
heat of the day. And he lived again in his dreams: Hawk flew wind
away from the savages toward the hills where his people lay rotting;
his mother and father and sisters and brothers waved to him as he
flew beyond them toward Sacred Spring.

Before the Spring, he knelt and asked what his people had done
that their homeland should be invaded by savages. But Sacred
Spring did not answer. Are we to submit? he asked, incredulous. Are
we to not fight back? The Spring gurgled, then belched forth red:
blood flowed from wounded Earth. But I am only one, he said, and
not even a warrior. Become a warrior, ordered Sacred Spring. I
have no weapons, he said. Then it came to him: he was Hawk and he
had the wind.

He awoke to find a cup of water and a metal plate with a few
pieces of dried meat and hard bread on it. He wanted to bolt the
food, but Hawk's battered face made chewing difficult, so he broke
both meat and bread into tiny pieces which he softened in his mouth,
then swallowed. Just as he finished his meal, he heard voices outside
the hut, and gruff laughter. There was one small, low window in the
dark hovel and suddenly a stream of urine sprayed through it. The
laughter grew louder, some words were shouted, then the voices
grew faint. Hawk peered out the window and saw three of the
savage warriors striding away, their blue uniforms dark as death
over the bright earth of the compound.

It was nearly night when several blue warriors threw open the door of his hut and pulled him out. Prodded to their chief again, Hawk felt strengthened from the food and able to breathe and draw life from the air. This time there were other human beings present, though they were of a rival clan. As the pale chief spoke, one of the human beings said to Hawk: "Now listen to this. I will tell you what their chief says." The man spoke poorly, but at least he could be understood. "The white chief says you and your clan have hurt many of his warriors. He says you are dangerous vermin. He says you must be an example. He says they will pull your neck with a rope until you are dead. He says their god will protect you." The human being who was not of his clan could not resist a comment of his own: "You and yours are lice," he added.

Hawk turned to face the other human being. "At least we have not become savages," he spat, and the other human being was ashamed and angry. He knew that Hawk, a boy not yet a warrior, had bested him. He said something to a savage in the strange tongue, and the blue warrior struck Hawk hard across the face. The other human being was even more ashamed when Hawk did not flinch.

Back in the wooden hovel, the boy again curled on the grass to sleep. His face hurt badly where the savage had struck him. He could neither open nor close his mouth. His head pulsed with pain each time his heart beat. He could not sleep and was sitting up when a very pale young savage visited him, accompanied by blue warriors. The savage held two pieces of wood tied together to represent the four sacred directions. The direction stick told Hawk that the savage was a shaman. So Hawk listened respectfully to words he could not understand while the pale shaman gestured and babbled. When the savage finally quieted, Hawk mumbled no, only that. The pale savage seemed to understand, and departed. He had been a weak shaman with no real power.

Hawk found himself feeling a strange kind of pity for these hopeless creatures who possessed no magic at all, no union with Earth or Sky, only the ability to hurt and kill. He could not even hate such creatures for they were beneath hate. They were sad and dangerous like a broken rattlesnake thrashing around wildly to kill

whatever neared it because it could not save itself. They had great
skill at destruction, but he could sense no life force in them.

Hawk flew wind again that night, flew high to the zenith where
Old Man of the Ancients resided; Old Man was growing impatient
with the savages. Hawk flew to the nadir and Earth Mother wept
angrily over her torn land and dead children. It was a bad dream
because the savages killed everything and everyone. And, in the
instant before he awoke, the shattered, bleeding face of the little girl
he had seen in the gully flooded him. It was a very bad dream, for he
knew he must kill a savage.

They came for him early next morning, a mass of blue-shirted
savages who bound his arms with leather straps, then led him around
a building into a square where it seemed all the pale villagers were
gathered around a wooden platform. As he was thrust up the steps,
he saw a rope—a rope for pulling his neck—draped over a cross-
beam. Hawk was placed beneath the rope and the savages' chief stood
at the front of the platform and spoke loudly to his people. At the same
time, the wan shaman stood directly in front of Hawk, muttering
tensely and senselessly into his face, holding his sticks in one hand.
Another savage knelt behind Hawk and began to bind his legs.
Hawk knew it was time, and he repeated to himself a warrior's song
he had been learning as part of his training:

> Let us see, is this real,
> Let us see, is this real,
> This life I am living?
> You Powers who dwell everywhere,
> Let us see, is this real,
> This life I am living?

He leaned forward and bit the shaman's pallid white nose, at the
same time kicking the man who sought to bind his legs. Then Hawk
darted across the platform and kicked the startled chief behind a
knee and the enemy leader crumpled directly in front of him. One
more kick with all his leg behind it and Hawk felt the pale chief's
head crumple. He had killed the savages' leader.

From all around him, blue savages fired their weapons, yet Hawk stood straight and tall, making no attempt to flee or dodge. Bullets smashed into his body, but they were too slow, for Hawk flew wind once more, high over the frantic scene and away, over plains and deserts, over brooding hills, over bleeding Sacred Spring. And Sacred Spring called to him as he soared: "Ho Warrior!"

A Dream Of Grand Junction

Wilma Elizabeth McDaniel

LEE ROY HICKS threw his winter cap and fleece-lined jacket in the corner of the front room and announced angrily, "There ain't one squirrel left in Barker Pasture. I cain't blame it on old Fife. He'd tree 'em if they was there."

He went to the potbellied heater and warmed his rough red hands, and looked toward the table in the end of the room.

His wife was patching a pair of overalls. She said in a high-pitched voice, "I spect you're hungry," then added, "there's some fried squirrel left from breakfast and a few biscuits."

Lee Roy looked hard at the pale woman who had been his wife for fifteen years. On their wedding anniversary, which he hadn't remembered, she said shyly, "Well, I've been married half my life."

Now, he told himself, she looked fifty, not thirty.

He cleared his throat. "Yeah, I figured that there would be some squirrel on the table. It would be a miracle if there was anything else."

He went to a washstand, poured water into a basin, and scrubbed his hands with lye soap. He wiped them on a floursack towel, observing, "My hands are as raw as beef. I sure need some gloves."

He sat down at the table, paused before turning over the upside down graniteware plate. He looked toward his wife with some embarrassment and said defensively, "You're the one that does the prayin' before we eat."

Nadine glanced up. "The Lord knows if you are thankful, whether you say anything about it."

"But you think I should say somethin' out loud, don't you?"

Lee Roy speared a piece of cold squirrel and began to munch on it. He took alternate bites from a large, cold biscuit, filling his mouth full, and chewed with mounting satisfaction.

He was on his second biscuit when they heard voices outside. He swallowed and said, "I bet you that's Rayda and Roleen. They probably got a letter from Grand Junction they want us to read."

The door was pushed open and Lee Roy's twin sisters rushed inside breathlessly.

They were husky ten year olds, with inflammatory black eyes and strong buck teeth, Rayda being the more forward and talkative.

She pulled off a warm stocking cap and handed Lee Roy an envelope. "Lee Roy, Justus is gonna work on a ranch that grows sugar beets. Don't that sound funny? We never seen a sugar beet in Oklahoma."

Lee Roy removed a sheet of lined paper from the envelope and read, "Dear Papa and Mama, we better write you as you will wonder what has happened to us. We moved since I wrote last. I got me a job on a sugar beet ranch, with my own house. Sure beats living in town paying rent. It is cold up here, but kind of dry cold and pretty nice. You tell old Lee Roy, if he was here we would have a good time. I bet he is hunting squirrels about now. Well, not too much news, Arta and the kids are well. Kiss the twins for me. Love to you all, Your son Justus."

Lee Roy paused and looked across the room at Nadine. He said, as if he could cry any minute, "I'd give anything in this world if I could be up there in Grand Junction with Justus."

Roleen asked, "Why did Justus move away from Depew anyway? We don't have no folks up in Colorado do we?"

Nadine finished patching the overalls, and laid them across the back of a rope-bottomed chair. She answered Roleen, "Honey, Justus never was satisfied to let things stay the way they was. He was half the size of other men in his body and twice their size in his mind."

Lee Roy reflected, "He done everything better than anyone else, even salutin' the flag at Green Ridge School. Mrs. Goad used to let him lead us."

He added, "He done it like he meant it."

Nadine recalled, "He was always a patriotic boy. I remember him singin' The Battle Hymn of the Republic with tears in his eyes."

Rayda looked intently at Lee Roy and asked, "Lee Roy, what makes you different from Justus?"

Nadine saw Lee Roy's face flinch with emotion. She said, "Lee Roy works more with his hands than his head," and got up from her chair.

She went to the stove and lifted the lid and said, "The fire's gettin' low. I'll chunk it up and boil over the coffee grounds."

The girls became restless. Rayda told Roleen, "Come on, let's go home. I want to see how old Prissy is doin' with her pups."

They left the house as abruptly as they had arrived.

Shamrock Road

Wilma Elizabeth McDaniel

I T WAS THE most beautiful road in the entire world. It had to be. I first saw it when I was three years old, comparatively fresh from the hands of the Creator. For the next three years, I lived beside it, or rather, mostly on it. Our tall unpainted sharecrop house was simply a last resort-refuge from torrential rain or pitch darkness.

Since my chores were light, feeding the cats and scattering corn to the chickens, I was able to be out on my beloved road early each morning. Looking east, I could follow its course to Preacher Owen's log house which sat off to the left. The road sloped down from that point and disappeared into a small valley, only to reappear at the top of a seemingly distant hill. There, it merged squarely with the Oklahoma sky. For two years, I believed that the road ran on until it actually touched the sky, and ended there. My theory was blasted when our brother Vernon drove us up the hill in a steaming, lurching Model T Ford. The road led to a tiny town called Shamrock, but the sky stretched on before us endlessly. I asked Vernon if it was the same sky that they had out in Oregon where our great Uncle Henry Finster lived. He said that it was the same sky all over the world.

This was the first of a series in disillusionment that I was to experience very early. The second was that people on my magic road had to be keenly concerned with whatever it took to put food in their stomachs. Gardens were vitally important, especially crops of corn and potatoes to provide cornmeal and the every day staple of fried potatoes.

The second summer on the road produced a bumper crop of potatoes from great shiney plants, and an equal amount of insects bent on eating their share. Papa didn't know anything about ecology, that ladybugs were a definite asset to gardens. He gave me an empty Prince Albert tobacco can and told me to pick as many ladybugs as I could. I parted the leaves and picked off dozens of the brilliantly colored bugs. The soil of the furrows was deliciously cool to my feet. I picked on. The ladybugs were dear to me; somehow, a few independent types escaped from the can before I could close the lid and soared away. When Papa returned from the barnyard, he took my can and dumped its contents into an old lard bucket. He doused the teeming bugs liberally with kerosene from a jug, saying that would take care of them. It wrung my heart. After Papa went about his work, I picked off a few magnificent green cabbage worms and privately relocated them in a lush spot under the berry vines. It had been a bitter lesson in survival.

Still, those very early years on the road were much like the first days after Creation as it was depicted in the Sunday School cards. I could know nothing of the ugliness and past failures of the human race that had preceded me. I had no reason to fear the future.

Egg Boat

Nora Dauenhauer

IN THE FALL of every year Qeixwnei and her family went trolling for coho salmon. The season for trolling usually opened mid-summer and the run became intense toward the end of the cannery season when the whole family went to the cannery to earn their money. Her father seined for the canning company while her Aunty Anny and sometimes her mother worked processing the catch from the salmon seiners. Because they worked for the cannery, they lived the summer season in the company houses.

Some years the catch of salmon seiners began to decrease before the seining season came to an end, but around this time coho trolling began to pick up. In order to get in on the favorable runs when the salmon began to migrate to the rivers for spawning, trollers had to be ready.

This was one of the times they were going to go fishing early. Her father had observed on their last trip that there were signs of coho, but he wasn't catching too much salmon in his seine. So he stripped his seine off the boat and began to replace it with trolling gear.

While Pop prepared the gas boat for trolling, the rest of the family packed their belongings from the company houses and transferred them to the boat. Everyone helped get everything aboard.

Mom packed things from their house while Grandma and Aunty packed things from theirs. Qeixwnei and her younger brothers and sisters carried things they could carry easily, and the little ones carried things like pots and pans.

The older boys were big enough to help their father get the boat gassed up and get fresh water for the trip. So they had plenty to do, too, beside helping Grandma and Aunty pack their belongings down to the boat.

When the New Anny was finally ready, they left port in the early afternoon and headed toward Point Adolfus. The tide was going out, and they got on the right current which would carry them fast.

It was on a similar tide the previous year while they were coming to Hoonah from Cape Spencer that Qeixwnei's father spotted a little square-ended rowboat floating on the icy straits water. He picked it up and he and the boys put it on the deck of the boat. They had it on deck when they stopped in Hoonah. Everyone saw it and commented on what a nice boat it was. Everyone noticed it wasn't one of the family's rowboats. When they arrived in Juneau, people noticed it too but no one claimed it. There wasn't a fisherman who didn't know another fisherman or about another's boat and no one knew who the boat belonged to.

So, Pop brought the boat up on the beach at their home at Marks Trail and started to work on it. He checked the boards to see if they were strong enough to hold the new materials he was going to apply to it and found that indeed it was strong enough and would hold them.

He began to renew it by stripping the old paint off. Then he caulked up the seams and finally put on some green paint left over from some other boat that had been painted before. He put a pair of oars in that didn't quite match. He tied an old piece of manila rope on the bow that could be used to tie it up with.

It was a good-looking boat. It looked just like the flower chalice of a skunk cabbage. And when he tried it, it had balance. It glided across the water very nicely. It was almost as wide as it was long. It was almost round and because it looked like an egg shell, they called it "Egg Boat."

Qeixwnei liked it very much and wanted to try it. She thought the boat was so cute. But when her father told her it was hers, she thought it was the most beautiful boat she had ever seen.

Her own boat! Why, she thought that it was going to be for one of her brothers. She could hardly believe the boat was hers. She was so happy she went around day-dreaming about it for the longest time.

Now that she had her own boat it meant she could go fishing on her own boat alongside her brothers, Aunty, and Grandma all by herself. It also meant she might catch a record-breaking salmon that she would fight for so long that she would get exhausted from just the thought of it.

Or perhaps she and her Aunty and Grandma would hit a school of fish like she heard some fishing people talk about. She would fill up her little boat, empty it, then go back out and fill it again.

Or perhaps she would catch her first king salmon, and she wouldn't care what size it was just as long as it was a king.

Her rowboat took her through many adventures during her day-dreaming. How exciting the next coho season was going to be. She was so happy.

And now they were actually going to the fishing ground. The boat moved along at a good speed. They all worked on their gear, giving it a last minute check for weak spots and sections that needed replacements.

Mom steered the boat while Pop checked the tackle he would use on the big boat. She ran the boat a lot, taking over completely, especially when Pop had to do work on the deck or started catching a lot of salmon. Sometimes she even engineered. There was no pilot house control, so Pop would ring a bell to signal "slow," "fast," "neutral," "backwater," and so forth.

The boys were playing some kind of a game on deck. They said their gear was ready. Qeixwnei's Aunty wound her line onto her wooden fishing wheel. Grandma was taking a nap. She had been ready for quite some time. She was always ready for things.

As for Qeixwnei, she had her tackle that her Aunty had helped her get together from discarded gear left by various members of the family. She and her Aunty had made a line for her while she was still fishing in her Aunty's rowboat. Her spinner was the one her father had made for her the previous year from a discarded spoon. It was brass metal.

Her herring hook, however, was brand new. It was the one her Aunty had given her for her own. She was ready to fish, completely outfitted with the rubber boots her brother loaned her that were slightly too large.

She was so excited she could hardly eat. The family teased her that she was probably fasting for the record-breaking salmon.

When they finally got near enough to see the fishing ground, there were a lot of power boats trolling and others were anchored. A lot of the hand trolling fleet was there too. Some of the hand trollers lived in tents out at Point Adolfus for the duration of the summer. When there were no salmon the fishing people smoked halibut they jigged from the bay over past Point Adolfus. Some of the people were relatives of the family.

When they finally reached the fishing ground, everyone was anxious to get out and fish. They all took turns jumping into their boats while Pop and the two boys held the rowboats for them while the big boat was still moving along.

Grandma went first, then Aunty Anny, then at last Qeixwnei's turn came. The boys followed in the power skiff that was converted from a tender boat from seining.

They immediately began to troll. Grandma and Aunty Anny went close to the kelp beds along the shore line. The boys stayed just on the outside of the kelp while Qeizwnei was all over the place place and sometimes dragging the bottom.

She didn't even know where her father, mother, sister and brothers were. She didn't notice a thing–just that she was going to catch her own salmon. Every time she dragged the bottom she was sure she had a strike.

Evening came and people began to go to their own ports. Grandma and Aunty waited for Qeixwnei for such a long time they thought she wasn't coming in for that night. When they finally got her to come along with them to go back to New Anny, all of a sudden she realized it was near dark and uneasiness came on her.

She had completely forgotten all about the kooshdaa qaa stories she had heard, where the Land Otter Man came and took people who were near drowning and kept them captive as one of them. She quickly pulled up her line and came along with her Grandma and Aunty Anny.

Everyone had caught salmon except Qeixwnei. It was so disappointing, especially when her brothers teased her about being skunked by saying, "Where's your big salmon, Qeixwnei?" The rest of the family said she would probably catch one the next day and she shouldn't worry. She slept very little that night. Maybe she never ever was going to catch a salmon at all.

The next day the fish buyer who anchored his scow said that there were fish showing up at Home Shore and that he was going over there to buy fish on his tender.

Pop pulled up the anchor to start off for Home Shore. But half way between Point Adolfus and Home Shore, the boat started to rock back and forth from a storm that had just started to blow. Chatham Strait was stuffed with dark clouds and rain. So they had to make a run for shelter instead of trolling that day—another disappointment for Qeixwnei, especially after standing on deck most of the way straining her eyes to see if anyone was catching any salmon.

They holed up all night. She heard her father getting up from time to time during that night. He never slept much on nights of a storm.

Daybreak was beautiful. It was foggy, but through the fog they could see that the sun was going to be very bright. Where the fog started to drop, the water surface was like a mirror except where the "spine of the tide"—the rip tide—made ripples of tiny jumping waves on one side and the other side had tiny tide navels. Sounds carried far. They could hear gulls, and a porpoise breathing somewhere, and splashing from fish jumps. 'It was going to be gorgeous.

They ate quickly and went off to the fishing ground. Once again they took their turns getting into their boats while the big boat moved along.

This day Qeixwnei stuck really close to her Grandma and Aunty.

They stayed on the tide spine, circling it as it moved along. She did
everything they did. They measured fathoms by the span between
their arms from fingertip to fingertip. Qeixwnei also measured her
fathoms the same way. She checked her lines for kinks whenever one
of them did theirs. She especially stayed close by when Aunty got
her first strike of the day. She had hooked onto a lively one.
Qeixwnei circled her and got as close as she dared without the
salmon tangling their lines.

Then Grandma got her first salmon of the day.

Qeixwnei had just about given up hope of getting a salmon for
that day when she got her strike. It was so strong that the strap that
holds onto the main line almost slipped from her hand. She grabbed
for it just in time.

Splash! Out of the water jumped the salmon! At the same time-
swish-the salmon took off with her line. The line made a scraping
hum on the end of the boat where it was running out.

In the meantime the salmon jumped out into the air and made a
gigantic splash. She could hear her Grandma saying, "My little
Grandchild! It might pull her overboard!" while her Aunty said,
"Stay calm, stay calm, my little Niece. Don't hold on too tight. Let
it go when it runs."

Splash, splash, splash, splash the salmon jumped with her line. It
was going wild. It was a while before she could get it near enough
to see that it was a coho and a good size one too. She would get it
close to the boat and then it would take off on the run again. Just
when she had it close enough to hit with her gaffhook club, it would
take off again. Several times she hit the water with the club instead
of the fish because it kept wiggling out of range. Each time the
salmon changed its direction the little boat did too, and the salmon
pulled the little boat in every direction you could think of. The boat
was like a little round dish and the fish would make it spin.

At long last the salmon tired itself out, and when she pulled it to
the boat it just sort of floated on top of the water. She clubbed it one
good one. It had no fight left.

She dragged it aboard and everyone around her yelled for joy with her. Grandma and Aunty looked as if they had pulled in the fish. They both said, "Xwei! She's finally got it!" Qeixwnei was sopping wet. Her face was all beaded with water.

It was the only salmon she caught that day but, by gosh, she brought it in herself. She sold the salmon and with some of the money she got for it she bought a pie for the family. What a feast that was! Everyone made pleasing comments about her so she could overhear them.

They mainly wished she didn't spend all her money on the pie and that she was going to start saving her fishing money for important things that a girl should have as she grew older.

It was great to be a troller. That fall was a very memorable one for Qeixwnei. Rain or shine she tried to rise with her Grandma and Aunty each dawn.

One day they all timed it just right for the salmon to feed. Everyone made good that day. There wasn't a fisherman who wasn't happy about his or her catch that day. Qeixwnei also made good. When her Aunty and Grandma lined up their salmon on the beach for cleaning, she also had her eight salmon lined up. What a day that was!

When they got to Juneau after the season was over, everyone bought some of the things they'd said they would buy once the season was over. Pop bought some hot dogs for dinner and a watermelon that Grandma called "water berry."

Qeixwnei bought herself a pair of new hip boots. What dandies they were! They had red and white stripes all the way around the sole seams. And they also had patches that read "B. F. Goodrich" on each knee. And they fit perfectly if she wore two pairs of sox.

Her mother told her they were a very fine pair and that they would wear for a long time. Now she wouldn't have to borrow her brothers' boots anymore. In fact, they could borrow hers from time to time. And she could use the boots to play fishing with boats she and her brothers made from driftwood bark at Marks Trail. And very best of all-she would wear her boots when she went with the family to get fish for dryfish camp on their next trip.

The Aftermath

W. M. Ransom

THEY TURNED RIGHT and he could tell by the noise, the railroad tracks, that they were riding through town. He was always impatient to get through town, up the long climb out on the Meridian Street hill. They crested the top and Monte shifted into high. A hint of afternoon sun warmed his face and the hands folded on his lap, and he guided Monte to the old one-room fishing cabin at Kapowsin.

"Hey," he said. "Come in for coffee."

It wasn't an invitation, and he said it as he stepped out of the car. By the time he reached the door and opened it, the car shut off, coughed a couple of times and died. He didn't need eyes to show him that Monte's car was in worse shape than the cabin.

There were no steps to the door, the shack was built right on the ground. An attempt at a porch was enough to keep the rain off while someone fumbled for keys, but the door was never locked. Or while someone kissed someone goodnight and left them at the door, but no one had been kissed under this porch in the rain. At least not in his memory. His uncle built that porch and he would tell Monte about that, but not this time and not here. The porch was a wreck. Both support poles were sunk into the ground and hadn't been treated. One rotted and settled so far that almost everyone who stepped under it ducked. Even Maryellen ducked, and she stood five-foot-one.

The door itself was a piece of plywood nailed to a two-by-four frame. There was no latch, just a hasp for a padlock. Instead of a padlock he hung a piece of kindling through it by a string. The gaps around the door were covered by ragged strips of cardboard stapled to the frame. The staples had long since worked loose, so most of the cardboard was held down by rusted nails pounded half in, then bent over.

Monte closed the door but it popped back open.

"There's a loop of string nailed to the wall there. Hook it over the nail on the door and it'll stay closed."

"Doesn't that door rattle a lot in the wind and keep you awake?"

"If I'm asleep, I stay asleep. If I'm awake, I listen. Either way, it don't bother me." He opened the door, stepped outside and filled his coffee pot from the faucet just outside the door.

"You don't have water inside?" Monte asked.

"Nope. No power, either."

He wondered, then, about all this sudden talking. He listened as Monte wandered around the cabin, fingering things, leafing through books, asking question after question. He was a little afraid of the talking. He wanted to tell this stranger all about himself. Maybe it was their mutual love of Maryellen that did it, but suddenly he wanted to explain the cabin and how he got there. How it got there and each book and how it was that he heard about each book and how he got it, bought it, earned the money to buy it, got whatever job in spite of his empty eyes, his daydreaming, his absences. He wanted to tell the substance of his dreams, his women and their houses that kept him away, and warm and quiet.

Then the coffee boiled over and he hadn't remembered building the fire or finding the coffee.

He set the cups on the tabletop.

"You want some milk?"

"Yes," Monte said, "you have some?"

He went to the cupboard behind the stove. Part of the cupboard was a hole in the wall with a few shelves and some screen around it. A cool breeze blew in from the bottom. He opened the carton and sniffed at the milk.

"Still good."

"Looks like a pretty good idea for a cooler," Monte said.

"Pretty fair," he said and dumped some milk into his coffee. "Poor design, right behind the stove."

"Pretty good idea," Monte said and dolloped some milk into his cup.

"Poor design, right behind the stove."

They sat quiet, sipping their coffee. They listened to the start of a light rain that built with the wind into a thick chatter, then faded and quit. He wished that Monte would say something, ask him something. He thought then that he couldn't live without the rain, the chatter of the rain. The only people who heard the monotony in the rain were monotonous people.

Monte broke the spell. "That rain was nice. The last place I had I lived in for three years. It was an attic apartment and the rain was fantastic. At Maryellen's, all you hear is the street."

He nodded. He helped her move into that apartment. He hated it, but it was cheap and it had a laundry room that Maryellen turned into a darkroom and studio.

"You helped her move into that place, didn't you?" Monte asked.

The coincidence of the question surprised him.

"She tell you?"

"No, I guessed. She told me her best friend helped her move and she was lucky to have someone so big."

He laughed, saw her there behind his eyes, telling Monte about it. Explaining how she couldn't leave the apartment because she needed her darkroom and there was no place for one at his place. And, too, the rent was much lower at her place.

She never lived with a man she didn't love. Though she'd lived with him in spite of his odd jobs. He didn't last long at any one thing, but he needed work of any kind, needed his body moving hard, all day or night regularly. What could he do if not work? Listen, walk, handle his books. He didn't care to travel. He had a fear of dying away from home. He thought of his own death matter-of-factly since the accident, but the particulars of it didn't disturb him. Except that he knew that if he died away from the country he was born in he would die wrong. And he didn't know what that meant either, since he didn't believe in a god that he could talk to, or any

other conscious life that he would go to after this one. He did see a
light at the end of a long dark funnel of cloud once, face down in the
street with glass and steel and footsteps falling with the rain around
him. But he didn't like to think about it except when snatches of it
came to him in dreams. Except one time with Maryellen, two miles
up McCoy Creek after a perfect day of sun, fishing, wading the
creek, good food, air and her. The moon was just leaving full and she
described the ball of it to him as it glowed through the top of their
tent. He stepped outside while she slept on, tired as a child, and he
felt old lady moon creep across the top of the canyon.

Then, later, that slamming pain in his face and head and shoulder,
the long warm tumble through a thick and pleasant air, and the light
moving his way, friendly and warm, the light of everyone he'd loved
floated towards him small as a high country moon, and he saw
himself there, face down in the gutter, people running back and
forth, red lights flashing and voices besides his face.

This one's dead, get the kid
and the board sliding underneath him and the cop's jacket thick
against his face smelling of leather, sweat and pipe tobacco and the
kid, slashed to pieces by broken bottles in the back seat screaming
and then the light, cold and hard against his face and the
click-buzz click-buzz and the steep table slippery and cold with
smears of his blood then the mask over his face that they stripped
back and it was the side of his scalp and the other mask that they
forgot to turn on and the black smother of night that he fought this
time and the nurse's yell *the tank the tank's off* then the *whish-
thuck whish-thuck whish-thuck* of the respirator, the dull poke of
needles and tubes and the smooth face of one pale red-haired nurse
glimpsed as he fell under the dark one last time.

So that night, high in the Cascades under moon and tent, he told
Maryellen that sometimes he was sure that he had died out there in
the rain on some black street. He told her all that he remembered or
thought he remembered of it, how he believed he wouldn't die now
unless he wanted to, and it was a long time before he dreamed it
again.

Then, as always, his coffee was cold and Monte was gone.

Report To The Nation: Claiming Europe

Carter Revard

IT MAY BE impossible to civilize the Europeans. When I claimed England for the Osage Nation, last month, some of the English chiefs objected. They said the Thames is not the Thames until it's past Oxford; above Oxford, it is two streams, the Isis and the Cherwell. So even though I'd taken a Thames Excursions boat and on the way formally proclaimed from the deck, with several Germans and some Japanese tourists for witnesses, that all the land this river drained was ours, these Oxford chiefs maintained our title was not good, except below their Folly Bridge at most. At least that leaves us Windsor Palace and some other useful properties, and we can deal with the legal hitches later. Also, just in case, I accepted a sheepskin from Oxford with B.A. written on it, and I didn't bother haggling. It will prove I was there, and next time if we bring whiskey we can bribe the Oxford chiefs—bourbon only.

So I said the hell with England for this trip and went to France and rented a little Renault in Paris and drove down past the chateaux to Biarritz, stopping only to proclaim that everything the Loire and Seine flowed past was ours. I did this from the filling stations, and I kept the sales-slips for evidence. Oh yes, I waved an arm as I was passing over the Garonne, in Bordeaux, so we now have the area of Aquitaine as I understand. The people there talk differently from those in London, but their signs are much the same—they use a lingua franca so to speak—and they recognized my VISA card and gave the Renault gasoline much like that in Oklahoma, so they aren't completely benighted. Whether they understood that France belongs to us now was not clear, but they were friendly and they fed me well, accepting in return some pretty paper and some metal discs with which they seemed very pleased; if they are this credulous we shouldn't have much trouble bargaining with them when we come to take the rest of France. It was so easy that I headed on down to Spain.

There, however, I hit some trouble. Everything was crowded because some ceremony that they hold, the first full moon after the spring equinox as I understood it, had filled their marketplaces and the trails and all their homes away from home—*todas completas*, as the Spanish desk-clerks everywhere kept saying. So it was back to France, the Spanish border-guards restamped our papers, no hassles even though I heard there'd been some bombings, as there had (I forgot to mention) in England. The Europeans kill each other pretty casually, as if by natural instinct, not caring whether they blow up women, kids or horses, and next day display the mutilated corpses on front pages or television screens. I mention this so that when we send another expedition over the people will be careful and not take it that everything is as friendly and peaceful as the Europeans would like us to think. They can surely be treacherous to us if they treat each other in this way.

After we'd doublecrossed the Spanish border, I thought maybe we'd slip back up a mountain pass at which the Christians once, they told us, had headed off some Saracens. Roland's Pass, they called it, Roncesvalles. Very nice it was, there was a swift clear stream rushing down the gorge and the road went snaking alongside and then got higher and higher, single-lane with bulges, like a snake that had swallowed eggs, for cars to pass each other, till finally we were way up on the side of the pass looking down two thousand feet on apple trees in bloom, and shepherds and white dots of sheep down below ignoring us. I waited to claim the country because I realized this was going to be a watershed and if I waited till the top I could get both France and Spain at once. At the top of the pass there was a giant radar station keeping watch on something, evidently not us though. We climbed out of the Renault, looked along the road to where some young men and women were picnicking on a saddleback, and decided it would be best to climb all the way to the top of a peak to see what were claiming. From the top we could see way over into Spain and back to France, a lot of mountain gorges with the mist in some of them, real windy but the sky mostly clear with just a cape of clouds blowing away from the Pyrenees peaks to the south of us. We looked down to where the border guards were stopping cars, checking for Saracens no doubt, and then we looked up and there were a pair of golden eagles circling, back and forth over the border guards, and there was a peregrine falcon that crossed fast from Spain into France, none of the birds showing their passports. So I claimed both sides of the Pyrenees for the Osage Nation, but reserved rights of passage for all hawks and eagles, and decided to include said rights also for doves and sparrows—feathers we may want from them once we go to dance there, no use restricting their crossing rights.

Having claimed this I went on down to see Narbonne, where we heard the Europeans spirit of inquiry had started and the instruments of torture were still displayed among the heads of Roman statues etcetera. They had very impressive old walls there, but the wind blowing through loopholes and whirling in the empty towers and chambers was bitter cold. The ramparts, however, gave us a terrific view over orange tiled roofs and terraced vineyards to villages (walled) on the hills around, each with its castle, pointing, like football fans chanting, "We're Number One." I went ahead and claimed those too, you never know when an ancient ruined castle might come in handy, and some day our kids might want to use one for a Forty-Nine dance. Then we drove down to Narbonne's beach and dipped our toes in the freezing foaming swells, so we could claim all shores these washed. I am a little worried though because these waters touch some lands that we'd do better selling off to other tribes—water not fit to drink, all kinds of people mad at each other, full of land mines and deserts that somebody is always claiming must be made to bloom or sown with salt.

On the whole though this was a profitable trip. We brought back several things of local manufacture indicating that the people could be made to clothe and feed us nicely — some dishes, some leather things. If our elders decide it's worth the bother and expense, possibly we could even teach the poor souls our Osage language, although if our faith and goodness can't be pounded into them we may just have to kill them all. I hope, though, they will learn — although I must confess, from what was learnable of their history and current attitudes, they do not seem capable of being civilized. Even, however, should they prove intractably savage, they can serve as bad examples to our children. They do not know how to use the land; for one thing — they insist on spreading oil and tar all over it. They dry out rocks and reduce them to a powder, transport them hundreds of miles, pour water on it and make it back into rock, and build their houses out of this stuff. They cut up cliffs and use the pieces to imitate aisles of tall forest trees, and they melt certain rocks and make transparent sheets of it, colored with certain powdered rocks, to imitate the colors of autumn leaves. This shows how ingenious they are, and how they misuse their cleverness, since the stories of their sacred ceremonies that are represented in these colored sheets could be told in the forests among the autumn leaves if they chose, saving the trouble of moving all that rock. I must admit though they get some pretty effects this way. It would be nice to have one of these shrines to look at now and then. They certainly have a lot of torture scenes in them, and these are the models for their spiritual life they say. That may explain the bombings that keep happening among them, and the threats of wiping out their enemies with so many different kinds of weapons. We could probably put together a nice museum, if our people wanted, with the skeletons of such victims, and the religious clothes and such — there are plenty of these inside the shrines I mentioned, and even though they seem to object to having these things dug up, I expect a few drinks of firewater will pacify them, and if not we can simply overpower them. But of course I don't know that we would want to collect such barbarous things; it's just a thought. We ought to have something to remember them by, in case we have to wipe them out as incapable of rising to our level, and we would easily turn one of their shrines into such a museum.

To conclude this report, I can say, in sum, that we have now got much of England, France, and Spain, and a good claim to all the lands with Mediterranean shores. I see no reason why we should not send as many of our people as might want to go, and let them take up residence in any of these places. It would at first be a hard and semi-savage life, and there would be much danger from the Europeans who in many cases would not understand our motives; as a chosen people, setting up standards, we would probably have to suppress some opposition, and at times it might be best to temporize. We will, however, as the superior race, prevail in the end.

But, hold on a minute. Our elders, I realize, don't want to do things in the way my report has been suggesting; they think that's too much like the Europeans did our people, and they think we ought to be more civilized. Well, they have a point, and we culture-warriors ought to listen carefully. So I have been thinking, maybe we shouldn't really bother with the military side of things. Maybe instead of sending people over here to take the land, and drive the people off, and starve those that wouldn't leave into submission, and show them how to live and worship by force if necessary, we would do better just to transport Europe over to us, and not try to counterpunch Columbus. And I have thought of a way to do this, because I did go on past those late staging areas from which Chris jumped off, and I got back closer to where there power came from, first in Rome and then in Greece, and even though I did not get to Damascus and Jerusalem and Mecca or to Peking, where what went around is coming around, I saw how we can cram most of Europe into a word-processor and bring it back to deal with on our terms, far more efficiently and cheaply than by trying to load all that geography on our backs the way Ameropeans have done. See, I

started by looking carefully at Vesuvius and the villas which it saved
by destroying, and the fine pornographic walls there, and the neat
body-casts in volcanic ashes, and some of the words that were left
here and there; geo-graphics made out of graffiti. These fitted
nicely into my preconceptions and cost very little to bring back to
Pawhuska, if anybody there should want them. And while we
admittedly don't have a volcano handy in Osage country, we do
have other things that show us how destroying has been used in
theory to save; you may recall my letter in the Osage Nation News
not long ago, reporting on rock shelters — and in case that isn't handy,
here's a copy:

                    Rock Shelters
              (for John Joseph Mathews)
        Up here, bluff-slabs of sandstone
                        hang out from the rim,
        painted bluegray with lichens, sheer
                over dusty level of a
              sheltered place; water sometimes
        down over places worn and knobby drips
                and darkens, softens earth to hold our
              lifeprints; buttercup and rock pink
              live where the hickory's branches fight
              the sun and wind for power, but mostly here's
        just humus: leaf-mulch deep and rustling
                between great boulders broken from rimrock sliding
              invisibly down the steep slope. The walk
                down through these to the creek that
        runs some of the year below here,
                thin and clear over silty sandstone's
        edges and angles, is short, steep, shady. Stoop
              back beneath this shelter, we're in dust,
                but in this damp earth just outside
              the overhang are mussel shells—
                                    worn

to flaky whiteness, rainbow of
iridescence long since dead. Here's charcoal too,
deep under the hanging slab. See,
                    we were
                              once here.

Moving with Doe Creek down
            to where it joins Buck Creek,
down this narrow shallow canyon choked
    with rocks you come out where
the trees loom higher, elm and pinoak columns
    rise and arch dark over earth
            loamy and loose and the creekbanks
of steep sandy clay, roots jutting over pools
muckbottomed winding down to Buck Creek and
        mingling where it moves from
            sandy shallows down to springfed depths
    and darkness.
                    Here, the winter
surrounded deer and turkeys, here lived plenty
        of beaver, muskrat, mink and raccoon, fox and
    bobcat and cottontail, coyote slinking, quail
        and squirrels, mice and weasels all with
small birds watching from the bush and grapevine, berry
            tangles, juncoes, waxwings, cardinals like
blood on snow, all sheltered here from
            the prairie blizzards north.

                    And southward, in the bend
    of Buck Creek level to the southern ridge a valley
        of bluestem grass thigh-deep under
    sunflowers nodding, meadowlarks flying and singing with
grazing buffalo, red wolves and coyotes trotting watching
            with pricked ears a hunter crawl with
        bow and arrows for a shot.

                    Now crossed
by asphalt road, wire fences, lanes to white farmhouses
        where no farming's done, grapes and lettuce and
    bananas on the polished table from Texas, from
        California, Nicaragua, the orange-fleshed
        watermelons that once lay in sandy fields by
            Doe Creek gone as truckloads of melons rumble
past from Louisiana into town where food is
        kept. To plant here, you buy. This land
was needed, we were told, it would be used. So oil is
        pulsing from beneath it, floats dead
    rainbows on Buck Creek and draws its brief trails
straight as a Roman road across the sky where people sit
        drinking and eating quietly the flesh of what
    has followed buffaloes to winter in
                    the valleys underneath on which
                        the travellers look down.
        This new world
            was endless, centered everywhere, our study
of place and peoples dangerous, surprising, never
        completed. Doe Creek tasted different
            from Buck Creek and our people still did not
        look all alike. How far, meant counting
                    the streams that must be crossed.
    The reasons why were everywhere, uncircumscribed;
stars twinkle, moon never does, they both
        were relative to whippoorwill and owl.
                            Greenwich did not
        keep time for us. The small stars now
move fast and send down messages of war
            to speech machines or pictures of
    pleasure to our living rooms, inviting us out into
        a larger endlessness with many
                    centers. Galaxies before long may
    be sold for profit, once the first space ship has

claimed one and the next has
come to kill all those before. Think
of walking on blue
stars like this one, new
plants, new beings, all the rock
shelters where we'll crouch and see
new valleys from.

Here is
my mussel-shell. Here is the charcoal.
We were here.

As you can see, it is simple enough to bring Vesuvius and the
Roman Empire back, and as for what evaporates in transit, it is
easier for our people to go over and enjoy the flavor of it there than
send our war-dancers over there to annex it at first hand and have
such troubles with the local savages as would be sure to break out. So
in case our elders don't think it is worth such troubles, here's Rome
in a pome.

Unfortunately, Greece is giving me a little more trouble getting
processed. We took a ferry over to Corfu, and then in the town
across from Corfu we rented a Volkswagen and drove it across
northern Greece, through the Pindus mountains, to Olympos. We
stopped a while in Meteora, to look at the huge rock mountain or
tower with all the caves which were lately used for religious
hermits. There were great black and white birds sailing in the updrafts around the heights of that place, and I thought they were
eagles but they turned out to be storks. This might explain the
guidebook's curious statement about how the medieval hermits
became so numerous — they "went into the rocks and multiplied," it
said, and there are old Christian legends about storks bringing
babies. But what we really wanted to do was drive in the mountains,
and I was particularly anxious to get up Mount Olympos, that being
the place where Greece's head diety was when Greece was doing
things that mattered. And so I traced the power back up along the

Vale of Tempe, under the mountain, and toward its source, since
they have a road that lets Volkswagens up clear to the top. We got
slowed down by a blowout and spent the middle part of a sunny
chilly spring day beside the greengray River Tempe, looking up at
Olympos, and repairing the tire, and eating honey and bread and
peanut butter and drinking Coca Cola. But we found we could drink
the spring water, showing the old gods are friendly there, and we
filled our empty plastic Coke bottles from Aphrodite's spring, and
Apollo's spring, and Dionysus' spring, and the Muses' spring—see, I
brought back some in this container, and the water fitted the sides of
our cowpond nicely:

To The Muses, In Oklahoma

That Aganippe's well was nice, it hit the spot—
            sure, this bluestem meadow
        is hardly Helicon, we had
            to gouge a pond, the mules
        dragged a rusty slip scraping
            down through dusty topsoil into
            dark ooze and muck, grating open
        sandstone eggs; but then the thunder
            sent living waters down, they filled
    the rawness with blue trembling where white
        clouds sailed in summer and we
            walked upon the water
                every winter (truth
        is this frozen allomorph of time), though it
was always more fun sliding. We'd go and
        chop through six-inch ice by
            the pond's edge, pry the
    ice-slab out onto the pond from its
            hole where the dark water welled
    up cold to the milk-cows sucking noisily,
            snorting their relish; and

when they'd drunk we shoved the ice-
slab over to where the bank
sloped gently, took
a running chute and leaped atop the slab real
easy and slid,
just glided clear over
the pond riding on ice — or flat
on the black windowy ice
looked down into darkness where fish
drifted, untouchable, below our fingers.
Ice
makes a whole new surface
within things, keeps
killer whales from seals just long
enough to let new seals be born before they
go down to feed or be fed upon.
—Come sliding now, and later we'll
go swimming, dive in with the
muskrats, black bass, water moccasins, under
this willow let the prairie wind
drink from our bare skin:
good water
fits every mouth.

I noticed that shepherds in the Greek mountains were very friendly and regret missing the chance to cement a relationship when one asked in sign language for a cigarette I didn't have — they have taken up our discovery of tobacco as offering, but denuminalized it which makes it hard on their lungs. This shepherd gave his name as Aristotles, and on the whole the mountain seemed worth claiming since its water—unlike that in Rome, full of Mussolini's Revenge—gods and muses still approve; so after changing tires we drove up Olympos. But we did not get quite all the way to the top, and this may be why I have difficulty getting Greece into the word processor. The blowout cost us quite a bit of sunlight and also reduced the Volkswagen to four healthy wheels, so we got worried that one of them might be gored by the road when it turned from asphalt to broken stone and dust about eight thousand feet up. Olympos is only something over ten thousand feet but very husky and sprawls a lot, with spurs and gorges and the road winding and zigzagging up one perpendicular ridge and over onto another one. It was when we got onto the dirt and rocky road, and from the edge of it looked down on eagles soaring over several thousand feet of updrafts, and a pine tree had fallen across the road and we had to drive around its tip by the cliff-edge, that we decided to claim only as much of Greece as this level of Olympos would allow us. So we did not get above the Aonian Mount and this may mean trouble for our epic Osage work at least in English, until the next expedition, but that is as the elders may wish.

The only thing that gave me pause when we decided to turn around was the noise of thunder. Since I am of the Thunder people I wondered if this was telling me to go on up, but then we noticed that some distance out toward the Aegean Sea, on the plains under Olympos, was where the thundering came from, and when I got out of the car and walked over to the rim and listened and looked, it became clear that those were cannons firing, and so I did not believe it was an oracle to go up after all. Later we found these were army exercises, and tanks firing, near the army base beneath Olympos. But at least in looking for the sound-source, it was possible to see that the view across the Aegean was fine as wine, and the peninsula where Mount Athos is situated was in plain sight over some aquamarine and amethyst distances which darkened to emerald and purple as the light began fading. We got back down into the twilight and joined the tanks going home, and so it would now be possible for any Osages to feel free to use whatever comes down from Olympos, such as epics, tragedies, democracy, honey and honeybees, odes, civil wars of people or gods or both, good water, idealism, and the like.

I don't think it is necessary to say much more about Greece. Athens we should not bother with; it is too much like Paris and

London, since everybody tries to be someplace else at the same time,
and the paths are all knotted up and covered with asphalt and smoke.
Like Paris and London, Athens is full of ruins, but theirs are harder
to get to and those in Athens are on the whole prettier and less
cluttered with people living in them. We went down, also, and had a
look at Argos, where Agamemnon took a bath the way Custer took
a ride, and then we drove across the Paloponnese to Olympia, the
scenic route through Arcadia where Death was the shepherds'
friend, and there were redbuds blooming among the fallen marble
columns at Olympia, nice to see the Oklahoma state tree there.
There was also a dead European adder, smashed and dried, lying on
one of the column-stumps where the lizards were frisking in bright
sunlight. I don't know why the poison snakes never invented, in
Europe, rattles to warn people, but this one clearly did not get in the
first strike. On the whole I would be for our claiming all the
Peloponnese, including Argos as well as Olympia too, because it
could be useful to us — what the hell, we might as well have pastoral
as well as epic and tragedy if we want to claim Europe for our kids.
And it is probably our destiny anyway, if our elders don't mind our
sounding so Ameropean, to get the whole thing anyhow. I sneaked a
piece of it into a lyric as a sample:

Over by Fairfax, Leaving Tracks
(for Mike and Casey and the kids)

The storm's left
this fresh blue sky, over
Salt Creek running brown
and quick, and a huge tiger
swallowtail tasting the brilliant
orange flowers beside our trail
Lightning and thunder've spread
a clean sheet of water over
these last-night possum tracks
straight-walking like a dinosaur in

the mud, and next to these we've
left stippled tracks from soles made
in Hong Kong, maybe with Osage oil.
Lawrence and Wesley pick blue-speckled flints
along our path, one Ponca boy
in braids, one part Osage
in cowboy hat.
Over the blue Pacific, green Atlantic we
have come together here; possum's
the oldest furred being in this New World,
we're newest in his Old World.
Far older, though,
and younger too, the tiger swallowtail has
gone sailing from those orange flowers to
sky-blue nectar: the wild morning glories
will spring up where he's touched, marking
the next year's trail.
Makes me wonder,
if archaeologists should ever dig these prints
with possum's here, whether they'll see
the winged beings who moved
in brightness near us, leaving no tracks except
in flowers and
these winged words.

Well, I am going to end this report for now, only adding that I hope some better fate befalls me than fell on the European conquistadores-you know how Cortez ended up running alongside the chariot of Charles the Fifth, crying about never having been given the empire he had conquered, and Balboa, Pizarro and the rest got hanged or assassinated. Anyhow Europe, being second-hand and badly used, ought not to be priced so high as Louisana when Jefferson took the land on which, as he maybe didn't know, our people happened to exist; and freeze-dried as in these words Europe won't be worth things of value. So don't let any of us offer

language, traditions, beadwork, religion or even half the Cowboy
and Indian myth, let alone our selves, this time. These words,
whatever has evaporated, will give its aftertaste, enough for anyone
wanting to steal a culture from under the noses of its guardians; they
wouldn't let me take the gold mask of Agamemnon but I did sneak
out with his story. Still, remember that Coyote himself could
outsmart himself and lose his beautiful fur. (Kept his wits though.
Wonder how things would have gone if it had been Coyote not
Oedipus up against that Sphinx. Europe with a Coyote complex ...
maybe it WAS Coyote!) Comedy is worth more than tragedy any
time where survival is at stake. Always tricky, of course, claiming
another continent, especially when you get it, which I hope we are
about to do; and then Zion's hill, and Sinai, though a few hundred
years of recycling may be needed first for those. Meantime, keep the
oil wells pumping, and let me know if you have any special orders
for pieces of Russia, China, Japan, or "India."

Yours,
Special Agent Wazhazhe No. 2,230

P.S. Speaking of Jerusalem, how retroactively can we claim a place?
I forgot, in passing through the Dordogne and Spanish areas, to
claim the caves at Altamira, etc., but here is a piece of metamorphic
rock from there that might get them back for us.

Stone Age

Whoever broke a rock first wasn't trying
to look inside it, surely,
just looking for an edge
or trying just to hammer with it, and it broke.
Then he saw it glitter,
how *bright* inside it was; noticed how things
unseen are fresh. Maybe he said
it's like the sky, that when the sun has
crashed down through the west

breaks open to the Milky Way so we see
　　farther than we are seen for once, as far
as light and time can reach and almost over
　the edge of time, its spiral track like agate
　　swirls in rock from when it still
　was water-stains, had not yet found its
　non-solution to the puzzle
of dissolution, keeping within its darkness
the traces of its origin as day keeps night and
night keeps stars. Pebbles, headstones, Altamira,
　dust-wrinkles over darkness.
　　What shines within?

The Sonofabitch And The Dog

Ralph Salisbury

"T HIS SONOFABITCH remembers everything."
I had never killed anyone before, but I knew how to do it the instant I had to.

Fist slammed against jaw bone. Throat twisted like a giant snake between hands.

His friends pulled at me. Hit me.

Too late. That mouth would never twist air again.

Instead of the firing-squad, they sent me to be a Behind-the-Enemy-Lines Soldier.

"This man remembers everything," the assignments officer said, remembering what he had been told. "And he's a bare-hands killer."

They explained that it was all right for all of us to call each other sonsofbitches, it didn't really mean our mothers, they said. They said we wouldn't let the enemy call us anything, we would kill them, but if we insulted each other we were only practicing like we did with our weapons.

We practiced before the sun and after the sun.

I learned knives, pistols, rifles, machine-guns, mortars, rocket-launchers, land-mines — compass, maps, radio — to fly a helicopter in case the pick-up pilot was killed. I learned the White people's language better than before. I learned the enemy's language.

"This sonofabitch remembers everything," the training sergeants said. They'd all heard my story, and they liked practicing.

"You sonsofbitches are good teachers," I said.

"He's never had a fight," my mother had told the soldiers who came for me. "He's never been with a woman. His father was killed the first year of the war. He's only seventeen."

"No problem," the corporal told my mother. "He'll be eighteen next year. If he lives that long. And this'll save our coming back for him."

I felt pretty good about all the things I learned.

"If they all caught on as fast as this sonofabitch catches on, we'd win the fucking war before the fucking year was over," my unit sergeant told the Inspecting Officer.

"Good man," the officer said. His decorations shined like bullets. he had white hair and a white mustache. There were little shining eagles on his shoulders. I guessed he was one of their important ones, very wise. "They tell me you're not only smart, they tell me you're also one mean, tough little sonofabitch," the old officer smiled.

I smiled back. "They tell me you are one super duper chickenshit sonofabitch, sir," I told him.

The sergeant made a little sound even though he was supposed to be at attention. I never knew a sergeant could make a mistake.

The Inspecting Officer didn't utter a sound for a long time. It was like it is before a big storm, the silence is big, as big as the wind is going to be. It was like that before I hit the city soldier and choked him to death.

Then the Inspecting Officer hit the sergeant in the stomach, but it was just a practice hit.

"You leave off instructing this man and send him on a mission," the officer said. "He knows too fucking much already."

Once I was assigned to a mission, they let me visit the city at night.

At first I felt nervous. It was because I remembered all the streets from the train station that the city soldier had said I remembered everything.

But now it was all right because my buddies went with me. We gave some of our money to women, and the women never asked who our family was or anything. It was very easy. No problem. I liked all this very well.

One night one of my Oriental buddies said something not very friendly to a white woman and later she called me a "sonofabitch Indian."

"Don't you call him any Indian. He's a soldier. And you're a whore," one of my Black buddies told her. He wasn't practicing. And she hadn't been practicing either. I didn't like it so well after that.

I finally learned that "bitch" meant female dog in the White language. Some soldiers had brought a mongrel pup onto the base one night when they were drunk and after everybody was sober the next day they thought they'd use the pup for target practice, but it kept offering to shake hands and standing on its hind legs and rolling over and covering its eyes with its little paws and finally they realized somebody, probably some little kid, had taught the pup these tricks and so they fed the pup and taught it to lap beer out of a mug and take a few puffs on a cigar and after it got big they even got it to take a mortar shell between its teeth and drop it down the tube; then they said the dog was a commando, and they named it "Commando."

When it thought some soldier was playing "fetch" and brought back the grenade he'd thrown, the sergeant-who'd just managed to throw the grenade a second time far enough-ordered an end to Commando's military training. The dog accepted this like a veteran soldier. He'd been almost close enough to fetch the grenade a second time, and after that he'd slink off whenever some innocent new soldier offered to throw a stick for him.

Commando still drank beer, but a smoking cigar would send him squirming out of his buddy's arms and off to the far end of the base. They taught Commando to go to town and taught him where to catch the bus to return to base after his night out.

"Poor old Commando is shell-shocked. He got that there combat-fatigue. He just ain't motivated no more. But he's still big on booze and bitches."

That was when I learned that "bitch" wasn't just a White insult word.

I came into training shortly before the grenade-fetching incident, but I wasn't on the grenade range and only heard about that, just as I'd only heard about Commando's puppy days.

"He ended his training about the same time you started," a buddy laughed. "Maybe we should all be as smart as this dog and freak out like he did—before some enemy wastes us."

We weren't supposed to talk like that, but sometimes when soldiers were drunk they did talk like that. I decided it was only practice talk.

We weren't supposed to fight when we went to town, and other soldiers from ordinary units were supposed to recognize a Behind-the-Lines-Soldier's uniform and leave him strictly alone, but one night when I was about to get on the bus back to base, a White soldier said to me, "Stand aside there, Indian, and let this gentleman on the bus ahead of you all." He meant wait for Commando, who was just about to follow me onto the bus.

My Black buddies grabbed the joking soldier, kicked him in the balls and left him writhing on the sidewalk.

"This man isn't an Indian, you sonofabitch, he's a commando, and don't you ever forget it."

Hearing "Commando," Commando ran up to the Black soldier and sat at attention as he'd been trained to do.

"At ease, Commando. Dismissed," the Black soldier laughed, and Commando strolled over, raised his hind leg in a jaunty salute and pissed on the head of the ordinary soldier, who was still writhing on the sidewalk.

Feeling the warm liquid, the soldier took one hand away from his crotch and hooked it over his head like a schoolkid expecting a hard cuff.

I felt kind of sorry for him, but I knew he hadn't been practicing when he called me "Indian" just as I knew the soldier I'd killed had not been practicing really but had really been saying something he'd been used to saying ever since he was small.

I knew, too, that the Black soldier wasn't right. I was a commando, yes, but I was still an Indian. But by now I had learned that words meant different things to different people at different times.

"Enemy."

I was only two days back from my first behind-the-lines mission. I'd killed seven people, six with my rifle, one with my knife. I'd been given a medal. And freedom to go to town every night for a week. All three of my buddies had been blown up by the same land mine.

"You get drunk for them. You get laid for them. Live it up," the Base Psychiatrist said. "It's the only way."

"Enemy."

Only Commando and I had been waiting at the bus stop, but it was dark there, as all streets were, blacked out to prevent attracting enemy bombing planes. I looked around to see who had joined us, but I saw only Commando's grinning teeth.

"That smart aleck soldier I pissed on was right," Commando said. "You're an Indian. You understand the earth. You understand nature. You understand animals. You understand what I'm saying, and you understand that I'm not just bullshitting you."

I was pretty sober in the chill night, and I thought Commando was correct in what he was saying, but I'd never heard a dog talk White language before. I'd been hearing my dead buddies' voices. And I wasn't sure in just what way I was hearing the dog. And it didn't seem right to answer back in an ordinary way.

"How old are you?" Commando asked.

"Seventeen."

"Do you want to be eighteen?"

"Hell, yes," I looked around, but I wasn't in any doubt about who I was answering. I just wanted to be sure no one had come up to hear me talking to a dog.

"Everybody keeps telling everybody how smart I am to learn

where and when to catch a bus," Commando said. "And they keep telling how fast you learn," Commando told me. "What's two Blacks plus one Oriental plus one seventeen year old Indian?"

I knew the silence was really his answer, but when Commando continued, "The cadre selected for one of the most dangerous missions on the list," I didn't argue.

"So what do you want to be, proud and stupid and dead, or humble and freaked-out and alive?"

When the bus pulled up, Commando trotted on first and went straight to the furthest back seat. I went back there, too, but there was no more talking.

Next day, instead of reporting for further combat-interrogation, I went to the only piece of earth that wasn't covered with concrete or grass cut short like a military-haircut—the firing range.

Spreadeagle in the sacred way, I gazed at shaggy white buffalo clouds and prayed while stones under me softened.

"Leave him alone," they said at first, "he's had a hard mission. He's just doing some Indian stuff. He'll get it back together."

But when target practice time came, and somebody said they should drag me off, the Range Sergeant said something else.

For hours, bullets twanged air over me, and I thought of the bullets that had driven my buddies to run into the mine-field, and I remembered Commando's first word: "Enemy."

After target practice, there was less reason to move me.

For seven days I fasted. For seven days I prayed.

When they marched me in, the Base Psychiatrist gave me a shrewd, knowing grin, and after the tests, he grinned again, pulled a card from a box and said that from now on I'd be the Chaplain's Assistant.

"Are you a Christian?" the Chaplain asked.

"No."

"No problem," he said. "Just do what you're told."

I do what I'm told. I remember every detail. And by now I'm eighteen.

Waterbugs

Peter Blue Cloud

F OX YOUNG MAN was sitting by a mountain pool watching waterbugs circling one another, first one way, then another. He thought they resembled half-shells of small black nuts. They moved so swiftly that it was hard to keep focused on them. The edge of the pool was shallow and the shadows of the waterbugs went faster than their owners, having to climb stones and plants.

Coyote was passing by and came over to sit by Fox Young Man. He looked at the pool to see what was so interesting. All he could see were waterbugs and water. "Uh, what you looking at, Fox Young Man?"

"I'm watching those waterbugs. They sure move fast. I wonder how they do it? Do you suppose they paddle around with legs? If they do, their legs must really move. Or maybe they have underbelly fins and a tail so thin we can't see it, huh?"

Coyote sat awhile watching. The waterbugs really were kind of fascinating. He motioned across the pool to where a stream entered. "See that grass over there? Well, it's a kind of salt grass that's covered with tiny bugs that live on the salt warts which grow around the roots. That's all those little bugs eat, of course, and that's why they live underwater, 'cause if they ever surfaced they'd probably turn into salt crystals.

"If you went over there, you would see little bubbles always popping from those bugs burping. Yes, those bugs are so small that we can't see them. They're called Carbonated Buggers 'cause there's so many of them.

"And those waterbugs, that's all they eat, those little Carbonated

Buggers. So they're always full of gas. And that's how they swim so fast. They just fart themselves in circles all day long. You can actually hear them farting if you stick one ear underwater, plug the other and close your eyes."

Fox Young Man looked at Coyote. "Coyote, I think you're making it all up," he said.

"No, I wouldn't do that. It's an old, old story. Coyote Old Man himself told it to me. It was back when World-Maker was creating everything. He was working so fast one time, without resting, that he got what's called "verbatim" which is when you get suddenly real dizzy and start talking to yourself. He got spots in front of his eyes swimming around.

"Now, because he was World-Maker, he figured that he'd created those spots for a reason. He was at a pool at the time, just making the first frog. So he took some of the spots swimming before his eyes and put them on Frog Person. But they weren't circling around on frog's skin, of course. They were just sitting there, but they looked okay so he left some on Frog Person.

"But he took the rest and turned them into waterbugs. And that's why so many pools of water look like eyeballs reflecting the sky and having waterbug spots swimming around in them. Yes, that's probably how it all happened."

Coyote got up then and walked away, saying over his shoulder, "Well, I gotta be going home for some mush. I guess I'll see you again if I ever run into you." So Coyote went over a hill, then circled back and looked at the pool from behind some brush. Sure enough, there was Fox Young Man with his head underwater, eyes closed and a paw covering one ear.

Coyote walked over the hill again and met Flicker. "You ever want to know about waterbugs," he told Flicker, "just go ask Fox Young Man. He'll tell you all about them."

"What?" said Flicker. "Coyote, what are you talking about?"

"Me?" answered Coyote, "Oh, I'm just letting you know how stories are born. That's all."

Miracle At Chimayo

Robert L. Perea

I LOVED TO LISTEN to Grandma Josephine's Lakota songs and Lakota jokes. I loved to hear the nicknames she gave to people. Lakota nicknames. She couldn't see my sisters so I described them to her.

They are attractive, but Grandma Josephine ignored that. My shortest sister became Gnugnushka Ptechela. Short Grasshopper. The one who weighed the most, although she wasn't really fat, became Tatanka Chepa. Fat Buffalo. The youngest and most talkative was named Wichinchala Hotanka. Little Girl With The Big Mouth. My sister who teaches school became Waonspekiya Mani—Teacher Who Walks—because she was forced to walk to school after her car broke down.

The first thing Grandma noticed about me was the way I spoke English. "You don't sound like no Indian." So I became Takoja Iyeska. Grandson Who Talks White or Grandson Who Sounds Like A White Man.

My mother, Grandmother Josephine, and I had come to Chimayo. Grandma had never been there before.

"Takoja," Grandma asked, "where are we going?"

"Just hang on to my hand," I answered as we entered the old church.

"Bienvenidos," said the old priest, taking Grandma's hand. She quickly pulled it back. "Ha visitado Chimayo antes o es este la primera vez?"

"Mi abuelita no habla Español," I said in the clearly enunciated

Spanish I'd learned while in the Peace Corps in Colombia. "Ella es India. Oglala Sioux de South Dakota."

"Perdoname," said the priest throwing up his chubby round hands and smiling. "Does she speak English? Tewa is the only Indian language I'm familiar with."

"Yes," I answered, holding Grandma by the hand and arm. Her skin felt softer than a baby's.

"How long has she been without sight?" asked the priest.

"I can talk for ma'self," interrupted Grandmother. "You don't have to ask my grandson."

"Why, but of course," said the priest.

"I been blind as a bat for 'bout ten years now," Grandmother said. "Can't see a damn thing." I couldn't help but laugh. The priest's face turned a bright red.

"I guess she can't see that I'm a priest," he said, nervously fingering his rosary.

"I know you're a priest," insisted Grandmother. "I may be old and blind, but I'm not stupid." This time, it was all I could do to keep from laughing.

"She doesn't mean to be rude," I said. The priest smiled nervously and nodded.

"Excuse us, father," I added. "Come on, Grandma, let's go find Ida." I knew exactly where my mother would be. At the back of the old adobe church scooping up healing dirt to use for her arthritis.

Grandma Joesphine and I came to a side room where crutches hung from the ancient earthen walls. Some had little notes attached to them thanking Dios for the healing dirt of Chimayo. Religious symbols covered the walls of the dark and cool room. Statues of Jesus, Mary, and saints, plus rosaries, candles. Some had been left by those who felt they'd been healed. Others had been put there by the priest. I led Grandma to the little room where my mother was.

"Careful, Grandma," I said, "there's a hole in the ground in front of you." I held her arm. I was amazed every time I touched her arm. Time had made her skin softer than anything I'd ever felt. Soft and smooth, like fine buckskin.

My mother was bent over the hole filling a glass jar with the dirt of the santuario.

"Lazaro, how's Mom doing?" my mother asked, standing up and brushing herself off.

"I need a beer!" Grandma Josephine said.

"Mom, you can't drink beer in a church," Mother said. "And besides, you shouldn't be drinking anyway."

"Ida, us old Indians need to have fun too," Grandma Josephine insisted. I laughed again.

"Les, did Mom meet the priest?"

"Well, sort of."

"Sort of?"

"Grandma's language got a little too colorful, so we had to excuse ourselves."

"Mom!"

"An ol' Indian can't say nothing around these priests," Grandma Josephine complained. "Just like that damn boarding school I went to. Always had to keep my mouth shut."

"But Mom," my mother said, "you know you're not supposed to swear around priests."

"I say anything I want on the res'," Grandma Josephine insisted. "I cussed around Oglala holy men. They never said a damn thing to me. Wichasha wakan," she added, turning to me. "That's how you say holy man in Lakota."

"Wichasha wakan," I repeated.

"Now, Mom, promise me you won't cuss anymore. This is a church," Mother repeated.

"Oh, alright," Gramdma Josephine answered.

"Shall we go to the gift shop," Mother suggested. "I've got my jar full of dirt."

"What you gonna do with a jar full of dirt?" Grandma asked.

"It's healing dirt," Mother answered. "If you rub it on you and have faith, it will cure all kinds of illnesses."

"Takoja," Grandmother Josephine said, turning to me. "Maybe that's what this ol' Indian needs instead of a cold beer."

"I don't believe that dirt performs miracles," I answered.

"Oh Takoja, the earth is very wakan, very sacred," Grandma Josephine said.

"The earth isn't wakan anymore," I said. "People buy it and sell it and pave it over."

"The earth is still sacred in Chimayo," my mother replied. "And it's still sacred on the reservation."

"I think I need a cold beer too," I said.

"Mini-peja," Grandma Josephine said. "That's how you say beer in Indian. Mini-peja."

"Mini-peja," I repeated, trying unsuccessfully to correctly pronounce the difficult "j" sound of the Lakota language.

There was a small gift shop in the front of the church. It was full of medallions, rosaries, crosses, postcards, and other religious articles for sale. Whenever we were in New Mexico, we visited Chimayo and my mother always followed the same routine. First, she knelt before the ancient Chimayo altar and prayed, then she gathered her dirt, and finally she bought religious articles at the gift shop. Afterwards, she would have the gifts blessed by the priest.

While my mother hunted through the religious articles hanging everywhere, Grandma Josephine started feeling for the door.

"Where you going, Grandma?"

"Get some fresh air."

"Let me help you find your way out."

"I don't need no damn help!" Grandma said. "I may be blind, but I'm not helpless."

Her tiny bent-over fingers wandered into the small graveyard in front of the church. She didn't have a walking stick, so she kept her hands in front of her.

"Takoja!" she yelled.

"Yes, Grandma."

"What's this?" She had her hands on a wooden grave marker in the shape of a cross. I walked to where she was standing.

"It's a grave, Grandma. You have your hand on a grave marker."

"I know that. What's it doing here?"

"You're standing in a graveyard, Grandma."

'Oh," she said.

"Let's go."

"You afraid of this place, Takoja?"

"Lakota people aren't afraid of death, are they?"

"Ma Lakota. Say that," Grandma Josephine said. "It means, 'I'm a Sioux Indian.' 'I'm Lakota.'"

"Ma Lakota," I said. "But I'm not. I'm afraid of dying like the Washichus are. I can't even talk about Vietnam."

"If dying scares the piss out of you, well, living ought to, too."

I laughed aloud, though nervously.

"You are Lakota," she said.

"But how will I learn not to be afraid of death?" I asked.

"'Hou' means 'Hello' in Lakota," she answered.

"I'm Mexican, too," I said in frustration.

"Mexicans are Indian people," Grandma Josephine said.

"But Grandma, most Mexican people know very little about Indian ways."

"Spiola," she answered. "That's how you say Mexican in Lakota."

"Spiola," I repeated.

Grandma Josephine wandered over to an unsteady pile of adobes. She must have thought it was a wall because she leaned against the adobes, knocking them over and falling down. I rushed to her.

"Are you okay?" I asked, helping her up.

"Why sure," she said. "But I think I made a mess. We better get outta here before the priest comes. He's liable to kick my butt for this," she added, laughing.

My mother was still browsing through the rows of religious articles. The merchandise of the gift shop didn't blend in with the hard earth and ancient adobe walls.

"Grandma?" I asked.

"What, Takoja?"

"Do you really think I sound like a white man when I talk?"

"Washichu," she said. "That's how you say white man in Lakota."

"I know."

"Takoja," Grandma Josephine laughed, "when we gettin' to Pine Ridge?"

"That's a long way from here," I answered. "Besides, we're going to spend a couple of days visiting Grandma Dolores."

"Where's she live?"

"In a little town in southern Colorado."

"What kinda beer does she drink?"

I laughed.

"She doesn't drink beer, but you'll like her anyway."

Grandma Josephine laughed.

"Lazaro, here's a cross and chain for you," my mother said, interrupting us. "Put it around your neck and we'll have the father bless it."

"Why don't you give it to Grandma Dolores?"

"I have one for her."

"You know I don't go to Mass anymore."

"Once a Catholic, always a Catholic."

"I thought it was, 'Once a Mormon, always a Mormon.'"

"Les, there's no need to get sarcastic."

"Takoja," Grandma Josephine said. She placed something in my hand. It was a small reddish arrowhead with a small hole in it.

"What's this, Grandma?"

"It's made from red pipestone. It's what the wichasha wakan uses to make the bowl of the Sacred Pipe."

"But I've never been to a Sun Dance," I said. Only recently had the Sioux nation been allowed to practice the Sun Dance again. The washichus had finally decided freedom of religion also applied to Indians.

"It doesn't matter if I've never been to a Sun Dance, does it." I'd answered my own question.

I put the red pipestone arrowhead on the chain with the cross my mother had given me. My mother smiled. "The priest is in his office."

"Grandma," I said. "We can get you a nice cold beer now."

"I don't want one."

I don't either, I said to myself, smiling at Grandma Josephine.

Tough Love

Paula Gunn Allen

IT WAS right there. Clawing and tearing. Trying to get out. He was aware of it, in a vague, unfocused way, and his hand often went to his belly, resting against his skin, pressing slightly to soothe it. The feeling was centered about an inch or less below his ribcage, almost a handsbreadth above his navel. It was almost painful, a not-quite burning tightness that he visualized as a small knot of tangled dark threads.

It had been with him for a long time. As long as he could remember. Something inside of him that wanted to get out.

He walked, dazedly, head hunched between his shoulders, dirty bare feet scuffing along the sidewalk, frayed paled jeans dragging on the cement with every step. He was dimly aware of the cold wind that blew against his bare arms and chest. He wore no shirt under the grease-stained leather vest he had shrugged into when he left his mother's place, and when he became aware of the cold, he cursed softly and methodically at the wind. Head and shoulders hunched he looked sideways, glowering at the west mesa that rose several miles away from him on his left. Clouds were piling up there and he thought he could smell snow. Tilting his head lower toward his left shoulder, he glared for a second at the tall peaks that made the eastern boundary of the city. Gray and towering, the peaks stood, completely oblivious to his glance and his rage.

He put his hands deep into his pockets where a few coins met his stiff, probing fingers. "Goddamn, lousy, fucking stupid town," he swore. "Motherfucking bitch whore town."

On the way home, they stopped in Santa Fe for some coffee. She decided to call her daughter from there, to say she was on her way in. "Okay," Lila said, "I'll get the place cleaned up by the time you get here." She giggled softly, then said, "I guess it's gotten kind of messed up since you left. But I'll get it all nice and shiny." She paused for a second and as Margaret started to say something, Lila said, "Guess what? Guess who blew in last night?" Margaret couldn't imagine and said so. "Charley."

"Charley?" Margaret grinned, then frowned. "What's he doing here. When did he get in?"

"I don't know," her daughter answered. "He came in this morning. I heard the doorbell and went downstairs and there he was. And Mother, he's got a girl with him, says they're married."

"Is he there now?" Margaret asked. Her mind was unfocusing. She didn't know whether to laugh with delight or weep with despair. So she made her voice louder, sounding cheered. "Let me talk to him."

"I can't," Lila said. "He's asleep right now. I guess they drove all night."

Relieved and disappointed, Margaret said only, "Okay, then I guess I'll see you both in a couple of hours. I should be home by six." She went into the women's room and splashed water on her face. She combed out her hair, noticing again her satisfaction with how white it had gotten, and refastened it with the beaded clip she had bought during the conference.

It's a really nice one, she thought looking with pleasure at the careful working of the tiny, gleaming beads. Somebody was paying attention when they made this one, she thought. And she grinned a small grin. She had gotten it for a good price, too.

Glancing once again in the mirror she straightened her flannel shirt under her belt. Not bad for an old lady, she thought, slapping her angular hip with long, boney fingers.

She walked through the crowded coffeeshop to the booth where the women she was driving back to Albuquerque with were sitting. The women, Leona Lucero and Alice Graham, had ordered hamburgers and coffee. They were talking in tired tones about the Indian Health conference they were returning from.

Alice Graham was a big freckled Comanche woman with long lightly curled hair and an habitually earnest expression. She reminded Margaret of a large, intensely loyal Irish setter.

Leona Lucero, Margaret's best friend and co-worker at the Alcohol Abuse Center in Albuquerque, was a short, pudgy woman who wore her thin flyaway hair in tight curls as though she had pin-curled it and then just removed the pins without combing it out. She was an Isleta and had two grown sons and a small daughter. Her husband had worked for the tribe until his recent death. Kidney failure. He had been a diabetic for years and had finally died because he didn't stay on the diet the doctor prescribed. He really hadn't been that old, only around forty-five.

Biting into her cold hamburger, Margaret turned her attention to the conversation. Leona was smiling broadly, her light, silky skin looking soft and youthful, her black eyes sparkling. "That Bill Pretty Bear," she was saying. "He's sure a good man."

I must have missed something, Margaret thought. She grinned slyly at her friend. "Bill Pretty Bear?" she said. "I didn't know you'd gotten something going with him!"

"You didn't?" Alice smirked. "Oh, our little Leona got her a great big snagaroo. Didn't you see her sneaking out of the powwow with that big gorgeous hunk?" She winked at Margaret. "They had their own special forty-nine. Just ask her."

Leona frowned at Alice. "We were talking about the workshop." She pulled her turquoise polyester blouse firmly to emphasize her respectability. "He had been talking about drinking and how it made him crazy, beating up on his wife, getting in brawls, the whole story. Did you hear his talk?" Leona turned her head entirely in Margaret's direction, so she had the back of her head to Alice. "He said he and some of his friends had started a rap group to try and stop the cycle. I was just talking to him about it, trying to find out more." She glanced over at Alice who was still grinning.

"I didn't get to that workshop," Margaret said, trying to soothe Leona's ruffled feathers and to head off Alice's joking.

But Alice was grinning wickedly at Margaret. "Course, you missed everything. First you were yelling at the poor old doc from California, then you were busy trying to score with that good-looking cowboy, so how could you know what was going on with Leona?" She nudged Margaret with her elbow.

Margaret grinned at her. "I wasn't just trying," she said. "You sound jealous, Alice. Didn't you find a sweetie this time? You're usually the one who's out dancing all night."

Alice finished her hamburger with one huge bite. "I did all right," she said, looking down at the table. "But I do my romancing more ladylike." Her smile was coy.

"More ladylike? I thought it was just more," Leona said. It was her turn to smirk. Margaret was beginning to giggle.

"Yep." Alice was laughing her short, barking laugh. "The more the better, I'd say, aiii."

When their laughter died down, Margaret turned to Leona. "I'm interested in what Pretty Bear was saying. Did you find out how the group went?" She thought uneasily of Charley sleeping at her apartment.

"Well, he said it went really good. They got into some serious conversations, and by helping each other talk about what was happening with them, they seemed to find ways to stop the violence."

"What about the drinking?"

"Oh, he says some of them are still on the bottle but none of them beat up their women anymore."

Margaret thought again about Charley. The girl he'd brought home. If he beat up on her. If he had learned how to control his rage. She shivered suddenly and took a swallow of coffee. "I wonder how I could get in touch with Pretty Bear," she said.

"Now, Maggie, he's already spoken for." Alice wasn't through trying to get Leona's goat. "Lee saw him first."

"I did not!" Leona snapped. "I mean, I'm not interested in Bill Pretty Bear."

Margaret knew that Alice's jokes were getting to Leona, and she also knew that Alice was letting her friend know that now that her husband was gone she was going to need some kidding and joshing

about her attractiveness. It was important that Leona not go too
deeply into the depression that had been hovering around her since
Jim had died. The women took care of each other that way, using
joking and jibing to convey love and concern. It worked. The one
who was getting the kidding got a chance to get mad, to snap, to
defend herself, to just get rid of some of the tension that came with
living and with the work they did.

"Bill Pretty Bear is a fine man," Leona continued to Alice. She
was getting indignant. "He's married anyway."

"Oh," Alice said. She patted Leona's hand. "That's a darn
shame." Her voice was sickeningly sympathetic.

Leona jerked her hand away. "Would you cut it out?" she
demanded. Turning to Margaret, she said, "I asked him if he could
do a workshop at our conference in November. He said he could.
You could talk to him then if you want to."

"You should invite his wife," Alice commented. "She's the one
who has something to say."

"What do you mean?" Margaret asked.

"I mean she must have quite a tale to tell, getting beat up by that
one. He must weigh nearly three hundred pounds."

"Oh, Alice," Leona shook her head reprovingly. "He's not that fat."

"Not fat," Alice agreed. "Huge. His hands are as big as sledge
hammers."

Margaret winced, remembering how it felt to be slugged by
someone so much larger. She felt sick. "They're still married?" She
looked at Leona.

"I guess they are. He said she was the one who made him see what
he was doing. He sounds like he really loves her."

"How'd she make him see it?" Margaret kept her eyes on her cup,
newly filled with coffee. She hoped she sounded nonchalant, but she
could feel her heartbeat speeding up, making her chest
uncomfortably full. She took a quiet deep breath, trying to slow it
back down to normal.

"One night they were fighting. He'd been out and was really
loaded. He'd gotten in a fight at the bar and been thrown out. He

came home in an ugly mood and was staggering around the house, crashing into furniture, cussing out everything. His wife had been in bed but the noise woke her up. She came out to the room he was in and saw he was bleeding. She asked him what happened, and he let her have it. In a second, he said, he was on her, pounding her head. She just stood there for a little bit, just taking it. Scared, maybe, that if she made any noise he'd kill her. Or maybe she was afraid to wake up the kids."

As she spoke, Leona's usually cheerful face sunk into a heavy sadness. She sighed, shaking her head almost imperceptibly, then went on.

"He said one of her eyes was cut. Blood was seeping out. She gave him this look. Cold and clear, like she was seeing him for the first time. Like she'd never seen him before. She started to moan. Not loud at first, just a low moaning that really shook him. He couldn't swing at her. He said it was like his hands had turned to solid lead. They wouldn't swing—he couldn't lift them. They were frozen. Then she turned around and grabbed something. A long, heavy piece of wood I think it was. She was still making that unearthly sound, that moan. She began to hit him as hard as she could. She began to chant something at him. It took him a minute to understand her, what she was saying. She was saying, 'You stupid, mean drunk. You stupid, mean, cruel drunk. You get out. You just get out.' He said she kept saying it, over and over, and hitting him. He was hurt, bleeding. But he didn't feel the blows—too drunk I guess. But he was just stunned, he said. That she'd say that to him. That it was true. He was just stunned because he understood just how he seemed to her. Finally, after what seemed a long time, he said, but was probably just a couple of minutes, he reached out and took the stick from her. She'd put quite a gash in his head and there was blood everywhere." Leona looked up, her voice brightening. "You know how those head wounds bleed."

"So then what happened?" Margaret was hardly breathing. Her head was pounding.

"Well, he saw that he was hurt, so he told her to take him to the doctor, to the emergency room. She said, 'Take yourself. We don't have any money for doctors, you drank it all.' And she just turned around and went back to bed."

"She did what?" Margaret was aghast. "She just left him standing there bleeding?"

"She did. She said he liked getting beat up. He liked to bleed. That since he liked it so much, he could spend the night bleeding for all she cared."

"Whew." Margaret found that she couldn't imagine anyone doing that. She didn't know whether she admired or despised the woman. "She must have been furious, to do a thing like that," she finally said.

"No, just fed up. The next day when he came back from the hospital she was gone. She'd packed up the kids and left. Some of the women—his relatives and hers—were there. They told him she wasn't coming back and that there would be no more wife beating. They had taken her where she'd be safe, and she wouldn't be back until he got some help. They said they were there to see to it that he didn't try to find her or hurt her again. They said a lot of things, and then they left.

"They said one thing that stuck in his mind. That they had all decided that if some of the men wanted to kill themselves on liquor, that was their choice. But that no one was going to help them destroy themselves anymore."

"Tough love," Alice said quietly.

"That's it," Leona nodded. "That's tough love."

He lay with his eyes shut tightly. Trying not to hear the sounds coming from the other room. The vacuum cleaner. The dishes ringing against each other as they were stacked to dry. The doors opening and slamming shut. The thin wail of rock music playing somewhere, downstairs or next door.

I'm sleeping, he said to himself, gritting his teeth so hard against each other his jaws began to ache.

He felt the warm back and butt of the woman who lay next to

him, heard her slow breathing. He tried to make his own breath go slow and deep like hers. He tried to keep his breath from matching time to hers. Otherwise she'd know he wasn't really asleep, he thought slyly, elated by his cunning, his greater control. He felt fear somewhere in his chest. Felt his pulse erratically pounding. The woman next to him began to snore lightly.

Jesus Christ, he thought, what am I doing here anyway? What the fuck am I gonna do now? He shifted his shoulders slightly, trying to ease the weight of them. He realized he'd been lying in the same frozen position since he had laid down. He wanted a beer. Or something. Some weed. His heart pounded, like it wanted out of his chest. He raised his hand slightly into the air, bringing it close to his face so he could make out the outline of the hand-tooled leather wristband he wore. He'd made it himself, carefully stamping the intricate pattern into the dark leather. Nobody knew what the pattern meant but him. The designs were his luck, his proof that he could be something and nobody would be able to understand it. Nobody. He snorted at the thought, sardonic.

He'd made the band while he was in the hospital. He'd taken months to work out the design, using a pencil stub he'd heisted from a buddy's bed and some cheap lined paper from a Big Chief tablet. He'd called the buddy Big Chief because it was also his tablet. "Hey, Big Chief," he'd say, "wanna help me with this masterpiece I'm working on?" Or in the late afternoons, bored and irritated by the pain, the sameness of the days, the hospital's niggling, bland unchanging routine, "Hey, Big Chief, wanna go out and tie one on?" He'd edge over to his buddy's side, punch his arm sharply and grin. Or he'd rib him about the tablet, slyly, saying, "Big Chief, you seen that new psychedelic tablet they got now? It's called Son of Big Chief. You ever have a hippie kid, we can call him Son of Big Chief! How 'bout it, man," and he'd chuckle, "Son of Big Chief, all dressed in day-glo feathers, just like his old man, hey."

The man had taken Charley's ribbing and slugs quietly. He'd seen a lot of action. Wouldn't ever walk again. Guess he was alright, Charley thought now. Yeah, he was an okay dude. Shouldn't have ribbed him like that I guess. But what the fuck, you gotta be tough in this world like I use to tell him. Poor old Johnny. Wonder if he ever went home. Wonder if he was one of them dudes shooting up Wounded Knee. Yeah, he snorted quietly so he wouldn't wake the woman sleeping beside him. Yeah, he was probably running guns in his wheelchair.

The door opened and someody came into the room. He looked up through slitted eyes, feigning sleep. He snored lightly, for effect. Through the dim light that slanted through the open doorway, he could see his mother standing beside the bed looking down at him. Her face appeared expressionless in the shadows. He felt his pulse begin to race crazily.

Oh Christ, he thought. Here we go.

It was hot at the clinic when Margaret got there. They turned off the air conditioning, she thought. Why they turned it off just because it was September was beyond her. It was still very warm during the day, too warm for anyone's comfort. It says right here in the federal policy regulations Issue 94 Section 365 Subsection 121-b, "Turn off the air conditioning on September 15," she thought sarcastically. It doesn't matter that it's still hot as blazes here in September, especially in this unventilated office. The rule says and the rule holds. She sighed, knowing she was in for a difficult day.

"How's it going, Maggie?" Alice looked up brightly from her desk. "How's Charley?"

"Fine, I guess. He's out looking for work. I hope he finds something pretty soon. It's kinda cramped at the apartment and tempers are getting a little short."

"Is he still drinking?" Alice looked concerned. She knew about Charley's problems with alcohol and his mother's worry about his drinking.

"I don't know. I guess not," Margaret said. She frowned and began to twist her rings. "He says he quit since he had that bad episode in L.A. But I don't know. He's had such a hard time of it. And that girl he married doesn't seem very happy living with us. I think she's ashamed of us, the way we live. She told me she wanted a civilized place to raise her baby in."

"She's pregnant?"

"Yeah. Didn't I tell you? Yes, she's due in a few months, January I think."

"Is she white?"

"Yes. Well, sort of. Charley says her mother has some blood-Chocaw I think. But her people have money. Her mother remarried some time ago, a C. P. A. I guess they have a nice home in one of the uptown areas."

"That must be hard on you. Do you like her?"

"I don't know. It's not up to me to like her, she's Charley's wife. But I think she's pretty strange. I guess she was on the streets when Charley met her. You know him, always picking up strays."

"She was a hippie?"

"I really don't know. I think she was hooking, doing a lot of heavy drugs. Who knows what these kids get mixed up with nowadays."

Alice looked sympathetically at Margaret. "Well, some of us got into some good messes when we were young. We survived. Maybe Charley's going to settle down now with a baby coming. Is he happy about it? Are you?"

"Oh, yes. We both are. I can't wait to have my own grandchild. Just the thought of it makes me feel, I don't know, really good. Excited. It seems more exciting and wonderful than when I was having my own. It's a strange thing. And Charley's making all sorts of plans, about getting a place for them, buying the baby things, you know. He looks really happy when he talks about the baby."

"Well, that sound like good news."

"Yeah, it does." Margaret sighed. She clasped her hands in her lap, leaning back in the desk chair she was sitting in. It turned slightly as she moved, angling her face away from Alice's gaze.

"You want to talk about it?" Alice's voice was low and warm. "You seem really down, Maggie."

Margaret was silent for a minute. Then she exhaled sharply and said, "I don't know, Alice. I just don't know. It's the things he tells

me, about how he's been living. We were up really late last night
and he was telling me about how he tried to kill himself in L.A. He
showed me his wrists. They're all scarred. I just feel so terrible, that
he was so far away and he did that and he was all alone."

"Why'd he do it, did he say?"

"He said it was because he was all messed up. Drinking all the
time, getting in fights, doing drugs. He slashed up his leather work
and was trying to break his tools. He says Polly came in to his room.
He was staying at some flop joint downtown in L.A. She came in and
stopped him from destroying everything that was left. And they
called the mental health squad, and they came and took him to
emergency and sort of patched him up. He said he didn't understand.
He'd always thought that if you slashed your wrists you'd die, and he
didn't."

"Well, if he was tearing up the place when he slashed them he
must have been making quite a racket. Sounds like he didn't really
intend to die, at least not that way."

Margaret looked at her friend's earnest face. They didn't speak
for a few minutes. She thought about what Alice was saying. Then
she continued. "I didn't hear from him in over a year. Didn't even
know where he was. He never wrote or called except once, and then
he was blasted and said such crazy things to me that I told him I
wouldn't listen to him or talk to him when he was like that. And I
hung up. He called back, collect, but I wouldn't accept the call."

Alice got up and crossed the room to the coffeemaker in the
opposite corner. She poured them both a cup, set Margaret's down
on her desk then sat back down at her own. She gazed silently at
Margaret for a few moments, then said, "Margaret, do you believe
that he tried to kill himself because you wouldn't let him talk crazy
to you?"

"I don't know." Margaret shrugged, then shook back her hair.
"Maybe."

"Well, maybe he's telling you about it now as a way of letting you
know he's still mad, but I don't think you are making his choices for
him, about drinking, or cutting his wrists, or getting into fights, or
for the better choices he makes either."

"No," Margaret took a sip of her coffee, setting the cup carefully back down. "No, of course I'm not making his choices. He is."

"But," Alice said, letting the word trail off, hanging it in the air.

"Well, but he's my son!" Margaret couldn't keep her face under control any longer. It crumpled like an old grocery bag. She put her hand up to her face to cover it. "I have to take care of him. I am responsible for him, I bore him, I raised him. Oh God, what did I do that he's so angry, so hurt!" She turned to Alice, fear in her eyes. "What am I supposed to do, let him die?"

The women were silent for a time. Margaret shuddered. She twisted her rings, sighing, trying to get her emotion under control.

"Here." Alice spoke softly, handing her a kleenex. She put her hand over Margaret's, letting her know that she understood Margaret's fear, her pain. "You can cry. You need to, don't you?"

Margaret nodded, voiceless. She took the kleenex and blew her nose. "I know the theories, damn it," she said, "I'm a counselor, for heaven's sake. But theory's one thing and my boy is something else. God, Alice, what am I gonna do!"

The phone rang. Alice answered it. "It's Leona," she said to Margaret, holding the phone away from her mouth. "She's gonna pick us up in about five minutes. We have that meeting with the new director of the rehab unit downtown. Then we have to go to lunch with those people who're putting the local health conference together. Then we have that consultation with the Arvisu family. Are you ready for all this?" She looked at Margaret, concern heavy on her friendly, earnest face.

"Sure. Might's well. It'll feel good to spend the day doing something I think I understand." Margaret smiled to show she was alright.

Alice hesitated, searching Margaret's face. Then she said, "Okay, I'll tell Leona." After she hung up she turned to Margaret. "Let's get together after work. I'll get Leona to join us. Let's go over to my place and just talk. No one will bother us there. How does that sound?"

Margaret hesitated, then realized that she really needed to talk this out if she was going to be of any use to Charley or herself. She stood up and picked up her purse. "Sure," she said. "I'd like that fine." She was glad they had a meeting right now. Maybe the clinic had its air conditioning on.

Lonely. He was so lonely. As though he was an arroyo, waiting for water that would never come. As though clouds forever moved over him, never blessing him with rain. He was parched and aimless. Dry and forever unfilled.

Not that he didn't try. He reached out over and over. Loved. Cared. He thought about the kitten he had taken in, the poor starving creature. How he had nursed it, crooned over it, held it close. How sweetly it had looked at him, small eyes blinking, claws softly kneading his chest, softly purring, content. How he had fed her cream even when he had nothing for himself to eat. If only he still had that small warm furry animal now. She had loved him and he had loved her.

He hadn't meant to hurt her. He was only so irritated when she kept mewing at him. For food, he guessed. She was so hungry and he didn't have anything to feed her. And it was the middle of the night. And she wouldn't let him sleep. He remembered the feel of her small body when he gripped her. How her bones and fur felt in his hand in that second he held her, raising his arm high behind him, how she had felt just as he let go.

She had landed against the far wall. He hadn't meant to use so much force. He had lost control. Then he stood over her, watching the blood coming up from her, dribbling out of her mouth onto the floor.

After he was sure she was dead, he took her outside. He couldn't bury her, there was no unpaved ground where he lived. He put her body in the trash can in the alley and went back upstairs to bed.

Polly was like that kitten. Soft and helpless. When he'd found her she was hungry. She wore torn jeans and a scanty top. She had an old lightweight windbreaker that was her only protection from the cold. Pretty though. She sure was pretty. So small and soft. She'd look up at him with her trusting eyes, smiling so softly. Just like the kitten.

He hadn't thought about that before. How she reminded him of his kitten. He wished he could remember the cat's name. If she had one. She had trusted him too. Too bad. He ached with unshed tears for the kitten, for Polly, for himself. He reflected how important it was for him to have a small creature relying on him. Looking at him with trust. Looking up to him.

He had taken Polly in. Fed her. Given her grass, beer, even good quality whiskey from his precious store of Black Jack. They'd been warmed by each other. Young faces gleaming in the half-light. He kept the light dim in his rented room in that crappy hotel he was living in then. In L.A. But it was good enough, he thought. It was okay.

After he'd been released from the hospital he'd drifted for awhile, then found that room and moved in. He'd gotten odd jobs, hawking and bouncing for strip joints, running bingo games, parking attendant. He'd made out alright. At least he'd had enough to take care of himself and have some party money. He'd planned to be a leather worker. Set up a booth maybe. Go around and sell his work. He was good at it. People were always wanting him to make them something. He thought he could make a good living at it after awhile. He'd been hopeful then. It seemed like the world was opening up. He would make it, he was sure.

Then something happened. He didn't know what. He had been drinking of course, but he'd always drank. Nothing new about that. But there he was, going into bars, walking up to strangers, punching them, belligerent. Hey man, you're screwy, he'd say. And more. But he didn't remember it all. He was drunk. But he knew he kept getting beat up. He kept losing jobs. Getting fired. Getting eased out. Everything would be going along just fine, then wham. Out on the street, buddy, out on the street. He'd call in to ask about the work schedule and they'd say, "You ain't scheduled, Charley." Just like that. "Why don't you come on in and pick up your check."

The worst time was the day he'd been so drunk he'd fallen down on the street. Head cradled on his arm, he'd decided just to stay there. He was comfortable, he'd thought. No need to move. Suddenly out of nowhere this Black dude was kicking his head, telling him to get up. Taunting him, calling him names. Saying he was a bum, he was ruining his life. Saying, "Get up, man, get the fuck up, motherfucker, get off your ass, man, GET UP," the whole time kicking him hard.

Charley had gotten up then, reeling. Trying to stand. Putting his hand out against the wall to steady himself. "Drunk on your ass, man," the dude had mocked, spitting. "Look at you, a damn drunk Injun, just like in the flicks. Whassa matter with you, man," he'd said, looking hard at Charley. "White man get you?" Charley had been too shocked to be mad. His head hurt where the dude had kicked it. He could barely focus his eyes. The man would go in and out of focus, blurring, looking like a bird flying up close somehow. His purple coat and light tan pants seemed to glow like his eyes, his mahogany skin.

He grinned when Charley finally focused on his face. A triumphant grin that broke into a huge knowing smile. "Man, thought that'd get you. Now go on out of here. Get yourself cleaned up, get some food. Go on now, split, man."

Charley looked at the man for a minute, trying to understand what he was saying. Then he lurched down the street back to his room. It was the bottom.

He'd sat there puking and crying. His rage washing over him like sheets of rain. Rocking back and forth on the edge of the bed, he'd sat, getting madder and madder. Raging at himself, at what he'd become, what he'd done. The Black man was right. He was a drunk Indian. He was a nogood bum. Just like they wanted him to be. But he was obedient. He obeyed them after all, didn't he? Enraged, he had gotten up and begun tearing his clothes up, slashing the furniture, smashing the lamps. He gouged and slashed his leatherwork with his knife. He broke his records. He smashed his cassette. He tore the tapes out of every plastic cartridge. When he had ripped everything in sight and smashed what he couldn't rip, he stood in the middle of the room, staring around. "It's no good, man," he said. "It's no fucking good." And he sat on the floor wet from the whiskey he'd poured on it, from his vomit. And he was filled with sorrow and revulsion. For his life. For what he lived. For what he was. He held out his wrist, raised the band to expose the veins beneath and took his knife to them, sawing hard, watching through narrowed tearing eyes as the blood came. Satisfied with the job, he switched hands, cut deeply into the veins in the other wrist. Then he put the knife down and waited for death. I should sing something, he thought. Heap big chief, noble Ind'in warrior. Should sing for my death.

Then he must have passed out because he didn't remember much after that. He remembered Polly's face, white with fear, her normally hazel eyes dark and huge. She was talking to him, telling him it would be alright, he'd be alright. They were in an ambulance, medics working on him or sitting near him, something. It was vague in his mind, obscured by exhaustion, booze, loss of blood.

Later she told him that she'd come in and he was trying to cut his wrist band in half. She'd taken it from him, wrestling him for it. She'd gotten it and the knife away from him and then called the ambulance. The social workers had come too, talked to him about being suicidal and did he want treatment. They'd stitched up the worst of his cuts and released him the next day, giving him a small card with the number he could call for emergency counseling or to make an appointment for psychiatric care. "I'm not nuts," he'd said. "I'm just fucking pissed off." He'd glowered at them, the two serious-faced white boys, longhairs, bearded and too thin, who were talking to him. He and Polly had left, gone back to his room.

Walking along the busy boulevard now, shivering in the cold wind that blew off the mesa, he thought about that time, his anguish, his despair when they'd gone up the three flights to his room and switched on the overhead light. What a mess. He'd torn it apart completely. He'd left nothing. He felt again the despairing ache in his gut, the tangled threads pulling tighter, snarling hopelessly. And the rage that grew out of the threads, a bright glow warming him.

The kitten, the room, now Polly. He looked bleakly out at the traffic moving past him. Polly. Swearing, he clenched his hands into tight fists. Punched at the air, at the traffic, at the memory of the past few hours. Polly bleeding, screaming at him. Clawing him with her pretty nails. Hating him. Running out the door screaming, "You'll pay, you bastard, you'll pay for this, I swear it, you no good rotten bastard. You wait. I'll get you, you just wait."

Then she was gone. He'd grabbed his leather vest and gone out behind her, slamming the door. Christ, he thought, I didn't lock it. Mom'll be mad as hell when she comes home and finds the whole place open. Shit. What the fuck am I gonna do now? How will I explain why Polly's gone? She thought I was getting a job. Doing fine. We talked about it last night. I told her all about how it's been with me. Oh God, Margaret, I'm sorry. Jesus H. Christ, I'm sorry. Your precious boy's nothing but a nogood bum, just like the man said.

He turned. Maybe I better go back. Straighten the place up a little. We musta torn the hell out of it. Yeah, he thought, I'll go on back. Polly will come back, she has to. She can't go any place with no money. She doesn't know anyone here except Lila and Mom. I'll go on back there and get cleaned up and maybe fix something to eat. There was a bottle of something under the sink in the kitchen. I saw it behind the soap. Bitch. Thought she was hiding it from me. Well, she'll never miss it. Not for awhile. I'll have a few and get things straightened up. When Polly comes home we can talk. It'll be alright.

He hurried now, back the way he'd come. His feet were icy from the cold. He thought about being inside, in his mother's apartment, warm and safe, making things work out, making everything come out alright.

The November wind bit through the thin fabric of her slacks. She shifted her heavy shoulder bag more securely on her shoulder, then shoved her hands deep into her pockets. She walked quickly through the parking lot, weaving among cars, trying to find the shortest way into the hotel. She was late.

She pushed open the heavy glass doors and entered the lobby. A blast of warm air hit her and she began to shiver. Damn, it's cold, she thought. She hurried down the corridor, looking for the meeting room. They'd been in session awhile, she knew. She felt resentful, pushed. Never where I'm supposed to be, she muttered in her mind.

Never on time. She dug into her bag for a cigarette, found one, lit it, not breaking her long stride. Crap. Bet they won't let me smoke in here, she thought as she pushed open the door of the meeting room and stood peering through it for a moment before she quietly slid into the room. She saw Alice against the rear wall, an empty chair near her. She sat down. "Hi," she whispered. "Hi," Alice answered, "thought you weren't gonna make it." Margaret nodded and shrugged. "Neither did I," she whispered.

Three men and a woman were sitting at the table at the head of the room. The woman was talking.

"She's the first speaker," Alice whispered, pointing on her program to the woman's name. The panel was titled "Getting Over Your Loved One's Drinking." It was about how everyone associated closely with an alcoholic was also involved in alcoholism

The woman was saying that parents, spouses, and lovers of alcoholics were also alcoholics even if they didn't drink. Margaret had heard it before but she was interested in something the woman said. It was about how alcoholics had a driving need to be in control of things and that they drank or lived with alcoholics as a way of meeting that need.

"Having a sense that you can have some control over the things that happen to you is a major step in getting over alcoholism," she said. "Trying to control someone's drinking is one way of expressing your need to control, but it's not a good way because it won't work. You can't control someone else's life so you might as well not try. What works is for the co-alcoholic to get control over her own life by finding real things to do that make her feel stronger. Making friends who respect and support her emotionally is one thing she must be encouraged to do. Finding work or other activities that she finds gratifying and rewarding is another. The main thing is for her to find out that she really functions whether or not her or his loved one is drinking."

She finished her remarks and the man sitting next to her stood up. "That's Bill Pretty Bear," Alice said in a low voice. "Isn't he gorgeous?"

Margaret grinned at her friend, then shrugged. "He's not my

type," she said. "He's married." Alice chuckled and nodded.

The man dwarfed the speaker's podium when he stood behind it, his great weight hulking over the crest of it. His huge hands nearly covered its edge. He wore several massive rings on each hand. Heavy earrings hung from his ears. He wore a wine-colored cotton shirt and a bandanna tied around his head Indian style. He spoke in a quiet, deep voice, leaning forward, giving the impression that he spoke to each person in the room personally. "I'm Bill Pretty Bear," he said. "I used to beat my wife. I thought that made me a big man."

He grinned, standing back from the podium for a second, letting the irony of that sink in. Several people laughed.

"I didn't know how big I was I guess," he said, leaning down over the podium again, grinning. "But my wife is a lot bigger than me, even if she's only five feet tall and weighs only ninety-five pounds. She's so big she makes me tremble." There was laughter scattered around the room as he said that. "And not because she wields a mean frying pan either."

Pretty Bear told the audience the story Margaret had heard. It didn't vary much from what her friends had said but it was moving, compelling, the way Pretty Bear told it. Margaret felt herself gripped with a longing to know Pretty Bear, to talk to his wife, the woman who had known what to do. But just hearing the tale strengthened her. She felt a calm growing out of her belly and moving through her chest and through her legs as she listened to his talk. The fragility of that huge, gleaming man stunned her into a silence more comforting than anything she'd felt for a long long time. She knew with perfect clarity when he was finished that things would be alright, and she felt herself sighing a deep, shuddering sigh.

The third speaker was a small man who sat in a wheelchair at the far end of the table. He had a microphone in front of him and did not go to the speaker's podium that was set on the center of the table. He introduced himself as Johnny Redding, a Vietnam vet. He spoke quietly, without the compelling power of Pretty Bear, telling about the war and his drinking, his wife's drinking, his daughter's. He was a counselor at his local Alcoholic Treatment Center and had been dry for three years. His daughter had left home after he and his wife had separated. He didn't know where either one of them was. He smiled while he spoke, a gentle shy smile. Sometimes his voice was so soft that Margaret couldn't hear what he said. But she saw the pain he had felt, was still feeling, and she understood. Especially when he spoke of his daughter.

"The worst thing," he said sadly, almost whispering, "is the feeling you have that she's in so much trouble because of you. That's the part that's been hardest for me to learn—not to use her drinking as an excuse to go off the deep end myself. I guess I gotta just keep on trucking," he said. "Keep dry and keep learning that people do what they have to do, even when those people are your children."

When he sat down there was quiet in the room for several minutes. Then people began to get up quietly, to find their coats and put away their note paper. A few went up to the table to talk to the speakers. Margaret got up. She lifted her bag to her shoulder, put her coat over her arm. "C'mon, Alice," she said. "I need some coffee." They made their way out through the people crowding in the doorway.

The Pebble People

Roger Jack

BEN ADAM SAT outside his grandparents' weathered old loghouse.

He liked to sit outside and listen to the sounds of the forest. Especially after one of his grandma's famous chicken and dumpling dinners. And he liked to play one of his favorite games—making rocks war dance. So he started looking for different-colored pebbles. Some were easily scraped off the surface of the well-worn path to the grandparents' loghouse, others he had to dig and scratch out of the earth.

Finally, he found the ones he wanted—black ones, white ones, red ones, yellow ones, and blue ones. Holding the pebbles on an open palm, Ben Adam talked to them. He spoke to the pebbles for a long time about the respect and discipline they should have while wearing the traditional clothing the Creator had given them. He talked of the symbols the old people said were in their dress. He spoke of how they should all try to conduct themselves with dignity. Ben Adam repeated the words of an uncle who had helped him dress for a war dance sometime before.

After several moments of serious meditation, he placed the pebbles on the bottomside of an overturned tin bucket, each according to its own size and color. He carefully placed the red, yellow, blue, white, and black pebbles into the circular grooves of the bucket in the formation of a bustle, the middlemost circle being the drum. Under his breath, he sang the ancient words of his favorite war dance song, but he didn't drum yet because he didn't want the dancers moved.

Ben Adam finished his silent song and again spoke to the pebbles. His message contained a prayer of thanksgiving that his people were alive to see another day and that this day was a day they had chosen to come together in celebration of tribal customs. He thanked all the dancers, drummers, and spectators. He asked the Creator to bestow special blessings upon them throughout the evening and as each of them travelled back to their homes.

Ben Adam asked for blessings on behalf of people who were sick and could not attend the dance. He prayed for those imprisoned by steel bars and by personal weaknesses. And he asked the people to remember those people who had died since the last time they had gathered. Ben Adam's words were very well selected and presented to the pebble people.

Following a moment of silence, he started singing a warm-up song. He drummed slowly on the bottomside ridge of the battered old bucket and watched proudly as the pebbles began to dance. At first they moved slowly about the grooves of the bucket according to the rhythm of the song. "For this slow beat the traditional dancers should be thankful," Ben Adam said.

The pace quickened. Ben Adam sang louder and drummed faster. The dancers hopped about fervently, like fancy dancers, their thunderous hoofbeats in tune with the drumming and their blurred colors lit the air. Some of the pebbles began falling off the edge of the bucket to the ground. Ben Adam drummed and sang as long as there were some pebble dancers left.

After only a few were left, Ben Adam announced to them, "This will be a contest song!" He drummed faster and faster and harder until all the pebbles fell off the bucket. Then, carefully, he picked up those that were the last to fall. "Gee, that was a good contest," he said.

He thanked the dancers and said, "One day there will be a big, big contest. Only those who are really good can come and participate in it." Ben Adam put the winning pebbles into marked jars to save. "The winners of the contest and my favorite dancers, I will take into the house and put away in my fishtank for the winter," he said to himself and the pebble people.

The Endless Dark of the Night

Robert J. Conley

THEY HAD JUST pulled out of their drive and onto the rocky, secondary dirt road which ran in front of their house, and Sky had only just straightened the wheels when the headlights of the pickup caught it standing in the leaves beside the road. It was a small red fox. Actually it was mostly gray, but as it was early March following a long and hard winter for eastern Oklahoma, the predominance of the winter coat was logical. It did not move. It stood there bathed in the pickup's lights, and it stared, it seemed to Sky, right at him.

"That was a fox," he said.

"A fox?" said Gay. "You sure?"

"It was a fox, all right. Just standing there looking."

Gay got real quiet. That worried Sky a little, because generally when she got quiet like that something was bothering her, and more often than not it would involve some belief from the old Cherokee ways-something, Sky thought, that she was afraid he would interpret as superstition. The silence didn't last long. It was broken by the kids.

"Did you say a fox?" said Chooj.

"That's what it was."

"Was it real big?" said Little Gay.

"No, foxes are little."

The conversation continued along those lines — kids' questions — and that was the end of it. But even while he was answering the questions, Sky was thinking other things. He thought of his wife's silence. And he thought of how unusual it was anymore to see a fox in the hills of eastern Oklahoma. He also thought about what the Indian doctor had told Gay when she went to him because of the problems they were having with the kids. He had told her that somebody might be bothering them. He had said to watch out for any unusual sounds or smells, or small strange animals around the house. Sky tried to put the fox out of his mind, but he couldn't. The picture remained vivid.

It had happened on a Friday evening, and the next day Sky and Gay were surprised by a visit from their good friend, Deacon. They hadn't seen Deacon for some time — in fact, he hadn't visited them since their move to the country. They were talking about life in the country, how good it was compared to life in town. Sky told Deacon about the time the little *yoneg* boy across the street from them had pushed Little Gay off her bicycle into a ditch and Gay had gone charging out into the middle of the street.

"You're nothing but white trash," she had shouted, shaking her finger in the little boy's face.

"I think the whole neighborhood could hear her," said Sky, "and there was nothing but white people all up and down the block. When she came back inside, I told her, 'We better move out of this neighborhood.'"

"Yeah," said Deacon, "it's a whole sight better to be living out like this here. Out with the deer and such."

"We've had deer right in our yard. Walking right down the drive here. And just last night I seen a fox right out here on the road."

"A fox?"

"Yeah. Right down this road out here."

"Well," said Deacon, "you know what the old Indians say about that-whenever you see a fox?"

"What's that?"

"They say that whenever you see a fox that somebody's gonna die."

Tsgili, thought Sky, but out loud he only laughed.

"That's okay," he said, "as long as it's somebody on my list."

But the new information kept bothering him. Gay hadn't heard, so Sky didn't say anything to her about it.

It was three days later when he was driving to work that he saw the fox again. It was in the same spot by the side of the road, but it was lying in the dry leaves on its side. It was dead. He stopped the pickup and stared at it for a moment, then tried to shake it out of his mind and drove on to work. Three more mornings he looked at the dead fox there beside the road as he went to work, and still he said nothing. Friday night, right on time, Gay's ex-husband, the kids' daddy, came to pick them up for the week-end. It was he, Sky was certain, who was behind the *tsigili*. It wasn't him but it was someone he was paying. That was certain. Ever since Sky and Gay had gotten together, they each had the feeling that someone was working on them. They were also fairly certain who was paying for it and why and that they were working in the most sinister of all the ways of Cherokee witchcraft—through the children.

Sky and Gay went to bed early Friday night and made love. Their love was always good, and they believed that it was a divine love, a pre-ordained love. It was something powerful. It was strong medicine. It was sacred.

On Saturday they drove to the home of Gay's mother and spent the day with her family there. It was late when they got home, so they slept late Sunday morning. It was early Sunday afternoon, a nice, warm Spring day, when they were behind the house. Gay was walking along where the water pipe drained out into the woods, and she had spotted a leak. Sky was across the yard by the back porch.

"Sky," Gay called. "Come here."

"Okay."

He stopped to light a cigarette, then walked toward her, but before he got halfway, he saw that she was pointing to the ground by the back fence. Sky walked a few steps closer, and then saw it-a dead fox. It was smaller than the other, and seemed to Sky to have been dead a little longer. It was lying on its left side, exactly as the other, and, like the other, there was no blood, no indication of what

might have killed it. It was strange. It was eerie. And it didn't seem
to fit any known patterns.

*If you see a tsigili, Sky recalled, in four to seven days, he'll die. The fox is
dead. Right where I seen him. But I always thought that meant if you seen him
in human form. Another thing. If a tsigili dies or gets killed while he's in some
animal shape, he's supposed to turn back into a man after he's dead. And that
down the road there's a dead fox. And then there's that second one. Sometimes
they go in pairs. But still it don't all fit.*

Sky had been so intent on the foxes that for awhile he had
forgotten some other things that didn't fit. Like the time they had all
been out walking—Sky, Gay and the two kids. They had just gotten
back into the drive and the kids had run ahead of them to the house.
They had gone around the far side of the house in the yard.

"Mama."

"Sky. Come here. Look."

When Sky and Gay had arrived in the yard, there had been
nothing there, but Chooj said, "It was a big owl."

"He was sitting right there," said Little Gay, and she pointed to a
spot in the middle of the yard.

"He just sat there looking at us."

That had all happened some weeks earlier.

Another thing had been the set of small animal tracks the kids had
found in the fresh snow one morning that winter. They had come
back into the house and told Sky. He had put a pistol in his belt and
gone outside to investigate. He had followed the tracks from the
small barn which stood away from and facing the house, through the
yard, up to the front porch. From there they circled the house going
clockwise and coming right up to the house at each bedroom
window. Sky hadn't been able to identify the small tracks.

And then there were the crows. On several different occasions, two
very large crows had flown into the yard and made their loud *ga gas* as if
they were taunting those in the house. Sky had gone outside with his
rifle, but they always flew before he got out to find them. Sometimes
they would come back, louder than before—purposeful, it seemed.
And Sky was always suspicious of them when they came around.

What is that damn tsigili? *Fox? Owl? Crow? Are there two of them? Are they dead? Or did they leave them foxes here to do something to us?*

The next few nights, as it often was, Gay's sleep was troubled with bad dreams. Sky called the Deacon.

"Well," said Deacon, "it sounds to me like someone's trying to do something to you, and he don't know too much about Indian ways. Or else maybe what you got's stronger than what he's got."

Sky felt a little reassured, but he still felt like he needed further explanations. He knew some Creeks at work, and as Cherokee and Creek ways are much the same, Sky told them the story of the foxes. The Creek woman looked serious for a few seconds after Sky had stopped talking. Finally, she spoke. "You better go see someone," she said. "Within the month. Don't let it go by."

"I don't want to go to a Cherokee doctor," said Sky. "You never know who the other guy might be using."

"I know a couple of good ones," she said. "I can take you to one of them."

No more was said. No definite plans were made. But Sky stayed home from work the next day. The kids were at school, and Gay had taken the pickup to work, leaving Sky with the little Vega. And he heard the crows. Sky went outside with his grandfather's .22, but the crows flew. He saw them in the field across the way through his living room window. He went quietly out the back door and around the house, staying close to the house and in the shadows of the trees. He saw one crow high in a tree top. It was a long shot, but Sky decided to take it. He put the rifle to his shoulder and sighted in on the crow, and he couldn't remember all the right Cherokee words, so he said them in English in a whisper.

> *Instantly, the Red* Selagwuchi
> *strike you*
> *in the very center of your Soul.*
> *Instantly.*
> Yu.

And as he pronounced the final syllable, he fired. The crow dropped. Sky thought that he had got it, but then it began to fly. Perhaps he wounded it slightly. Perhaps he missed it completely, only frightening it away. *You can only kill a* tsigili *with a special doctored bullet.* He kept watching, and a few minutes later, saw two large crows through the trees on the other side of the field, flying down low, close to the road just about where the fox would be.

He went back inside and got his .22 six-shooter. He put the belt over his head, his right arm through the belt, so that the pistol was hanging on the left side of his chest, the butt toward his right. He lit a cigarette, put the pack and lighter in his shirt pocket and took the rifle in his right hand. He went out again, this time through the front door, and he got in the Vega, started it, and drove up the road to about the place where he thought the crows had been, but he saw nothing there — nothing except the fox. He backed down the road, stopped to pick up his mail, then backed down the drive and parked in front of the barn. He opened the door but stayed inside and started to read his mail.

He had read all the way through the classified ads in the newspaper when he heard the crows again. He put the paper aside and looked out across the field. There were two of them, and one was just settling down on a large rock at the base of a tree. Sky got out of the car and laid the rifle across its top. He took careful aim and repeated the ritual chant.

CRACK!

The crow jumped straight up and yelled.

AI!

It sounded almost human to Sky. It flew. His shot must have hit very close to it and stung it with dirt. Both crows were gone.

Sky went to the field to look for any evidence that he might have wounded the crow, but he couldn't find any. He sat down beneath a tree in the field to wait for them to come back.

"Come on, you damn *tsigili*," he said. "Come on."

He waited for an hour there in the field, but the crows did not come back. He did see them from time to time, but they circled far around the field.

"Damn *tsigili*. Son of a bitches."

He gave up and went back into the house.

"Probably just some damn ordinary old crows, anyway," he said.

"What's happening to me? I know there's someone messing around here, but I'm starting to see *tsigilis* everywhere. I can't let this happen to me. I need to go see a doctor."

When Gay and the kids got home, Sky didn't tell them about the crows, but he spent the evening in a deep sulk, and Gay wondered what was bothering him. That night, when he went to bed, Sky could hear, perhaps only in his imagination, he did not know, the faint *ga gas* of crows somewhere out in the endless dark of the night.

She Sits on the Bridge

Luci Tapahonso

WHEN NELSON was still running around and drinking years
ago, he was coming home from Gallup
hitch-hiking late at night
and right by Sheepsprings Trading Post—
you know where the turn to Crystal is?
Well, he was walking near there
when he heard a woman laughing somewhere nearby

It was dark there
(there were no lights at the trading post then)
he couldn't see anyone but he stopped and yelled out
    Where are you? What happened to you?
but she kept laughing louder and louder
and then she started to cry in a kind of scream.

Well, Nelson got scared and started running
then right behind him—he could hear her running too.
She was still crying and then he stopped   she stopped also.

She kept crying and laughing really loud
coming behind him and she caught up with him.
He knew even if he couldn't see her.
She was gasping and crying
right close to him—trying to catch her breath.

He started running again faster and off to the side
he saw some lights in the houses against the hill
and he ran off the road towards them
then she stopped and stayed on the highway
still laughing and crying very loudly.

When Nelson got to the houses
he heard people laughing and talking
they were playing winter shoe games inside there.
But a little ways away was a hogan with a light inside
he went there and knocked
                Come in   a voice said
An old man (somebody's grandpa) was there alone
and upon seeing him said
                Come in!   What happened to you?
and started to heat up some coffee.
Nelson told the old grandpa about
the woman crying on the road.

        You don't know about her? he asked.
        She sits on the bridge sometimes late at night.
        The wind blows through her long hair.
        We see her sitting in the moonlight or
        walking real slow pretending to be going to Shiprock.
        We people who live here know her and
        she doesn't bother us.
        Sometimes young men driving by pick her up—
        thinking she wants a ride and after riding a ways
        with them—she disappears right in front of them.
        She can't go too far away, I guess.

That's what he told Nelson
stirring his coffee.

Nelson stayed there in the hogan that night
and the old grandpa kept the fire going until morning.

The Journey

Duane Big Eagle

I HAD KNOWN the train all my life. Its wailing roar rushed through my dreams as through a tunnel and yet I had never even been on one. Now I was to take one on a two thousand kilometer journey half way into a foreign country!

This particular adventure was my fault, if you can call being sick a fault. Mama says finding fault is only a way of clouding a problem and this problem was clouded enough. It began when I was thirteen and I still have tuberculosis scars on my lungs but this illness was more than tuberculosis. The regular doctors were mystified by the fevers and delirium that accompanied a bad cough and nausea. After six months of treatment without improvement they gave up.

Papa carried me on his back as we left the doctor's office and began our walk to the barrio that was our home. Mama cried as she walked and Papa seemed weighted by more than the weight of my thinned-down frame. About half way home Papa suddenly straightened up. I was having a dizzy spell and almost slipped off his back but he caught me with one hand and shouted, "Aunt Rosalie! What a fool I am! Aunt Rosalie Stands Tall!" Papa started to laugh and to dance around and around on the dirt path in the middle of a field.

"What do you mean?" cried Mama as she rushed around with her hands out, ready to catch me if I fell. From the look on her face, the real question in her mind was more like, Have you gone mad? "Listen, woman," said Papa, "there are some people who can cure diseases the medical doctors can't. Aunt Rosalie Stands Tall is a medicine woman of the Yaqui people and one of the best! She'll be able to cure Raoul! The only problem is she's married to an Indian in the United States. But that can't be helped, we'll just have to go there. Come on, we have plans to make and work to do!"

The planning began that day. We had very little money, but with what we had and could borrow from Papa's many friends there was just enough for a child's ticket to the little town in Oklahoma where Rosalie lived. I couldn't be left alone in a foreign country so Papa decided simply to walk. "I'll take the main highway north to the old Papago trails that go across the desert. They'll also take me across the border undetected. Then I'll head east and north to Oklahoma. It should be easy to catch occasional rides once I get to the U.S. When I arrive I'll send word for Raoul to start."

Papa left one fine Spring morning, taking only a blanket, a few extra pairs of shoes, bow and arrows to catch food, and a flintstone for building fires. Secretly I believe he was happy to be travelling again. Travel had always been in his blood. As a young man, Papa got a job on a sailing ship and travelled all over the world. This must have been how he learned to speak English and also how he met Mama in the West Indies. Myself, I was still sixty kilometers from the town I was born in and even to imagine the journey I was about to take was more than my fevered brain could handle. But as Mama said, "You can do anything in the world if you take it little by little and one step at a time." This was the miraculous and trusting philosophy our family lived by, and I must admit it has usually worked.

Still, the day of departure found me filled with a dread that settled like lead in my feet. If I hadn't been so light-headed from the fevers, I'm sure I would have fallen over at any attempt to walk. Dressed in my best clothes which looked shabby the minute we got to the train station, Mama led me into the fourth-class carriage and found me a seat on a bench near the windows. Then she disappeared and came back a minute later with a thin young man with sallow skin and a drooping Zapata mustache. "This is your second cousin, Alejandro. He is a conductor on this train and will be with you till you get to Juarez; you must do whatever he says."

At that time, the conductors on trains in Mexico were required to stay with a train the entire length of its journey which perhaps accounted for Alejandro's appearance. He did little to inspire my confidence in him. In any case, he disappeared a second later and it was time for Mama to go too. Hurriedly, she reminded me that there was money in my coat to buy food from the women who came onto the train at every stop and that there was a silver bracelet sown into the cuff of my pants to bribe the guards at the border. With one last tearful kiss and hug, she was gone and I was alone. The train started with a jerk which knocked me off my bench and I began my journey upside down in a heap on top of my crumpled cardboard suitcase. I didn't even get a chance to wave goodbye.

I soon got used to the jerking starts of the train, and unsmiling Alejandro turned out to be a guardian angel which was fortunate because my illness began to get worse as the journey went along. Many times I awoke to find Alejandro shuffling some young thief away from my meager possessions or buying me food at the last stop before a long stretch of desert. He would bring me things too, fresh peaches and apples and left-over bread and pastries from the first-class carriages where he worked. Once, in the middle of the desert he brought me a small ice-cold watermelon, the most refreshing thing I'd ever tasted—who knows where he got it?

To this day, I'm not sure exactly which of the things I saw through the window of the train were real and which were not. Some of them I know were not real. In my delirium, a half days journey would pass in the blink of an eye. Often I noticed only large changes in the countryside, from plains to mountains to desert. Broad valleys remain clearly in my mind and there were many of these. Small scenes, too, remain—a family sitting down to dinner at a candle-lit table in a hut by a river. And a few more sinister ones— once between two pine trees I caught a glimpse of one man raising a large club to strike another man whose back was turned. I cried out but there was nothing to be done, the train was moving too fast on a downgrade and probably couldn't have been stopped. But then, did I really see them at all? My doubt was caused by the girl in the dark red dress.

I think I began to see her about half way through the journey to

Juarez. She was very beautiful, high cheekbones, long black hair and very dark skin. She was about my height and age or maybe a little older. Her eyes were very large and her mouth seemed to have a ready smile. The first time I saw her, at a small station near a lake, she smiled and waved as the train pulled away. Her sensuality embarrassed me and I didn't wave back. I regretted it immediately. But she was back again the next day at a station in the foothills of the mountains, this time dressed in the white blouse and skirt that the Huichol women wear.

She became almost a regular occurrence. Sometimes she was happy, sometimes serious and most of the time she was wearing the dark red dress. Often I would only see her in passing; she'd be working in a field and raise up to watch the train go by. Gradually, my condition grew worse. My coughing fits grew longer and I slept more so I began not to see the girl so much, but the last time I saw her really gave me a shock. The mountains of the Sierra Madre Oriental range are very rugged and are cut in places by deep gorges called barrancas. The train was in one of these gorges on a ledge above the river and was about to go around a bend. For some reason, I looked back the way we had come and there, imbedded in the mountain with her eyes closed, was the face of the girl, thirty feet high! For the first time, I noticed the small crescent-shaped scar in the middle of her lower lip.

The vision, or whatever it was, quickly disappeared as the train rounded the curve. I sank back on to the bench with a pounding heart and closed my eyes. I must have slept or perhaps I fell into a coma because I remember very little of the last part of the trip. I awoke once while Alejandro was carrying me across the border and delivering me to a friend of his on the train to Dallas. How I got from Dallas to Oklahoma I may never know because I remember nothing. But it happened. And finally, I awoke for a minute in my father's arms as he carried me off the train.

Then, there was a sharp pain in the center of my chest. And a pounding. Rhythmic pounding. A woman's voice began to sing in a very high pitch. My eyes opened of themselves. At first I couldn't make it out, arched crossing lines, flickering shadows. I was in the center of an oval-shaped lodge built of bent willow limbs covered with skins and lit by a small fire. A tall woman came into view; she was singing and dancing back and forth. Somehow I knew this was Rosalie Stands Tall, the medicine woman. The pain hit me again and I wanted to get away but hands held me still.

Papa's voice said in my ear, "She is calling her spirit helpers, you must try and sit up." I was sitting up facing the door of the lodge. There was a lizard there and he spoke in an old man's voice, words I couldn't understand. Rosalie sang again and there was a small hawk there. The pain rose up higher in my chest. There was a coyote in the door and his words were tinged with mocking laughter. The pain rose into my throat. There was a small brown bear in the door, his fur blew back and forth in the wind. The pain rose into the back of my mouth. I felt I needed to cough. Rosalie put two porcupine quills together and bound them with leather to make a pair of tweezers. She held my lips closed with them, painfully tight. A pair of wings beat against the top of the lodge. I needed badly to cough. There was something hot in my mouth, it was sharp, it was hurting my mouth, it needed to come out! IT WAS OUT!

I awoke in bed in a small room lit by a coal-oil lamp. There was a young woman with her back to me preparing food by the side of the bed. She had very long black hair. She put the tray down on the table beside the bed. As she turned to leave the room, I saw a small crescent-shaped scar in the middle of her lower lip. I started to call her back but there was no need. I knew who she was. An immense peacefulness settled over me. It was warm in the bed. Papa sat on the other side of the bed. He seemed very happy when I turned and looked at him. He said softly, "Raoul, you have changed completely. You're not anymore the young boy I left in Mazatlan." I wanted to tell him everything! There was so much to say! But all I could get out was, "Yes, I know, Papa, I've come on a journey out of childhood." And then I went to sleep again.

The Talking That Trees Does

(from a novel-in-progress entitled *Daughters of Lot*)

Geary Hobson

BEFORE I COMMENCE, I just want to say this: I take a long
time telling you all about these kin—these aunts and uncles and
grandparents and great-grandparents and cousins and all—and the
land hereabouts and its shapes and looks back then and all its changes
and all its going-ons...

All that land you see across the bayou
yonder and some of it on this side, counting where we're sitting
right now, used to belong to our folks. All along Emory Bayou, clear
down to where it cuts and runs into Muddy Bayou, and then on
north a ways nearly to Black Bayou, and then on due west some
almost to Coldstream, nearly all the land that Eustace Tanner claims
title to now and rents on shares to people like the Hewitts and
Renfros and Wades—that whole portion, which is a shade-bit more
than a section, used to be held in the name of our people. Back then,
at the time I'm going to tell you about, Uncle Andrew Thompson
held title to it but it wudn't just his. What I mean is, he didn't own it
all to hisself. The way we all looked at it, it was more Aunt Minnie's
and Aunt Velma's and even to say that ain't entirely correct neither.
What I mean to say is, it belonged to us all, not to one, or even two,
but to *all*. All of us that was kinfolks and lived on it and spent our
time on it and knowed it as ours. In them days there was a whole
slew of little cabins and clapboard houses belonging to Thompson
and Squirrel kin scattered throughout the section and it was mostly
woods then. It was ours and it was like an island surrounded by a
whole sea of newcomers who moved in and built their houses and

started their farms and set up stores and cotton gins and churches and
such-like all around us. The way we looked at it, that was alright,
long as we was left by ourselves. And for a long time that was the
way it was.

I was born out west around Simms Bayou, over where some of
your mother's folks are still living. Matter of fact, a whole lot of that
land out there used to be ours too. Some kinfolks out there still own
some of that land, but what they got left ain't much. It's all just a
turnip patch now, upside what it used to be. Same as it is over here. I
don't remember my mama any. She died of the typhoid fever when I
was two and I never knowed my daddy neither, except that he was a
white man. Don't ask me how I know that or why it's even
important, if it is, even. I might get around to telling that but I doubt
it, since I think it's a separate story all to itself. I was took and raised
by Mama's folks, my Grandma and Grandpa Sanford, until they up
and died too. First it was Grandma that died and then a few months
after that, Grandpa passed on too. They lived right by Grandma's
folks, the Lamleys, on a dirt road that run alongside Simms Bayou
pert-near all the way to Bayou Bartholomew. When Grandpa
passed away or went, as he used to say, "back into the earth," I was
took and raised by my Uncle Achan. He was one of Grandma's
brothers.

There was four of them in Uncle Achan's house on Simms Bayou,
not counting me, and they was all old folks and Uncle Achan's
bachelor or widowed brothers and sister. There was Uncle Achan,
who was sixty-something and head of the place, and his younger
brothers, Joe and Zeno, and there was their older sister, my Aunt
Gustine, who was in her seventies. They all talked French to each
other, but I never picked up none of it. They come from around
Arkansas Post and sometimes they would talk about all the property
their mama and daddy had had over there long before Arkansas
became a state. Quapaw they was mostly, even if you wouldn't of
thought it of them because of that French they talked and the way it
looked to me like they tried to act when other folks not kin to them
or me come around to visit. I'll give you some for instances. Aunt

Gustine used to set a real pretty tea set out for evening visitors, and this to folks who wouldn't of been able to tell the difference between store-bought tea and stumpwater. She never done this to put on airs, I don't 'spect, but just to try and keep up some kind of sign of what their folks' ways had been like at the Post when they was all little kids growing up there. And there was Uncle Zeno and his realfine five-dollar gold watch that he was proud as all git out of. Five dollars for a gold watch was some big doings in them days. He used to carry it around in a little homemade watchpocket that Aunt Gustine had fixed up for him on his britches, even when he hunted and fished or chopped corn or cotton. They was a stand-offish bunch that generally kept to theirselves, in a whole lot of ways like my Aunt Minnie and Aunt Velma that I'm going to tell you about directly.

I never minded living with them even if I did have to do a right fair amount of fetching and toting for them — as Uncle Andrew one time said about it — and never got to be around any kids my own age. Except for some corn, Uncle Achan and them didn't farm any. They had some horses and hogs, but like us when I lived with Uncle Andrew, they let their stock run loose in the woods until they needed them. Uncle Achan and my other uncles just hunted and fished mostly, just like our granddaddy Jed used to do. Of course, Jed was directly descended from them and he had the same kinds of ways they had.

I stayed with them for two years and I learned a lot about fishing and hunting. I also learned most of my American from them because I couldn't talk it very good when I was littler and living with Grandma and Grandpa Sanford. Grandpa Sanford talked Cherokee to me and to Grandma too. She learned it during all them years she lived with Grandpa. Uncle Andrew used to come over there from time to time to see how us all was doing. Mainly, though, I think he come just to see me. Finally, one time when he come over, he talked to Uncle Achan and Aunt Gustine about me coming back over here and going to school. Why I was pert-near twelve years old and wouldn't of knowed anything about schooling even if it was to of snuck up on me and bit me in the butt. Uncle Andrew told about how his daughter Letty was learning to read and write real good and that I ought to learn it too. Me, I was all for it. He said they had a surveyor feller with the new railroad that was running by Coldstream who was teaching the younguns thereabouts their ABCs and stuff. Said the man wanted to git out of railroad work because he hated traveling around and that he wanted to set up a full-scale school at Coldstream. So, anyway, it was decided by Uncle Achan and Aunt Gustine and Uncle Andrew and them other Lamley uncles that I ought to come over here and live with Uncle Andrew and Aunt Elvira and learn my ABCs with my cousins and the other kids. And that was how I come to live over here and here I been ever since.

Well, that schooling part went okay for a few months and then that surveyor feller, Mr. Bailey, was up and transferred out by the railroad to somewhere else and that was the end of my schooling. But at least I had my ABCs by then and could read a smidgin and figure some figures and from then on out I went on and learned more by my own self after I growed up.

That great-big cypress over there, where the bayou starts to turn this way? Well, up that rise from it, that's where Uncle Andrew's house used to be, and from where we're sitting now you couldn't of seen it in them days for all the trees. That house was pretty big even for them days. It was log-built with four rooms connected by a dog-trot to four more rooms. It had a wide front porch and a little bitty back porch and the whole thing was set high up on cypress blocks and covered on the outside with cypress shingles. There was a lot of out buildings too, a barn, a cow shed, a corncrib, and a pigpen. Now you can't hardly see a single sign of none of it, for shore none of the oak and gumball trees that covered the whole place. But if you look close from here, you can see a couple of apple trees that's gone wild mixed in that thicket that runs alongside that ditch going into the bayou. That's all that's left of the fruit orchard Uncle Andrew had in his backyard. One time about ten years ago, I walked around up there, looking at the plowed ground, and I picked up a handful of them old-timey square nails. They was all bent and eat up with rust and not good for nothing anymore. But I still got them in a coffee can that I keep on my bedstand.

Now this bayou here, I spent many a day in there when I was little, getting my tail end wet frogging after crawdads and shiners, and when I got bigger I trapped and fished and hunted all up and down it, clean down to Muddy. I have took many a coon and possum and rabbit out of them bayou woods and snagged many a bass and cat and buffalo with my trapboxes and trotlines. Now you look out there and what do you see? Nothing but a handful of cypress and a soybean field that stays too damp most of the year-round for that fool Eustace Tanner to get much more than a sorry crop out of. That Tanner. He's a sight. Like most of his kin, he's a man that's so stingy and selfish and shifty that he has to lock his tools up every night so he won't steal them off of hisself. It was all a sight better when it was all bayou woods down there.

Uncle Andrew was looked on as our chief around here when I was a boy, but we never called him that. I mean we never made a point of just flat out calling him chief. He just was. He was your great-great granddaddy, and he wudn't actually my uncle at all. What he was, he was a cousin. But I called him uncle all the same and even sort of looked up to him like the daddy I never had. He farmed quite a bit of cotton and corn and had some livestock that run wild in the woods until we needed some beef or ham or a horse to ride. People used to say that he was better at farming than most of the white farmers around here even, and you might not believe it but that's saying something for shore since it's been my notice that white people always act like they invented farming and things like that. Uncle Andrew was married to Elvira Squirrel, who was Quapaw Indian and close kin to the Lamley and Tyrell folks. Uncle Andrew, as you know, was close to being a full-blood Indian hisself. He was almost half-Chickasaw and full half-Cherokee. Him and Aunt Elvira had two girls. There was Letty, who was eight when I come over here to live with them, and there was Marandy, who was already a grown woman and married and with a family of her own. Marandy and her husband lived further off down the bayou a ways, but still in yelling distance of our house. Uncle Andrew and Aunt Elvira had a boy too, I think I heard one time, but he died when he was little and so I never knowed him.

This was all Thompson land that Uncle Andrew farmed. It belonged to his and Aunt Minnie's and Aunt Velma's daddy, and they say that just before he died, he — old Alluk, their daddy — put it all in Uncle Andrew's name because in them days women couldn't hold title to land. Matter of fact, Indians wudn't suppose to neither. I heard it told that old Alluk got around that prejudice by his out and out oneryness and by out-whiting the whites. He donated money to both the Coldstream Baptist Church and the Coldstream Cumberland Presbyterian one that has long since gone out of business, and he never even set foot in neither one of them. This was before the Methodist one come along that Aunt Elvira and Marandy joined up with. Old Alluk bought this section sometime back in the 1840's and moved here from Bonaparte. It was after he died and Uncle Andrew and Aunt Elvira got married and started their family that all the assorted Squirrel and Tyrell kin started moving in over here.

But even if all the outside folks counted Uncle Andrew as our leader, it was really my two aunts, Aunt Minnie and Aunt Velma, who was the real head of our folks. Since Arkansas law in them days had it that no woman — not even two women together — could own land in their own name, it was all in Uncle Andrew's name. Them aunts was old women even when I was a boy and they lived off down hereabouts on the bayou, off to theirselves. Two old-maid aunts they was, always good to me and passable pleasant to most other folks around here, but still at the same time they kept off by theirselves mostly. When I first come over here to live, they was medicine women and they did midwifing and stuff like that for all the folks around here. Over at Simms Bayou, Aunt Gustine and Uncle Achan was medicine people too, but they wudn't educated to it like Aunt Minnie and Aunt Velma was. And that wasn't all. Aunt Minnie and Aunt Velma was makers of spells and fixers of bones, what they used to call "putter-inners" and "taker-outers." This meant they was in a special kind of class as healers and was looked up to by mostly everybody around. And it wudn't just our folks that come to them for doctoring either. Sometimes white folks and niggers come to see them, too, when they needed help.

Back then, there wudn't no doctors—school trained white doctors I mean—around here like there is now. Some of the plantations started hiring doctors a little later on, but when I first come over here there wudn't none. The closest white doctor I knowed anything about was over at Delta City and he was a half-blind old drunk who was just as apt to saw you in two as to cut your britches leg off if you was to go see him to have him do something about your bad leg. They tell a story about how he doctored a cow with a whole mess of calomel when he got called out to somebody's house one time. I don't remember whose house and whose cow it was. The story goes that when that doctor got there and asked where the patient was, the man whose house he was at said, "She's on back there in that-ter back room, Doc," and so when the doc went on back he made a wrong turn or something and instead of going into the bedroom he winded up at a kind of lean-to shed they had there—a milk stall I 'spect it was—that was built on the back of the house. "She," so the doc must of thought, was the white-face cow they had tied back there and not the man's wife who was in the bedroom the whole time. Well, the doc guessed that the cow's belly was a little too swole up so he dosed her up real good with some calomel. They say that for a whole week that cow shit like a tied coon. And they also say that he never did git around to doctoring that sick woman.

So there was no doctors to speak of in these parts. Not unless a person wanted to go to a cow-doctoring old drunk over on the river at Delta City and that about twelve miles away. That, or travel sixty mile by train to Pine Bluff, but even then to go by train to Pine Bluff, you would of had to go clear out to Monticello to catch the train. Or if a boat was handy, and I guess this would of been the most likely thing to do, you could go down and then cross the river to Greenville where two or three school trained white doctors was. But folks around here in them days wudn't likely to do things that way. They was all-white, colored, Indian—pretty hard-working folks, farmers and loggers and hunters and fishermen, folks not known to have much in the way of cash on them or a whole lot of time on their hands for traveling. So when it come to patching up torn-up bodies and dosing whooping cough and such-like, why they had to make do with what they had. My two aunts was Indian medicine-makers, taught by their own aunt who was, so I been told, a full-blood Deer Clan Cherokee woman who come into these parts from the old country back east when the government started pushing Indians off of their lands, and they knowed a heap about doctoring and so folks just naturally come to them for help.

Aunt Minnie and Aunt Velma was Cherokee. Well, they was and they wudn't. What I mean is their mama was Cherokee, Deer Clan, like that older medicine-maker sister of hers whose name I never knowed except that I remember that an older cousin of mine sometime just called her Deer Woman and that she was a Sendforth. Their granddaddy, Aunt Minnie's and Aunt Velma's, was an Indian who somehow got his name listed on the government enrolling census as Sendforth because I 'spect he likely considered hisself and his family too as them that was sent forth from their homeland. Anyhow, that's where my name come from. My granddaddy, the son of the Sendforth I'm talking about, he changed it to Sandford, and according to Uncle Andrew, it was my mama who spelled it Sanford, dropping one of the "d's." I guess maybe I'm expected to change it up some too, since it seems like that's what the tradition calls for. Only I won't. I'm satisfied with it just the way it is. Always remember this: we ain't the people our granddaddies and grandmas was. I know that real good and so I guess I just don't have the gumption to change my name any like they done.

As I done said, Aunt Minnie and Aunt Velma's daddy was old Alluk Thompson. He was a Chickasaw man from Mississippi and he come into these parts about the time Arkansas become a territory, settling down first at Bonaparte, then over at Simms Bayou, and then finally over here. Now Bonaparte, in case you don't know it, was a pretty good-sized river town back then, like Delta City is now, only even bigger, and it was knowed far and wide for its saloons and bawdy

houses and gambling dens. It was kind of like the way the south side of
Pine Bluff is these days, except that it would of made Pine Bluff look
like a Sunday School class if the two was to be put upside each other and
looked at. Bonaparte is long gone. When I was still just a little-bitty
squirt, it was washed away. I can still remember when it happened.
There come a big flood and it was entirely washed off the face of the
land. All its buildings and streets and stores and pest-houses and filth
and meanness was swept clean away by the Mississippi. I 'spect
Bonaparte might be found somewheres down in the Gulf of Mexico
now, mayored over and sheriffed over by big catfishes talking
Mexican. Wouldn't faze me a bit to hear it.

Now, old Alluk's wife died while they was still living in
Bonaparte, a long time before the flood come, and when she did, he
come up and moved to Simms Bayou where there was other Indian
folks living, taking with him when he moved Aunt Minnie and Aunt
Velma, who was just little girls then, and a whole passel of assorted
kinfolks. Old Alluk stayed at Simms Bayou just about a year, long
enough to sell off his holdings in and around Bonaparte. Then he up
and moved over here, buying this section when there wudn't no
more than a handful of people in the whole township. That old aunt
come with them, too, and she was by that time a kind of substitute
mama to Aunt Minnie and Aunt Velma as well as their medicine
teacher. The story goes that she hated old Alluk like rat poison, but
that she come along on the move to help bring up the girls and Uncle
Andrew, too, who was just a little-bitty kid then, and even then she
wouldn't live in the same house with him. She lived off by herself in
the woods a ways and, as I heard it, would never set foot in Alluk's
house as long as he was around and would never talk nothing but
Cherokee to them girls and Uncle Andrew, or for that metter to
other folks neither when she even bothered to talk to other people at
all. I can just barely remember that older aunt, who I calculate
would of been my great-great aunt. She was always a shadowy
person to me, just like my memory of her is now, and I remember
her as the oldest person I think I ever seen or even knowed about. So
even if Aunt Minnie and Aunt Velma was almost half-Chickasaw as

well as being half-Cherokee, they was really more Cherokee in their
ways because of that older aunt's influence on them. That woman
just straight out took them girls away from their daddy, but like
some older folks was in the habit of saying when I was a boy, that
had been the best thing that could of happened to them. There had
been some talk, all a long, long time before I was even borned, that
my aunts had been wayward and wild some before they moved away
from Bonaparte and Simms Bayou and come over here, especially
with that white-trash element there was around at Bonaparte.
Whatever the story was, that old aunt took over care of them and
brung them up proper in a good Indian way. She, who had spent just
about all her whole life taking care of them or some other Thompson
or other kin and never getting married to nobody, just like her nieces
in their time would never wed nobody either, left her impression on
them girls just as sure and certain as a candle mold does when you go
and pour a dab of hot wax on it.

                                             ... because I believe that
all this forever afterwards will be the key to who you going to be and
what you make out of yourself to be. It ain't no real never-mind at
all whether you stay living around here the rest of your life, or
whether you move off to somewheres else. You this place and this
place is you. Don't ever forgit it, son.

Maybe He Is A Born Storyteller

Wilma Elizabeth McDaniel

W E HEARD a relative talking about Sartis Winn. He said, "That kid is the biggest liar for his age in the whole state of Oklahoma, probably in the world. Why if he accidentally told the truth, he'd lie out of it. His mother ought to rename him Windy."

The relative's cousin asked rather shocked, "That's pretty strong. What did he tell?"

"What did he tell? I'll tell you. He came from school the first day and described everything that happened. He said the first thing the teacher done was to call the roll. She rolled up a paper and hit each kid on the head when she called his name. Sartis said that was why it was called calling the roll. He also said the teacher made the first graders draw a map of North America and work ten problems in long division. Don't look at me like that. He said it, and that's not all. He told his mother that the teacher made everyone go outside at recess and rake the yard, pump water, and gather wood for winter. He also told his mother that when the kids opened their lunchboxes, their chicken and fried pies were gone, and the boxes were full of corncobs and cockleburs. You tell me that kid ain't no liar, or maybe is a born storyteller."

Return Of A Native Dreamer

Wilma Elizabeth McDaniel

OSCAR TETLEY came back to Depew and walked around the old frame house where he had lived as a child in the early 1930's. A sign read, "Condemned. Do not Enter."

The waitress at The Knife and Fork Cafe was very helpful. She said, "Yeah, they're going to tear that old house down as soon as the city gets around to it." She poured his coffee and asked, "Did you use to live here?'

"Yes, I learned most of what I know right here. Part of it in the green frame house, and part of it in the red brick grammar school."

The waitress said in amazement, "Why, my dad graduated from that school in 1934. Maybe you remember Homer Hamlin?"

"Oh my, yes. We graduated the same year. How is Homer?"

"Daddy died of a heart attack when he was only forty years old. He never left here, stayed on and farmed Grandpa Hamlin's old place."

Oscar lingered and had a piece of pie. He said, "I hate to think about the old house being demolished. If I had my druthers, I'd go there and live with kerosene lamps, and a few mice for company. Now, I know that sounds looney, but it gave me such a jolt to see the place again, and it was condemned."

He stirred his coffee and smiled. "Well, the old Depew water tower is the same anyway," and he made a wry face, "and so is the bad tasting water."

The waitress said, "People come back from other states and tell us the same thing. I don't notice it because I never have been away."

Pilgrims

Roxy Gordon

WHEN THE INDIANS came to town, Charlie Tabor, the barber, called old Dock Middleton and asked him to come by the barber shop. Then Charlie Tabor needed an excuse to keep the Indians at the barber shop till Dock Middleton could get there, so he told the Indians they'd have to wait until Pink Isaacs came to town to give them permission to go out to Bead Mountain. Pink Isaacs did indeed own Bead Mountain but nobody needed permission to visit the place. Charlie Tabor called Pink and Pink said it was a curious story but he guessed it was true. Bead Mountain was called Bead Mountain, after all, because of all the clay Indian beads that used to lay scattered about. Pink said he wouldn't mind meeting the Indians and taking them but he was, that day, too damn busy pulling rusty pipe on his windmill, and he said to tell them to feel free to camp there if they felt like it.

Charlie Tabor had taken charge of the Indians that morning because he'd been the first to see them. He'd been walking to the barber shop about 7:30 and he'd seen them parked down by the Home Creek bridge where they'd spend the night. He didn't know they were Indians, but Charlie Tabor was always bound to check anything, so he'd walked to the bridge. At first he'd guessed they were Mexicans, but Mexicans weren't apt to be traveling about in touring cars and certainly not apt to be camping beside Home Creek. So as Tabor walked up on them, he'd decided they must be gypsies.

There were four of them, two men dressed in denim overalls, a woman, and an old man wearing a dirty, shapeless wool dress suit.

When Tabor saw that the old man was wearing braids, he realized with surprise that these had to be Indians. Charlie Tabor had never before seen an Indian. He'd come to west Texas as a young man from Alabama thirty years after the last Indian had gone.

So Charlie Tabor had introduced himself and spoken of the fine morning, and the younger of the two men in overalls answered him carefully and none-too-happily.

"You people traveling, are you?" Charlie Tabor had asked the young man and the young man had said they were. Charlie Tabor asked where they'd come from and the young man said Oklahoma. Charlie Tabor asked where they were going and the young man seemed hesitant to answer. Charlie Tabor, who was bound to do his best to understand everything, had decided there was something about these Indians camped on Home Creek that he needed to know.

Charlie Tabor never was a man without words, so he had talked. He had talked nonsense, passing the time of day, commenting on the weather and how the creek was low, and he supposed he'd go up to the Blue Hole one of these evenings and catch some perch. The young man appeared confused; the old man paid no attention. The other man in overalls, he seemed to listen.

The two in overalls had stood by the car while the old man squatted by the dying breakfast fire as if to soak up heat though it was August and the old man was wearing a woolen suit. The woman cleared dishes.

The man who seemed to listen had finally spoken. He said, "My name is Amos Horn. This is my son; he's called Brian. And this is my father. That woman there, she's my old woman."

Charlie Tabor had introduced himself and asked again, "You folks just traveling?"

Amos Horn said, "We brought my father. This is the country where he was born and lived. He was a child over by that big mountain." Amos Horn had pointed east and Tabor guessed he meant Santa Anna Mountain. Twelve or fifteen miles east, Santa Anna Mountain was the only hill in that part of Texas which might deserve the name mountain.

"We camped there a few days," Amos Horn said, "and then my

father wanted to come here to another place." Charlie Tabor had glanced at the old man who still paid no attention. "There is another mountain over that way," Amos Horn said as he pointed to the southwest. "He says it's the other side of these hills." Low wooded hills banked the south side of the creek. Tabor guessed he meant Bead Mountain. It wasn't a mountain like Santa Anna Mountain, but setting as it did on the prairie alone, it was a widely noted landmark and could be seen from miles in any direction. Bead Mountain was maybe four miles away, on the other side of the breaks of Home Creek. Being down in the creek bottom, they couldn't see it.

So Charlie Tabor had decided to situate them in his barber shop till he could check all this over more carefully, and he'd told them he'd call Pink Isaacs, the man who owned Bead Mountain.

Amos Horn and Brian sat on straight wooden benches in the barber shop and the old man and the woman waited in the car while Tabor did his calling.

Dock Middleton didn't need a haircut and he couldn't figure out why exactly Charlie Tabor was anxious to get him to the barber shop. Charlie Tabor was a man who liked to talk but there were enough loafers in Valera that Tabor never lacked for conversation. Dock Middleton, nevertheless, pulled on his boots and took out for the barber shop.

Dock Middleton was seventy-two years old. He'd lived in western Texas all his life. His childhood had been spent on the Llano in the hill country and he'd come to Coleman County to cowboy when the range was still open and run by the big cow outfits. He'd lived here ever since, first cowboying and later raising cows himself down on the Colorado — except for a time in the early seventies when he'd joined the Frontier Battallion of the Texas Rangers to chase Indians and horse thieves.

The Ranger service, that was the reason Charlie Tabor had wanted Dock Middleton in his barber shop — not the Ranger service itself but the mold of mind it seemed to have given Dock Middleton. And, particularly, it was a conversation Dock Middleton had carried on in the spring; that conversation, Tabor's memory of it, had led Tabor to call. Middleton and an old doctor named Zeller had been sitting on the wooden benches, killing time, when Dock Middleton had complained about a pain. He'd said he guessed it was his liver hurting him. The old doctor asked him where exactly was the pain and Dock Middleton had pointed out a patch of midriff which Doctor Zeller told him couldn't possibly be the liver because that wasn't where the liver was located and he was a doctor and he ought to know. But Dock Middleton had strongly disagreed. He'd said he didn't know much about doctoring but, by God, he'd damn well cut open enough dead Indians when he was a Ranger that he knew exactly where lay the liver.

Charlie Tabor had been amused and a bit shocked to hear the old man say such a thing. It was an image he couldn't grasp, this skinny cowboy-hatted old man, two generations earlier butchering the dead bodies of human beings. It was a curious thing to Charlie Tabor. And Charlie Tabor, the man who checked everything, naturally remembered that conversation when he saw the Indians that morning down by Home Creek.

Burned Black Horn had never been greatly sentimental, and it was not sentiment that had led him to wish a return to the localities of his childhood and young manhood. It was, instead, a mystery which sent him back. Burned Black Horn was not of a philosophical turn of mind either. He had little need to understand the universe or his place in it. Indeed, had his universe not turned itself upside down so unbelievably, he would have spent the balance of all his days with no mysteries at all, with everything fitting exactly in the place it should have fit. But nothing fit anymore; the universe which should have fit right-side-up was right-upside-down. Burned Black Horn had been much younger when things flip-flopped but, then, he had seen no particular mystery. It had been the whitemen who were out to turn it and if the whitemen could have been destroyed, then the universe would have stood upright. The People were, in the end, unable to stop the whitemen, so the universe had had no protectors. But, of course, as a young man Burned Black Horn had not really thought in such terms at all. What he really had thought was something like this: The Tejanos have killed my relatives at The Place Where Salt

Seeps and, therefore, I must kill me some Tejanos. And this thing
that he had thought had meant the exact same thing as if he had
planned some defense of a right-standing universe.

It was after Burned Black Horn had passed middle age that he had
begun to have flashes that something was more dreadfully wrong
than he had suspected. True, many of his relatives and friends had
died a long time ago at the hands of the Tejanos and the army and,
true, he and his surviving relatives and friends had been in most ways
confined and kept from the haunts and pursuits of earlier days. But
still the Wichita Mountains where the Burned Black Horn family
camped was a good place and the Burned Black Horn camp was full
of his friends and relatives and many descendants. Burned black
Horn was never very hungry — those Wichita Mountains provided
better than the white agent provided.

And in the part of his self that listened, Burned Black Horn heard the
same murmuring of that-which-is-and-was-and-will-be that he had
always heard. Burned Black Horn was neither particularly philosophical nor, in the mumbo jumbo terms of the whiteman's explanation of
religion, was he particularly religious. It was just that part of his self
that could hear always clearly heard the sweet murmur of that-which-
is-and-was-and-will-be. This was what Burned Black Horn heard
every moment of his life until one bad hot August when he was past
middle age and then he didn't hear anything at all.

Burned Black Horn wouldn't have been able to say that he'd lost
the murmur in the part of his self that heard. And he wouldn't have
been able to say that at along last, these years later, the universe was
truly turned upside down. But after a generation of silence in the
part of his self that heard, he had said to his son, Amos, "I want to go
back to the places I lived when I was a boy."

Dock Middleton was called Dock because his full first name was
Dockery which had been his mother's maiden name. Most every
new acquaintance assumed he was a doctor. Dock didn't much care.
God knows he'd done his share of horse and cow doctoring and he'd
cut bullets and a stray arrow or two out of men and set more than one

old boy's broken leg. But Dock Middleton didn't in any way consider himself a doctor. In most ways, it never occurred to Dock Middleton to consider himself anything. He was just old Dock Middleton, a cowman too old and stove-up to work cows—old Dock Middleton whose wife, Audrey, died in 1912, who had two sons, one in San Angelo trying to sell real estate and one in Eldorado raising sheep, an old man who played dominos and wasn't any too clean.

Dock Middleton was an old man in Valera, Texas during the Great Depression, right now hobbling on his bad left leg—that leg damaged these forty years since one of Clay Mann's bad horses fell on it—hobbling beside the deserted blacktopped highway into the center of town toward Charlie Tabor's barber shop. Dock Middleton had by now ceased to wonder why Charlie Tabor had phoned. Dock Middleton never had much truck with mysteries. He was not a religious man, but he'd been raised a good hard-shelled Southern Baptist and that is a religion largely without mystery.

He hobbled into Charlie Tabor's barber shop and sat down quickly to take the weight off his bad leg. There were two Mexicans sitting on one of Charlie's benches and a couple more in a car parked outside, the only stray automobile parked in downtown Valera. Charlie Tabor was cutting old man Lawlis' hair. He introduced Dock to the Mexicans. "This is the Horn family," the barber said. "They're Indians from up in Oklahoma." Dock looked them over and, by God, they weren't Mexicans. They were right enough Indians. Tabor pointed his scissors toward the strange automobile. "That old man out there, he was born and raised around here." Dock Middleton squinted his near-sighted eyes to see Burned Black Horn with his braids and dirty, black woolen suit. They were right enough Indians and it had been many a year since Dock Middleton had looked upon any Indian.

"The old man out there," Charlie Tabor said, "he used to live around Bead Mountain and he wants to go out there. Pink thought maybe you'd show them the way." Dock looked at Charlie Tabor and he thought: Pink didn't think any such thing. Charlie Tabor had to stick his nose into everybody's business and if there wasn't no business, Dock thought, then Charlie'd make some up.

Amos Horn shook hands with Dock Middleton and introduced his son. Dock Middleton looked at both their faces and he was reminded of things he had not in years remembered. He was reminded of no particular event; he was, instead, reminded of the way it had been, of the way it had felt then.

In the spring of 1873, Dock Middleton was camped not ten miles from Valera with Captain Maltby's company on Home Creek when word came from Camp Colorado that Ross Hubbard had lost sixteen horses and had trailed a band of a dozen Indians south along the Mukewater. So the company broke camp and headed for the Trickham country hoping to cut their trail. Seven or eight miles north of Trickham, they cut trail. A rock house was still smoldering. The house belonged to a man named Stoddard. Dock Middleton knew him by sight but Dock Middleton didn't recognize him. Stoddard was scalped and disemboweled. Hot coals from the house fire had been heaped into his belly cavity. Stoddard's boy, who was maybe fourteen, was dead and scalped, a mesquite limb thrust through his nose. A baby lay in a mass of gore. It would have been much better if the baby's mother had been dead but she wasn't-yet. She wouldn't die for another three or four hours.

Burned Black Horn sat in the backseat of the touring car with his daughter-in-law and stared straight ahead. Burned Black Horn was a study in blankness; Burned Black Horn was a master of blankness. He did not approve of his son's continual insistence on dealing with local whitemen. No whiteman needed to tell him how to find the landmarks of his past. He was quite sure he knew this land better than any whiteman could. Still now, Burned Black Horn knew every landmark, minor and major, between Chihuahua and the Kansas plains. The Comanche Crossing of the Pecos was as familiar to him still as was his son's horse pasture on Cache Creek. Whitemen, quite imponderably, professed the strange notion of owning this land but never seemed to know the land they professed to own. In the old raiding times, raiding parties had little trouble hiding within plain sight while white pursuers passed them obliviously by. The whitemen rarely seemed to even notice the land—that was the army whitemen and bands of outraged stockmen who would chase the raiders. The son-of-a-bitch Tejanos Diablos— the Rangers—they were something else. The son-of-a-bitch Tejanos Diablos, they were hard to hide from and they were bad to fight. Burned Black Horn remembered his relatives at The Place Where Salt Seeps; he remembered when he and the other raiders had come in from Mexico only hours too late. He remembered how the old men's bodies had been castrated, how the women's breasts had been cut off. He remembered how his uncle had had no skin at all. The son-of-a-bitch Tejanos Diablos would skin dead people and make bullwhips and quirts and sometimes moccasins from their hides.

Amos Horn had been born to his father's middle age and he knew little of the life the old man had lived in this country. Amos Horn was a Methodist preacher and a fairly successful cattleman. He got along with whitemen. Any affection he had for the old life was akin to racial memory and, as in most first generations after immigration, his racial memory was dim and usually not very important. He loved his father though—and respected him—so when the old man had asked to return to Texas, he'd felt compelled to undertake the trip. Amos Horn had enjoyed the trip. He enjoyed seeing sights he'd not before seen. He even enjoyed dealing with the whitemen. He enjoyed watching their initial surprise turn to a kind of amazed friendliness when they'd talked with him for a few minutes. These Texas whitemen seemed surprised that an Indian could talk to them-and certainly surprised that he could be a Methodist preacher. A white Methodist preacher in the town of Santa Anna at the foot of the mountain had taken them home for supper, and, so far as Amos Horn knew, it was the only time in his father's life that the old man had sat at a whiteman's table.

Amos took the old whiteman out to the car. They'd drive to the mountain, but they had to wait a few more minutes for the barber to finish cutting the other old man's hair. The barber wanted to go along. The barber, thought Amos Horn, was a man bound to involve himself in everything. Amos Horn noticed nothing out of the ordinary about the old whiteman who was to guide them. He looked like any other old white cowboy, like many an old man Amos Horn had bought cows from and sold cows to. The old man limped like many another stove-up old cowboy.

"This is my father," Amos Horn said to Dock Middleton, motioning toward Burned Black Horn. "And this is my old woman," he said, motioning toward his wife who was named Elsie and was an Osage Amos had met when she'd come to Cache as a young girl with her brother who was a great breaker of horses.

Dock Middleton did not glance at Elsie Horn; his eyes snagged on the face of Burned Black Horn.

Dock Middleton was not a philosophical man and he did not think in philosophical terms. And thus the thing that came to him now had no exact words to define it, but a new thing did come to Dock Middleton that morning in the street in Valera and if he could have defined it, he would have asked himself finally at the age of seventy-two, stove-up and no fancier of mystery: How did I come to be the human being that I am? What was the thing that made me who I am? What enigma has formed this old man without enigma? Dock Middleton, had he been another man than Dock Middleton, might have asked these questions but Dock Middleton was Dock Middleton and so his eyes hung on the face of Burned Black Horn.

And this was the thing that Dock Middleton really thought. He thought without anger or even resentment: What are these people doing here? We fought them and we beat them. We drove them north of the Red River. What reason brings these people back here? What right do these people have here?

Burned Black Horn looked at Dock Middleton and he thought, Well, this one is no Methodist preacher.

Brian Horn wished he'd never come on this trip. In his own way, he'd wanted to come as badly as had his grandfather. Like most of the second generation after immigration, Brian had a passionate regard for pre-immigration people and places. He'd wanted to see the places of his grandfather's young manhood. He'd wanted some way to grasp the reality of his grandfather as a raider and hunter and killer and man of place. He had been sorely disappointed. The countryside was scarred by countless hardscrabble dry-land farms and maintained by sad, almost pathetic whitemen who wore looks of defeat in their shapeless clothing and in their desperate eyes. In the mythology of Brian Horn's childhood, this land of the Penateka was a glorious place of great wars and warriors. Brian Horn could only see the southern edge of a worn out dustbowl, the pathetic end of a westering whiteman condemned forever to patched overalls and the ass-end of a flea-bit mule. Good God, it was worse than Oklahoma.

Elsie Horn was having a nice enough time on their trip. She saw her husband was enjoying himself and that made her happy. Elsie Horn was a woman without many needs, physical or emotional. She had never shared her husband's passion for the Methodist religion; she cared little for any religion. Elsie Horn had seen both her mother and father die of measles despite the best ministrations of an Osage medicine man. He had called powerfully for the intervention of the spirits. Had any spirits existed, Elsie Horn had reasoned, they likely would have responded. None had. Elsie had not been distraught to discover there were no spirits; she had not even been surprised. But Elsie Horn did truly love her husband and her son and whatever things they needed, she needed. So she was glad to have come; she was glad to see her husband enjoying himself. Elsie Horn had no idea if her father-in-law was enjoying himself. Burned Black Horn had lived in her household for seventeen years, yet she understood almost nothing of what he thought. Elsie had never spoken to her father-in-law, for he spoke only Comanche and she understood almost no Comanche. Her husband and virtually everyone she knew spoke English to her. She supposed she had no talent for picking up other languages, but she cared little.

Amos Horn could understand and speak English well. But, like most people meeting Dock Middleton the first time, he misunderstood Dock's given name. In translating it to Burned Black Horn, he told his father that Dock Middleton was a doctor. Amos Horn was a bit surprised that Dock Middleton should be a doctor. The old man was obviously a cowman, but Amos Horn guessed that among these Texans who were widely known as cattlemen anyway, even a doctor might be a cowman.

Burned Black Horn was not so surprised. He was, in fact, somewhat pleased. He'd seen whitemen's doctors before and never had they impressed him as doctors. They were nervous men with shifty eyes or else they were fat, clumsy red-faced men. None of them seemed possessed of the power he expected in a man deemed doctor. But this one did seem to be doctor material.

Dock Middleton wasn't too sure of Charlie Tabor's motivation, but he was certain that Charlie Tabor had arranged this strange trip. His initial impulse had been to beg off, beg previous business, beg illness. Then he'd looked again out the barber shop window at Burned Black Horn outside in the touring car and that thing had come to him, that ill-defined mystery had seized itself upon him and he'd ceased to care about Charlie Tabor and Charlie Tabor's manipulations. Now he stood a bit uncomfortably beside the touring car while Amos Horn spoke to Burned Black Horn in Indian, explaining, Dock Middleton assumed, who he was and what was to happen now.

Charlie Tabor didn't know what would happen. That was the fun to Charlie Tabor. Charlie Tabor wasn't a bad man, nor did he mean badly with the games he played. He was a man who found the dynamics of human existence eternally intriguing. And he was a man who found no reason not to sweeten the intrigue. Cutting old man Lawlis' hair, Charlie Tabor examined what had happened up to now this morning and he was pleased.

Burned Black Horn paid no attention at all to Charlie Tabor. That whiteman was a man who chattered like a woman. He was a man who knew not the essential dignity of silence. He was like too many whitemen.

Though Burned Black Horn spoke no English, he had never known a time when whitemen were not about. Even in his earliest childhood there in the Penateka camp by Two-Flows Creek in the shadow of Santa Anna Mountain, even then there were whitemen and rumors of whitemen all about. The men of his band raided south to

the whiteman's town of San Antonio and along the San Saba and
sometimes even so far south as the coast of the ocean. They brought
back whiteman's things—rolls of red cloth they loved, and umbrellas
and tall silk hats. Already when Burned Black Horn was a young
man, the existence of the whiteman had imposed a kind of
definition, a kind of border onto the lives of the People. But always,
the center held; no one guessed the whiteman might even approach
the center—no one could possibly have guessed the whiteman might
indeed someday destroy the center. Such change had Burned Black
Horn seen in his life. But Burned Black Horn was not one to dwell
upon the obvious.

Amos Horn drove the touring car and Charlie Tabor sat in the
middle with Dock Middleton next to the door. In the backseat, Elsie
Horn sat between her son and her father-in-law. Charlie Tabor no
longer even pretended that Dock Middleton had any real function
here. Charlie Tabor, himself, directed Amos Horn southwest, off
the highway, down into the Home Creek breaks, across the bridge,
not the same one they'd camped beside but another, newer iron
bridge with timber flooring. Then they followed, roughly, Bead
Mountain Creek up out of the breaks onto the prairie and suddenly
the mountain loomed before them, the only real landmark on a
horizon of miles and miles of rolling prairie.

Burned Black Horn was not a religious man, but even to a man of
little religion, the sight of the mountain was suddenly affecting.
Burned Black Horn remembered how it had been that afternoon
those many years, those generations ago. He remembered how he'd
come walking up out of the breaks, not here, but south several miles;
he remembered how the mountain had looked then and it was much
the same as now. He had walked resolutely, carrying a blanket.
Comanches carried blankets when they went seeking; they had little
use for penitence. He had walked to that place, that center, that
place of spirits, that place where the dead were buried standing up
facing east, facing east to face the sunrise over Santa Anna Mountain.
He had gone to that place of spirits and of his people's dead. He had
gone to beg for nothing because Comanches did not beg. He had not

gone to prostrate himself; Comanches never prostrated themselves. He had gone to ask, respectfully and determinedly.

He had climbed the mountain and he'd spread his blanket on the east rim to face the sun to rise come morning. Four days and four nights, Burned Black Horn had sat there. And, of course, as he had never doubted, the center had held; a message had come. In twilight, a single buffalo, an old bull expelled from the herd, had approached the foot of the mountain. It had looked up, straight at Burned Black Horn, and there had appeared around its head an aura, a halo of fiery orange. Burned Black Horn had become then Burned Black Horn.

Burned Black Horn had lived in that country not much longer after that. The army had come, and the Rangers, to gather the Penateka to go live up on the Brazos reservation and though some Penateka went, many, including Burned Black Horn, scattered themselves among other bands far north out of reach of the army. Burned Black Horn went to the Naconis band of Peta Nacona which soon rejoined the Kwahadis, and thus Burned Black Horn was among the last to come into Fort Sill, coming in with Quanah, Peta Nacona's son. Quanah ultimately set up this camp on Cache Creek and, following his friend, so did Burned Black Horn.

The two of them, Quanah and Burned Black Horn, remained steadfast friends for all of Quanah's life. Quanah took well to the whiteman's way and became, among the whitemen, one of the best known Indians in America. He toured county fairs lecturing and went wolf hunting with Teddy Roosevelt while Burned Black Horn stayed in his own camp, never seeing whitemen for months at a time, never learning English.

Charlie Tabor directed Amos Horn off the road near the base of Bead Mountain and they drove across open prairie to park as closely to the mountain as possible. The car stopped and no one moved. "Well," Charlie Tabor said, "well, we're here." No one moved. "Well," Charlie Tabor said, "we'll have to hoof it now." For another moment still, no one moved. Then Amos Horn opened his door; then the others. Then they hoofed it. None of them doubted the old man wanted to climb the mountain; Bead Mountain was always meant to be climbed. There was never satisfaction in standing at the foot of Bead Mountain. So with hardly a pause, they climbed. Amos Horn and Brian helped Burned Black Horn; one took each arm, half lifting, sometimes pulling. They worked their way up the steep little mountain.

Neither Brian nor Amos had any real idea what this particular place might mean to Burned Black Horn. They had known since the beginning of the trip that this place was awfully important to him. Amos Horn never really wondered why. All the places on this trip were landmarks of his father's long ago; that was enough for him. Brian Horn had wondered a lot and still he continued to wonder. Brian Horn wondered at it all. Brian Horn was a young man beset by mystery.

Brian Horn was an educated young man. The Indian Department had sent him away east to school with the full cooperation and support of his father. Amos Horn knew that a man needed schooling. Brian Horn had spent the last summer before his schooling—eastern schooling at the age of fourteen—like all his available time, in the presence of Burned Black Horn. The old man had not been convinced there was any such need for whiteman's schooling, but he had kept away from discussion of it. As he was about to leave, Brian had expected some kind of advice, some word from his grandfather. None had come. Burned Black Horn was not one to give advice. Brian Horn had always wished his grandfather could be a little less taciturn. Brian Horn was a young man in need of some center.

Dock Middleton had no one to help his climb and his bad leg gave him hell. He'd be damned if he'd hold up the others, so he gritted his teeth and shifted his weight with each step—and he hurt.

Charlie Tabor was impatient to reach the top. He realized that in his many years in this country, despite the fact that he'd grown used to Bead Mountain on the horizon, he'd never before climbed it. He was anxious for the top not only for whatever might happen among this bunch but just to see what was up there.

Amos Horn climbed because he climbed; Elsie Horn climbed because her family climbed.

Burned Black Horn climbed because, in old age, to a man who

had no understanding of, nor need for mystery, there had come a mystery; there had come a mystery more important than any other that might come to a man. How could it be that that-which-is-and-was-and-will-be could have, all along, been a mistake? That old buffalo bull, he had stood there unmoving in failing light and he had looked directly up at Burned Black Horn. The old buffalo bull's head had been bathed in unearthly fire and Burned Black Horn had smelled burning hair. He had seen and smelled a thing no man had ever before seen or smelled in such a way. So, it had had meaning.

But, Burned Black Horn, truth to tell, being neither a religious nor a philosophical man, had taken his vision home and had lived with it all those years, all those generations, with no real idea upon this earth what it had meant. It had been a vision, a thing expected and needed to keep the universe upright, to re-affirm for him the center, and for all those years, that had been enough.

But then that thing had happened; the part of him that could hear had gone deaf. So he'd begun to wonder; a mystery had come to a man who was not meant for mystery. In another time, in an earlier time of his life, Burned Black Horn might have gone to some kind of medicine man; he might have gone to some old holy man to ask for guidance and for help. But that was another time. The medicine was gone; the medicine men were gone. How could a man go to a wise old man for help when that man needing help was by far the oldest man for many a mile around?

Burned Black Horn thought of the old white doctor and he glanced at him; he watched the old white doctor painfully climbing. This was a doctor of the people who lived here now, the people who saw the eastern sun rise here everyday now. Maybe this old doctor himself had spoken with the spirits of this place.

Burned Black Horn thought those things and he knew there was no way he could use his son, Amos, as a translator to ask the old white doctor. Perhaps, he thought, he could use his grandson. He thought, when we reach the top and both of us old men are no longer suffering this climb I will ask Brian to translate for me to the old white doctor. And, for the first time in his long life, Burned

Black Horn wished he himself could speak the English language of the whitemen.

Dock Middleton could walk no longer. The pain was unbearable and he was exhausted. When they were a bit more than half-way up the mountain, he sat down. Charlie Tabor sat down beside him. The others paused, puffed a bit, looked around, and then they all sat down. They were all silent in their own exhaustions, too silent for Charlie Tabor. Charlie Tabor, who was never a man without words, spoke to Dock Middleton. He asked, "Does all this country here look about like it used to?" Dock Middleton, who was in pain and without breath, looked at Charlie Tabor and could hardly restrain himself.

"I guess it does," Dock Middleton said.

No one would say anything and Charlie Tabor was a man who abhored silence. He tried to think of a relevant thing to say. "Were there buffalo here?" he asked Dock Middleton.

Dock Middleton was close to calling the barber a damn fool, but Dock Middleton didn't say things like that so he answered him; he said, "Yeah, I remember when there was buffalo here."

Then, they climbed to the top of the mountain.

It was the east side of Bead Mountain they climbed so that when they reached the top, a flat table of several acres sprinkled with mesquite bushes and salt cedar trees, they paused, heaved breath, and turned, almost as one, to look east.

Blue Santa Anna Mountain trembled gently in the heat rising across the prairie. A few puffy white summer clouds floated in an immense faded blue bowl of sky.

There was absolute silence on top of Bead Mountain. The entire group of pilgrims stood themselves silently. And then slowly, they turned to survey the circle of prairie around.

North, they could see a low range of wooded hills, dark grey-green from a growth of liveoak that fringed them. To the west, only rolling prairie so far as they could see. To the south, almost beyond vision on such a shimmering summer day, the blue-green breaks of the Colorado. A mile away that direction, south, buzzards floated slowly, marking some place of death. No other animal nor human thing could they see, no other movement.

Dock Middleton was still irritated; he was disquieted he supposed by the barber's silly questions. Yet it was not the barber's questions. This disquiet had begun at the sight of Burned Black Horn. Dock Middleton was suffering from some old uneasiness. What had it been like? What was it like now? Dock Middleton was not a philosophical man, but with the oppressive heavy, silent weight of late summer upon him, he suffered silently great-growing uneasiness.

Amos Horn thought the view from the top of Bead Mountain was quite nice. It reminded him a bit of the prairie south of the Wichitas where ran Cache Creek. Elsie Horn was glad to be no longer climbing. It was a fine place to be to her though, and she was glad to be here. She sat down.

Brian Horn was not much affected by this place. It had been much the same on top of Santa Anna Mountain; it was much the same at home in Oklahoma. Still, he sought to see whatever it was that might be seen. Brian Horn was, like many another displaced and homeless refugee, a profoundly philosophical and religious man.

He surveyed the electric vacuum of hot August Texas prairie and he wished mightily that he might see as his grandfather saw. So he turned to look at Burned Black Horn.

And he saw there had come upon Burned Black Horn a strangeness; he was, somehow, not the same. Burned Black Horn was always a composed man, but now he might be more composed. He was a man who affected blankness, but now he might be much more blank. Brian ceased to study the countryside; he studied his grandfather. Then, as if by command or design, Burned Black Horn turned stiffly to face his grandson.

"I want you to do something for me," Burned Black Horn said to him. "I want you to ask the old white doctor something for me." At Burned Black Horn's sudden voice, all the others turned toward him. They all waited. But Burned Black Horn, try as he might, could think of no way to make the question he wanted his grandson to ask Dock Middleton. He shifted his eyes to look into Dock Middleton's face.

Dock Middleton guessed that Burned Black Horn had meant to direct some statement at him. He tried to drag up the bits and pieces of Comanche language he'd once known. He tried to understand what Burned Black Horn wanted of him.

Having no need for mystery, Elsie Horn, who could understand none of Burned Black Horn's words, first understood that the word hardly mattered.

Amos Horn was surprised at his father's request and he was anxious at the desperation he heard. When he looked at Burned Black Horn, like Brian he was startled at the strangeness he saw. As Burned Black Horn turned his gaze to Dock Middleton, Amos followed. And then Amos Horn too understood. A man of practical and universal humanity, a man who earnestly believed that any mystery could be reduced to parable, Amos Horn saw that Burned Black Horn and Dock Middleton were now as mirror images to one another.

Brian Horn waited for his grandfather to finish and he wondered what on God's green earth it could be that the old man should ask with such urgency. Brian Horn looked from one of the old men to the other, and then he, too, caught the wordless thing that passed between them. It was a moving and memorable moment for Brian Horn. For the first time in a long, long time, he lost his own sense of loss and expectation.

Caught up as he was in great mute union, Brian Horn understood, or at least, without clear definition, began first to suspect, that mystery itself was its own answer.

Only poor Charlie Tabor the barber didn't understand. His eyes careened from Dock Middleton to Burned Black Horn and back to Dock Middleton and back to Burned Black Horn. What in the world was happening? What in the world was happening? A man who tolerated no mystery, he was swept up in a swirling, desperate rush he could not hope to understand.

Only Approved Indians Can Play: Made in USA

Jack Forbes

THE ALL-INDIAN Basketball Tournament was in its second
day. Excitement was pretty high, because a lot of the teams were
very good or at least eager and hungry to win. Quite a few people
had come to watch, mostly Indians. Many were relatives or friends
of the players. A lot of people were betting money and tension was
pretty great.

A team from the Tucson Inter-Tribal House was set to play
against a group from the Great Lakes region. The Tucson players
were mostly very dark young men with long black hair. A few had
little goatee beards or mustaches though, and one of the Great Lakes
fans had started a rumor that they were really Chicanos. This was a
big issue since the Indian Sports League had a rule that all players
had to be of one-quarter or more Indian blood and that they had to
have their BIA roll numbers available if challenged.

And so a big argument started. One of the biggest, darkest Indians
on the Tucson team had been singled out as a Chicano, and the
crowd wanted him thrown out. The Great Lakes players, most of
whom were pretty light, refused to start. They all had their BIA
identification cards, encased in plastic. This proved that they were
all real Indians, even a blonde-haired guy. He was really only about
one-sixteenth but the BIA rolls had been changed for his tribe so
legally he was one-fourth. There was no question about the Great
Lakes team. They were all land-based, federally-recognized
Indians, although living in a big midwestern city, and they had their
cards to prove it.

Anyway, the big, dark Tucson Indian turned out to be a Papago. He didn't have a BIA card but he could talk Papago so they let him alone for the time being. Then they turned towards a lean, very Indian-looking guy who had a pretty big goatee. He seemed to have a Spanish accent, so they demanded to see his card.

Well, he didn't have one either. He said he was a full-blood Tarahumara Indian and he could also speak his language. None of the Great Lakes Indians could talk their languages so they said that was no proof of anything, that you had to have a BIA roll number.

The Tarahumara man was getting pretty angry by then. He said his father and uncle had been killed by the whites in Mexico and that he did not expect to be treated with prejudice by other Indians.

But all that did no good. Someone demanded to know if he had a reservation and if his tribe was recognized. He replied that his people lived high up in the mountains and that they were still resisting the Mexicanos, that the government was trying to steal their land.

"What state do your people live in," they wanted to know. When he said that his people lived free, outside of the control of any state, they only shook their fists at him. "You're not an official Indian. All official Indians are under the whiteman's rule now. We all have a number given to us, to show that we are recognized."

Well, it all came to an end when someone shouted that "Tarahumaras don't exist. They're not listed in the BIA dictionary." Another fan yelled, "He's a Mexican. He can't play. This tournament is only for Indians."

The officials of the tournament had been huddling together. One blew his whistle and an announcement was made. "The Tucson team is disqualified. One of its members is a Yaqui. One is a Tarahumara. The rest are Papagos. None of them have BIA enrollment cards. They are not Indians within the meaning of the laws of the government of the United States. The Great Lakes team is declared the winner by default."

A tremendous roar of applause swept through the stands. A white BIA official wiped the tears from his eyes and said to a companion, "God Bless America. I think we've won."

A Good Chance

Elizabeth Cook-Lynn

I

WHEN I GOT to Crow Creek I went straight to the Agency, the place they call "the Fort," and it was just like it always has been to those of us who leave often and come home now and then: mute, pacific, impenitent, concordant. I drove slowly through the graveled streets until I came to a light blue HUD house.

"I'm looking for Magpie," I said quietly to the little boy who opened the door and looked at me steadily with clear brown eyes. We stood and regarded one another until I, adult-like, felt uncomfortable and so I repeated, "Say, I'm looking for Magpie. Do you know where he is?"

No answer.

"Is your mother here?"

After a few moments of looking me over, the little boy motioned me inside.

"Wait here," he said.

He went down the cluttered hallway and came back with a young woman wearing jeans and a cream-colored ribbon shirt and carrying a naked baby covered only with rolls of fat. "I'm Amelia," she said. "Do you want to sit down?"

The small, shabby room she led me into was facing east and the light flooded through the window making everything too bright, contributing to the uneasiness we felt with each other as we sat down.

"I need to find Magpie," I said. "I've really got some good news for him, I think," and I pointed to the briefcase I was carrying. "I have his poems and a letter of acceptance from a University in

California where they want him to come and participate in the Fine Arts Program they have started for Indians."

"You know then that he's on parole, do you?" she asked, speaking quickly with assurance. "I'm his wife but we haven't been together for a while." She looked at the little boy who had opened the door, motioned for him to go outside and, after he had left, she said softly, "I don't know where my husband is but I've heard that he's in town somewhere."

"Do you mean in Chamberlain?"

"Yes. I live here at the Agency with his sister and she said that she saw him in town, quite a while ago."

I said nothing.

"Did you know that he was on parole."

"Well, no, not exactly," I said hesitantly. "I haven't kept in touch with him but I heard that he was in some kind of trouble. In fact, I didn't know about you. He didn't tell me that he was married though I might have suspected that he was."

She smiled at me and said, "He's gone a lot. It's not safe around here for him, you know. His parole officer really watches him all the time and so sometimes it is just better for him not to come here. Besides," she continued, looking down, absent-mindedly squeezing the rolls of fat on the baby's knees, "we haven't been together for a while."

Uncomfortably, I folded and refolded my hands and tried to think of something appropriate to say. The baby started to cry as though, bored with all this, he needed to hear his own voice. It was not an expression of pain or hunger. He rolled his tongue against his gums and wrinkled his forehead but when his mother whispered something to him he quieted immediately and lay passive in her lap.

"But Magpie would not go to California," she said, her eyes somehow masking something significant that she thought she knew of him. "He would never leave here now even if you saw him and talked to him about it."

"But he did before," I said, not liking the sound of my own defensive words. "He went to the University of Seattle."

"Yeah, but . . . well, that was before," she said as though to finish the matter.

"Don't you want him to go?" I asked.

Quickly, she responded, "Oh, it's not up to me to say. He is gone from me now." She moved her hand to her breast. "I'm just telling you that you are in for a disappointment. He no longer needs the things that people like you want him to need," she said positively.

When she saw that I didn't like her reference to "people like you" and the implication that I was interested in the manipulation of her estranged husband, she stopped for a moment and then put her hand on my arm. "Listen," she said, "Magpie is happy now, finally. He is in good spirits, handsome and free and strong. He sits at the drum and sings with his brothers; he's okay now. When he was saying all those things against the government and against the council, he became more and more ugly and embittered and I used to be afraid for him. But I'm not now. Please, why don't you just leave it alone now?"

She seemed so young to know how desperate things had become for her young husband in those days and I was genuinely moved by her compassion for him and for a few moments neither of us spoke. Finally, I said, "But I have to see him. I have to ask him what he wants to do. Don't you see that I have to do that?"

She leaned back into the worn, dirty sofa and looked at me with cold hatred. Shocked at the depth of her reaction, I got up and went outside to my car. The little boy who had opened the door for me appeared at my elbow and, as I opened the car door, asked, "If you find him, will you come back?"

"No," I said, "I don't think so."

I had the sense that the little boy picked up a handful of gravel and threw it after my retreating car as I drove slowly away. When I pulled around the corner I glanced over my shoulder and saw that he was still standing there, watching my car leave the street: he was small, dark, closed in that attitude of terrible resignation I recognized from my own childhood and I knew that resignation to be the only defense, the only immunity in a world where children are often the martyrs. That fleeting glimpse of my own past made me even more certain that Magpie had to say yes or no to this thing himself, that none of us who knew and loved him could do it for him.

II

"Home of the Hunkpati," proclaimed a hand-lettered sign hanging over the cash register at the cafe. It could not be said to be an inaccurate proclamation, as all of us who perceived the movement of our lives as emanating from this place knew, only an incomplete one. For as surely as the Hunkpati found this their home, so did the Isianti, the Ihantowai, even the Winnebagoes briefly, and others. Even in its incompleteness, though, it seemed to me to be *ne plus ultra*, the super-structure of historiography which allows us to account for ourselves and I took it as an affirmation of some vague sort. In a contemplative mood now, I sat down in a booth and ordered a cup of what turned out to be the bitterest coffee I'd had since I left Santa Fe: "Aa-a-eee-e, pe juta sapa," I could hear my uncle saying.

I thought about the Hunkpati and all the people who had moved to this place and some who were put in prison here as great changes occurred, as they strove to maintain an accommodation to those changes. The magic acts of white men don't seem to work well on Indians, I thought, and the stories they tell of our collective demise have been "greatly exaggerated" or, to put it into the vernacular of the myth-tellers of my childhood, "Heh yela owi hake"—this, the appropriate ending to the stories which nobody was expected to believe anyway.

I was thinking these things so intently I didn't notice the woman approaching until she was standing beside the booth saying, "They gave me your note at the BIA office. You wanted to see me?"

"Yes," I said from the great distance of my thoughts, having nearly forgotten my search for the young poet I wished to talk to about his great opportunity. As I looked up into her sober intent face, it all seemed unimportant and for a moment I felt almost foolish.

Remembering my mission, I said solicitously, "Thank you for coming," and asked her to sit down across the table from me.

"Are you Salina?"

"Yes."

"This place here didn't even exist when I was a child," I told her. "The town that we called 'the Fort' in those days lay hidden along the old creek bed and the prairie above here was the place where we gathered to dance in the summer sun."

"I know," she said. "My mother told me that we even had a hospital here then, before all this was flooded for the Oahe Dam. She was born there in that hospital along the Crow Creek."

We sat in thoughtful remembrance, scarcely breathing, with twenty years difference in our ages, and I thought: Yes, I was born there too, along that creek bed in that Indian hospital which no longer exists, in that Agency town which no longer exists except in the memories of people who have the capacity to take deeply to heart the conditions of the past. And later my uncle offered me to the four grandfathers in my grandmother's lodge even though it was November and the snow had started, and I was taken into the bosom of a once-larger and significant, now dwindling family, a girl-child who in the old days would have had her own name.

Abruptly, she said, "I don't know where Magpie is. I haven't seen him in four days."

"I've got his poems here with me," I said. "He has a good chance of going to a Fine Arts school in California, but I have to talk with him and get him to fill out some papers. I know that he is interested."

"No, he isn't," she broke in. "He doesn't have those worthless, shitty dreams anymore."

"Don't say that, Salina. This is a good chance for him."

"Well, you can think what you want," she said and turned her dark eyes on me, "but have you talked to him lately? Do you know him as he is now?"

"I know he is good. I know he has such talent."

"He's Indian," she said as though there were some distinction I didn't know about. "And he's back here to stay this time."

She sat there all dressed up in her smart gray suit and her black shiny fashion boots, secure in her GS-6 Bureau secretarial position, and I wondered what she knew about "being Indian" that accounted for the certainty of her response. Was it possible that these two women with whom I had talked today, these two lovers of Magpie, one a wife and the other a mistress, could be right about all of this? Is it possible that the drama of our personal lives is so quiescent as to be mere ceremony whose staging is unpredictable? Knowable? In the hands of those who love us, are we mere actors mouthing their lines? Magpie, I thought, my friend, a brother to me, who am I and who are they to decide these things for you?

Near defeat in the face of the firm resolve of these two women, almost resigned with folded hands on the table, I looked out the window of the cafe and saw the lines of HUD houses row upon row, the design of government bureaucrats painted upon the surface of this long-grassed prairie, and I remembered the disapproving look of the little boy who threw gravel at my car and I found the strength to try again.

"Would you drive into Chamberlain with me?" I asked.

She said nothing.

"If he is Indian as you say, whatever that means, and if he is back here to stay this time and if he tells me that himself, I'll let it go. But Salina," I urged, "I must talk to him and ask him what he wants to do. You see that, don't you?"

"Yes," she said finally. "He has a right to know about this, but, you'll see ... "

Her heels clicked on the brief sidewalk in front of the cafe as we left, and she became agitated as she talked. "After all that trouble he got into during the protest at Custer when the courthouse was burned, he was in jail for a year. He's still on parole and he will be on parole for another five years — and they didn't even prove anything against him! Five years! Can you believe that? People these days can commit murder and not get that kind of a sentence."

She stopped to light a cigarette before she opened the car door and got in.

As we drove out of "the Fort" toward town, she said, "Jeez, look at that," and she pointed with her cigarette to a huge golden eagle tearing the flesh from some carcass which lay in the ditch alongside the road.

I thought: as many times as I've been on this road in my lifetime, I've never seen an eagle here before. I've never seen one even near this place . . . ma tuki.

III

Elgie was standing on the corner near the F & M Bank as we drove down the main street of Chamberlain, and both Salina and I knew without speaking that this man, this good friend of Magpie's, would know of his whereabouts. We looked at him as we drove past and he looked at us, neither giving any sign of recognition. But when we went to the end of the long street, made a U-turn and came back and parked the car, Elgie came over and spoke. "I haven't seen you in a long time," he said as we shook hands.

"Where you been?" he asked as he settled himself in the back seat of the car. "New Mexico?"

"Yes."

"I seen the license plates on your car," he said as if in explanation. There might have been more he wanted to say but a police car moved slowly to the corner where we were parked and the patrolmen looked at the three of us intently and we pretended not to notice.

I looked down at my fingernails, keeping my face turned away and I thought: this is one of those towns that never changes. You can be away twenty minutes or twenty years and it's still the same as ever. I remembered a letter that I had read years before written by a former mayor of this town, revealing his attitude toward Indians. He was opposing the moving of the Agency, flooded out by the Ft. Randall Power Project, to his town:

> April 14, 1954
>
> Dear U.S. Representative:
>
> I herewith enclose a signed resolution by the
> city of Chamberlain and a certified copy of a

resolution passed by the Board of County Commissioners of Brule County, So. Dak. The
County Commissioners are not in session so I
could not get a signed resolution by them.

As I advised you before, we have no intentions
of making an Indian comfortable around here,
especially an official. We have a few dollar
diplomats that have been making a lot of noise
and trying to get everyone that is possible to
write you people in Washington that they
wanted the Indians in here, but the fact is 90
per cent of the people are strongly opposed to it
and will get much more so, if this thing comes
in. Anybody who rents them any property will
have to change his address and I wouldn't want
the insurance on this building. We do not feel
that this town should be ruined by a mess like
this and we do not intend to take it laying down
irregardless of what some officials in
Washington may think.

(Signed: H.V.M., Mayor)

That same spring, my uncle Narcisse, thirty-seven years old,
affable, handsome with a virtuous kind of arrogance that only Sioux
uncles can claim, was found one Sunday morning in an isolated spot
just outside of town with "fatal wounds" in his throat. This city's
coroner and those investigating adjudged his death to be an
"accident," a decision my relatives knew to be ludicrous and
obscene. Indians killing and being killed did not warrant careful and
ethical speculation, my relatives said bitterly.

The patrol car inched down the empty street and I turned
cautiously toward Elgie. Before I could speak, Salina said, "She's
got some papers for Magpie. He has a chance to go to a writer's
school in California."

Always tentative about letting you know what he was really thinking, Elgie said, "Yeah?"

But Salina wouldn't let him get away so non-committally. "Ozéla," she scoffed. "You know he wouldn't go!"

"Well, you know," Elgie began, "one time when Magpie and me was hiding out after that Custer thing, we ended up on the Augustana College campus. We got some friends there. And he started talking about freedom and I never forgot that, and then after he went to the pen it became his main topic of conversation. Freedom. He wants to be free and you can't be that, man, when they're watching you all the time. Man, that freak that's his parole officer is some mean watch-dog."

"You think he might go for the scholarship?" I asked, hopefully.

"I don't know. Maybe."

"Where is he?" I asked.

A truck passed and we waited until it had rumbled on down the street. In the silence that followed, no one spoke.

"I think it's good that you come," Elgie said at last, "because Magpie, he needs some relief from all this," he waved his hand. "This constant surveillance, constant checking up, constant association. In fact, that's what he always talks about. 'If I have to associate with wasichus,' he says, 'then I'm not free; there's not liberty in that for Indians.' You should talk to him now." Elgie went on earnestly, eyeing me carefully, "He's changed. He's for complete separation, segregation, total isolation from the wasichus."

"Isn't that a bit too radical? Too unrealistic?" I asked.

"I don't know," he said, hostility rising in his voice, angry perhaps that I was being arbitrary and critical about an issue we both knew had no answer. "Damn if I know — is it?"

"Yeah," said Salina, encouraged by Elgie's response. "And just what do you think it would be like for him at that University in California?"

"But it's a chance for him to study, to write. He can find a kind of satisfying isolation in that, I think."

After a few moments, Elgie said, "Yeah, I think you're right." A long silence followed his conciliatory remark, a silence which I didn't want to break since everything I said sounded too argumentative, authoritative.

We sat there, the three of us, and I was hoping that we were in some kind of friendly agreement. Pretty soon Elgie got out of the back seat, shut the door and walked around to the driver's side and leaned his arms on the window.

"I'm going to walk over to the bridge," he said. "It's about three blocks down there. There's an old, white two-story house on the left side just before you cross the bridge. Magpie's brother, he just got out of the Nebraska State Reformatory and he's staying there with his old lady, and that's where Magpie is."

At last! Now I could really talk to him and let him make this decision for himself.

"There's things about this though," Elgie said. "Magpie shouldn't be there, see because it's a part of the condition of his parole that he stays away from friends and relatives and ex-cons and just about everybody. But Jeez, this is his brother.

"Wait until just before sundown and then come over," he directed. "Park your car at the service station just around the block from there and walk to the back entrance of the house and then you can talk to Magpie about all this."

"Thanks, Elgie," I said.

We shook hands and he turned and walked down the street, stopping to light a cigarette, a casual window shopper.

IV

Later, in the quiet of the evening dusk, Salina and I listened to our own breathing and the echoes of our footsteps as we walked toward the two-story house by the bridge where Elgie said we could find Magpie. We could see the water of the Missouri River choppy and dark as it flowed in a southwesterly direction, and the wind rose from the water, suddenly strong and insistent.

The river's edge, I knew, was the site of what the Smithsonian

Institute had called an "extensive" and "major" archeological "find" as they had uncovered the remains of an old Indian village during the flooding process for the Oahe Dam. The "find" was only about a hundred yards from the house which was now Magpie's hiding place. The remains of such a discovery, I thought, testify to the continuing presence of ancestors, but this thought would give me little comfort as the day's invidious, lamentable events wore on.

Salina was talking, telling me about Magpie's return to Crow Creek after months in exile and how his relatives went to his sister's house and welcomed him home. "They came to hear him sing with his brothers," she told me, "and they sat in chairs around the room and laughed and sang with him."

One old uncle who had taught Magpie the songs felt that he was better than ever, that his voice had a wider range, was deeper, more resonant, yet high-pitched, sharp and keen to the senses at the proper moments. "The old uncle," said Salina, "had accepted the facts of Magpie's journey and his return home with the knowledge that there must always be a time in the lives of young men when they move outward and away and in the lucky times they return."

As she told me about the two great-uncles' plans for the honor dance, I could see that this return of Magpie was a time of expectation and gratitude. Much later, I would see that this attitude of expectancy, a habit of all honorable men who believe that social bonds are deep and dutiful, was cruelly unrealistic. For these old uncles and for Magpie, there should have been no expectation.

Several cars were parked in the yard of the old house as we approached, and Salina, keeping her voice low, said, "Maybe they're having a party. That's all we need."

But the silence which hung about the place filled me with apprehension, and when we walked in the back door which hung open, we saw people standing in the kitchen. I asked carefully, "What's wrong?"

Nobody spoke but Elgie came over, his bloodshot eyes filled with sorrow and misery. He stood in front of us for a moment and then gestured us to go into the living room. The room was filled with people sitting in silence, and finally Elgie said, quietly, "They shot him."

"They picked him up for breaking the conditions of his parole and they put him in jail and . . . they shot him."

"But why?" I cried. "How could this have happened?"

"They said they thought he was resisting and that they were afraid of him."

"Afraid?" I asked, incredulously, "But . . . but . . . Was he armed?"

"No," Elgie said, seated now, his arms on his knees, his head down. "No, he wasn't armed."

I held the poems tightly in my hands, pressing my thumbs, first one and then the other, against the smoothness of the cardboard folder.

Amen

Linda Hogan

H E WAS BORN with only one eye and maybe that's why he saw things different than most people. The good eye was dark. The sightless eye was all white and lightly veined.

"There's a god in the light of that eye," Sullie's mother said.

Sullie only saw the old man's eye once in her life. It was the night of the big fish and she thought it was more like a pearl or moon than like an eye. And it was all the more unusual because Jack was, after all, only an ordinary man. He had an old man's odor and wasn't always clean.

He carved wood and fished like all the men. With his small hands he carved tree limbs into gentle cats, sleeping dogs and chickens. And he carved chains to hold them all together.

"It's the only way I can keep a cat and dog in the same room," he joked.

Sullie kept most of his carvings. She watched the shavings pile up on the creaking porch until a breeze blew them into the tall grass or weeds. On a hot windless day they'd fall onto the gold back of the sleeping dog or on its twitching ear. She sat at old Jack's feet and watched and smelled the turpentine odor of wood. His unpatched eye was sharp and black. She could see herself in it, her long skinny legs folded under, her faded dress, dark scraggly hair, all in his one good eye. The other eye was covered, as usual, with a leather patch.

Even then he had been pretty old. His skin was loosening from the bones. He was watching with his clear and black eye how the sky grew to be made of shadows. And some days he didn't have room for one more word so they sat in silence.

The night of the big fish people had been talking about Jack. He wasn't at the picnic and that was a good invitation to gossip.

"Jesse James was part Chickasaw," said Enoch. "Pete has one of his pistols. Word has it that Pete and Jack are related to the James brothers."

Gladys waved her hand impatiently. She leaned her chair back a little and stuck her chest out. "Go on. That old man?"

"That old man was a pallbearer at Jesse James' funeral, yes sir."

"They wouldn't have had an Indian at the funeral, would they?" she asked.

"Look it up. Besides, in his younger days he wore a coal black shirt, even when it was hot. And he had one of them there Arabian horses no one else knew how to ride. And a concho belt made out of real silver. Had a silver saddle horn, too."

Will smiled at the other men. He removed his hat and rubbed back his thick black and gray hair. "That's right. Rumor has it his own brother stole that saddle and belt."

People still kept watch for it, for the stirrups dangling like half-moons and the hammered conchos down the sides. There had also been the horsehair bridle he brought back from Mexico. It was red, black and white horsehair with two heavy threads of purple running through it. The purple dye had come from seashells. Greek shellfish, someone had said and Jack liked to touch the threads and feel the ocean in them, the white Greek stucco buildings, the blue sky. He liked the purple thread more than all the silver. Almost.

"You wouldn't have crossed him in those days. He won that horse in a contest. The trader said if anyone could ride it, they could have it. Jack got on and rode it. He sure did. And then the trader said he couldn't give it to Jack. 'I'd be broke,' he said. So Jack said, give me fifty dollars. The man said he didn't have that kind of money. Jack pulled out his pistol and said, 'If I kill you, you won't have no worries about money or horses.'"

Everyone nodded. A couple of old folks said, "Amen," like good

Baptists do. A cheater was a bad man. Jack's brother killed a man for cheating him out of thirty-eight cents. It didn't sound like much but there wasn't much food in those days and the thief had been an outsider. The old folks then also had said, "Amen." They had to feed their own. Not much grew out of the dry Oklahoma soil except pebbles. Word had it that this was just a thin layer of earth over big stone underground mountains. Close to the hot sun and the corn-eating grasshoppers.

And even Sullie had lived through two droughts, a dozen or more black and turquoise tornadoes rolling through the sky, and the year that ended in October. That year cotton grew up out of soft red soil and it grew tall. At first the old people praised the cotton and said "Amen" to the ground. But it kept growing until it was tall as the houses, even the houses with little attics. It stretched up to the wooden rooftops, above the silvered dried wood.

Jack went out in the mornings looking for signs of blossoms. Every morning he stood at the far end of the field and sang a song to the cotton. Sullie snuck out behind him and hid in the tall green plants. She heard parts of the song and silence and the cotton whisper and grow. No pale flowers ever bloomed. No hint of anything that would dry and burst open with white soft cotton inside. Jack went out daily. He stood and sang. He walked through the plants as if his steps would force the stems to let out frail blossoms.

Sullie's mother watched from the door. She dried her hands on the back of her skirt. "I don't think nothing's going to work." She whispered to Sullie and it was true because when October came the taller than houses plants froze, turned transparent and then dried a dull yellow. And the banks closed. And the new red mules died of bloat. And Sullie learned to keep silent at the long empty table.

"He even shot his own brother-in-law for beating up his sister. At a picnic just like this one."

"Amen," the women said, good Baptists. They nodded their round dark faces in agreement.

"After that he'd never sit by a window or go in a dark room. Why, he wouldn't even go in a barn unless it had two doors because he was sure the law or someone from the family would get him."

"He was mean, all right, a man to be feared. You'd forget he had such tiny little hands. And he only wore a size two shoe. Don't know how he ran so fast or handled them guns. And all the time turning his head like a cock rooster to make up for the missing eye."

It grew dark and several men went down to the lake to jack fish. They shined big lights into the water and it attracted fish the same way it paralyzed deer or other land animals. They wouldn't have done it if Jack had been there.

Sullie went down to the water. She was almost a teenager and she liked to watch the big men. She liked their tight jeans and shirts and hats. The women didn't like girls following the men but they forgot about her soon, they were so busy talking about new cotton dresses, their own little children sleeping now on blankets on the hillside. And later they'd talk about woman things, men, herbs, seeing Eliza George the old doctor woman who healed their headaches and helped them get pregnant. Sullie would be back in time to hear about Miss George and how to get pregnant.

But for now she watched the lights shine on the water. And some underneath showing up like sunset. A few miles away in the dark she saw the passing headlights of trucks. She sat in a clump of bushes and trees for a while, then went down to the dark edge of the lake. The men couldn't see her. They were blind to darkness because of the bright lights in their eyes.

She waded in the warm water. The hem of her dress stuck to her legs. She went a little deeper. She stubbed her toe and felt something move and give way. Whatever it was made a large current and she felt frightened. It was cool and slippery and swam like a large fish. Then it stopped. She reached her hand into the water, wetting even her hair, but it was gone. She felt nothing except the fast motion of water.

She smelled the water. She swam a little and looked at the light the women kept on the table, and the black trees.

She heard voices of the men out in the center of the lake. "Over there," someone said. And the lights swayed on water.

Jack walked down to the lake. Sullie started to call to him but then kept still. In the moonlight she saw that he wasn't wearing his eyepatch. And he walked stiff like maybe he was mad. So she kept silent and waded a little further into rocks and weeds and darkness near the shore.

He didn't have a boat or canoe and he stood a moment at the edge of the dark water. Then he dunked himself and stood again. Sullie saw his knobby shoulders beneath the wet shirt, the bones at the neck. Then he submerged himself in water and swam toward the other men. There were only a few splashes, an occasional glimpse of his head rising out of the water.

Before he reached the men with lights, Sullie heard them all become noisy at once. "Lordy," one of them said. The water near them grew furious and violent. One small canoe tipped and the lights shone off all directions.

Sullie waded out again to her chest to watch, forgetting about the women's talk. She heard the men's voices. "I could put my hands in that gill slit." Someone else said, "Watch his fins. They're like razor blades." They were pulling something around, taking ropes out of the boats when Jack arrived. Sullie didn't hear the conversation between Jack and the other men but she saw him breathing hard in one of the boats and then he was gone, swimming again toward shore, her direction.

"Pry it out of those rocks," Enoch yelled. The men were jubilant, dredging up the old fish with only one eye. It was an old presence in the lake and Jack must have known about it all along. His absence had given the young men permission to fish with illegal light.

He came up from the water close to Sullie and walked through the rocks and sand out into the night air.

Sullie followed Jack a ways. In the darkness there was a tree standing in moonlight, the moon like a silver concho. Jack's hands were small and the light outlined the bones and knuckles. They were spotted like the sides of the ancient fish.

She held herself back from the old man. His shoulders were high and she remembered how he had made cornbread on the day of her birth and fed her honey so she'd never be thin. Sullie's mother had been surprised that Sullie knew this. "Who told you?" she asked.

"Nobody."

"You remember it on your own? Babies are supposed to be blind."

"I just remember, that's all."

And now he stood breathing in the dark. And there were yucca plants at his feet. After the first freeze they would scatter a circle of black seeds on the earth like magic. Like the flying wisteria seeds that had hit and scared Sullie one night. So much mystery in the world, in the way seeds take to air and mimosa leaves fold in delicate prayer at night.

"Who's there?" he said.

"It's me." Her voice was weak. She was afraid to go near him, afraid to run off. He turned and the sight of his eye made her pull her breath too fast into her lungs. It was bright as the moon and the lanterns on water. He watched her a moment and then turned. He looked toward where the cotton was growing this year, toward a few scattered houses with dark windows. Fireflies appeared while he stood. And the sounds of locusts and crickets Sullie hadn't noticed before.

"Let's go back to the rest of the folks," he said.

And they walked, the skinny wet girl, the skinny wet man. The women shut up when they saw them coming. The men didn't notice. They were dragging the rope-bound old fish up on the shore and all the children were awake and running and splashing the water.

Its fins slowed. The gills quit opening while they cut at it and cleaned it of red and yellow ropey intestines and innards. Dogs lapped at its juices.

In the moonlight the sharp scales were scraped off like hunks of mica in a shining glassy pile.

The smell of fish cooking. The dogs eating parts of the head. So large, that dull-colored thing. They'd all talk about it forever. Something that had survived the drought, the famine, the tornadoes and dead crops. It grew large. It was older than all of them. It had hooks in it and lived.

Sullie refused to eat. She pushed her dish away. Her mother hit the table with a pot. "Eat," she said.

Jack's one eye looked far inside Sullie. She was growing old. She could feel it. In his white gaze, she grew old. She grew silent inside. She pulled the plate toward her and looked at the piece of fish, the fried skin and pale bones of it.

"Eat it," Jack motioned with his fork, his own cheeks full of the pink meat. "Eat it. It's an Indian fish."

"Amen," said the women just like they'd always been good Baptists.

Contributors

PAULA GUNN ALLEN is the author of *Shadow Country, Star Child, A Cannon Between My Knees, Coyote's Daylight Trip,* and *The Blind Lion.* Her heritage is Laguna. She has published poems and articles in *A, American Indian Culture and Research Journal, Contact II, New America, River Styx, Sinister Wisdom,* and *The Remembered Earth,* and others. She lives in El Cerrito, California.

SALLI BENEDICT (Kawennotakie), Director of the Akwesasne Museum as well as a writer, is Mohawk of the Akwesasne Reserve in New York. "She Carries A Good Word" has authored and illustrated two bilingual book, *Tsiakotsiakwin* and *Kanennakekwa,* which are intended to teach reading in Mohawk.

DUANE BIG EAGLE, statewide Affirmative Action Coordinator for the California Poets in the School Program, is of Osage descent. His work has appeared in many magazines including the *Chicago Review, Sun Tracks, The Nation,* and *The Remembered Earth.* His first book was *Bidato* and his latest is *Birthplace, Poems & Paintings.* He lives in Petaluma, California.

PETER BLUE CLOUD is Turtle Clan of the Mohawk Nation at Caughnawaga. He has had six books published including the recent *Elderberry Flute Song* and *White Corn Sister.* He has had many poems and stories published in journals and anthologies and has co-edited *Coyote's Journal.* About his Coyote stories, he says, "I keep writing them cause when I do readings, it's Indians who laugh most." He lives in North San Juan, California.

JOSEPH BRUCHAC III, Abenaki, has published books of poetry including *The Good Message of Handsome Lake, Entering Onondaga,* and *Translator's Son.* Presently, he is working on a book about contemporary American Indian poets and the theme of survival. He lives in the Adirondack foothills of upstate New York in Greenfield Center.

ROBERT J. CONLEY, Cherokee, is Director of Indian Studies at Morningside College in Sioux City, Iowa, where he lives. Stories and poems have been published in *Pembroke Magazine, Scree, The Belly of the Shark, The Remembered Earth,* and other publications. He has edited *Poems for Comparison and Contrast, The Shadow Within* and other books. He is the author of *21 Poems* and *Adwosgi, Swimmer Wesley Snell: A Cherokee Memorial.*

ELIZABETH COOK—LYNN, Associate Professor of English and Indian Studies at Eastern Washington University, is Crow Creek Sioux. Author of *Then Badger Said This*, she has had poetry and stories published in *South Dakota Review, Prarie Schooner, Sun Tracks,* and other publications. She lives on the Spokane Indian Reservation in Wellpinit, Washington.

NORA DAUENHAUER, Tlingit, has authored numerous traditional texts in the Tlingit language as well as poems in the *Greenfield Review, Northward Journal, NEEK, Raven's Bones Newsletter,* and other publications. A teacher and scholar of her Native Tlingit language, she lives in Anchorage, Alaska.

LOUISE ERDICH grew up in Wahpeton, North Dakota and is Turtle Mountain Chippewa. Her work has appeared in *Dacotah Territory, Ms., Redbook, Shenandoah, North American Review, Chicago Magazine,* and other places. Ms. Erdrich is a 1983 recipient of a National Endowment for the Arts fellowship in fiction and has been a winner of the Nelson Algren Prize. She lives in Cornish, New Hampshire.

JACK D. FORBES was born in California but writes that his heritage is the "long trail of Indians from the east coast, driven little by little towards the west" and his tribal background is Renape, Lenape, and Saponi. He wrote his first story at eighteen but discouraged by a college English teacher's remarks quit until he was forty-five. Now he's making up for lost time.

ROXY GORDON who lives in Dallas, Texas is author of *Some Things I Did* and has edited *Fort Belknap Notes* and *Picking Up The Tempo*. His work has appeared in *Village Voice, Rolling Stone, Country Music, Texas Observor,* and many literary journals. Of Choctaw heritage, he makes his living as an artist, presently producing Art-Magic Mailart Series.

GERALD HASLAM is the author of the novel, *Masks,* and the short story collections, *Okies, The Wages of Sin,* and *Hawk Flights.* Of his heritage, he writes, "In my case, a mestizo great-grandfather from Chihuahua — Mom's side — and a Choctaw half-blood great-grandmother on my Dad's. My kids, on the other hand, are one eighth Cree since my father-in-law is a half-blood. We Americans are all mixed up." He lives in Petaluma, California.

GORDON HENRY, working on a Masters in Creative Writing at Michigan State University, is Missippi Band Objibwa. He has lived on the White Earth Reservation in Minnesota, Guam, California, and presently in East Lansing, Michigan.

GEARY HOBSON, Cherokee-Quapaw-Chickasaw, teaches at the University of New Mexico. He edited *The Remembered Earth: An Anthology of Contemporary Native Amerian Literature.* Currently, he has a book of poetry and a novel, *Daughters of Lot,* in manuscript and ready for publication. He lives in Albuquerque, New Mexico.

LINDA HOGAN, Chickasaw, is the author of *Calling Myself Home, Daughters, I Love You,* and *Eclipse,* which is due to be published by the

UCLA American Indian Studies Center Press. She recently completed a novel. Linda was the editor of the Indian women's issue of *Frontiers*, and she lives in Idledale, Colorado.

ROGER JACK, a member of the Colville Confederated Tribes, is a graduate of the Creative Writing program at the Institute of American Indian Arts in Santa Fe. His work has been published in *New York Quarterly* and *Spawning The Medicine River*. He lives in Nespelem, Washington.

MAURICE KENNY, Mohawk, is co-editor of *Contact/II* and publisher of Strawberry Press. Among his many books are: *North: Poems of Home, Dancing Back Strong The Nation, The Smell of Slaughter,* and *Blackrobe: Issac Jogues.* His work has appeared in *The Remembered Earth, On Turtle's Back, A Nation Within,* and other places. He lives in Brooklyn, New York.

JUDY LA FORME writes, "I am Mohawk by birth. I was born and raised on the Six Nations Reserve near Brantford, Ontario in Canada." Further, "I have wanted to write for a long time but lacked the confidence and motivation to put my thought and feelings on paper. Not to mention having no idea how this is done." She has published a story in *Sinister Wisdom*. She lives in Fresno, California.

LARRY LITTLEBIRD, Laguna-Santo Domingo Pueblo, writes for film and television. Currently, he is producer-writer, in partnership with WTTW-TV in Chicago, of "Going For The Rain," a two 90-minute film series based on the work of Simon J. Ortiz. He is also an actor and a poet. He lives in Santa Fe, New Mexico.

WILMA ELIZABETH MCDANIEL writes that she was "born in Creek Nation, Oklahoma, 1918, made Dustbowl trek to California in 1936. Did a lot of hard thankless, practically payless work, always a poet and story teller, have written twelve books of poetry, four books of stories, one novella, one play." She has been published in numerous magazines and journals. She lives in Tulare, California.

DUANE NIATUM whose tribal heritage is Klallam is the author of four volumes of poetry. His last, *Songs For The Harvester of Dreams*, won the American Book Award from the Before Columbus Foundation. He was editor of the major poetry anthology, *Carriers of the Dreamwheel* and has published essays and short fiction in magazines and anthologies. Most of the time he lives in Seattle, Washington.

ROBERT L. PEREA, born in Wheatland, Wyoming, is of Oglala Sioux heritage. He has published his stories in *The Remembered Earth*, *Cuentos Chicanos*, *Thunderbird* and *Mestizo/DeColores Journal*. Living in Phoenix, Arizona, he teaches at Phoenix Indian High School.

W.M. RANSOM is author of *Finding True North & Critter*, *Waving Arms At The Blind*, and *Last Rites*. He has also co-authored *The Jesus Incident* and *The Lazarus Effect* as well as publishing in *New Mexico Magazine*, *Prairie Schooner*, *Rocky Mountain Review* and other places. His heritage is Arapaho and he lives in Port Townsend, Washington.

CARTER REVARD, who teaches at Washington University, was "born in Pawhuska and grew up in an Osage and white family in the country between Pawhuska and Bartlesville." In 1952, having won a Rhodes scholarship, he writes, "I was honored by my grandmother with an Osage naming ceremony and was given the name Nompewathe. I am grateful for the stories and for the earth and time to which my people have brought me." Carter lives in St. Louis, Missouri.

RALPH SALISBURY, Cherokee, is Professor of English at U. of Oregon who has authored *Ghost Grapefruit & Other Poems*, *Pointing At The Rainbow*, *Going To The Water*, and *Spirit Beast Chant*. Stories and poems have appeared in *New Yorker*, *Poetry Northwest*, *December*, *TransAtlantic Review* and other places. "I like to think of myself as in the tradition of the tribal poet, with a spirit vision and a sense of responsibility toward my people," he writes from Portland, Oregon where he lives.

LESLIE MARMON SILKO, author of the acclaimed novel, *Ceremony,* is Laguna. A much published writer, having poems, stories, articles appear in *Chicago Review, Fiction's Journey: 50 Stories, Rocky Mountain Review, The Best American Short Stories,* and other journals and anthologies, she is a winner of a 1981 MacArthur Foundation award. Living in Tucson, Arizona, she is completing a novel.

MARY TALL MOUNTAIN was "born in Alaska's bush on the Yukon River" to an Athabascan heritage. Living in San Francisco, she writes, "I must live beside water. San Francisco is a beach town of mist and rain and it's near the inland deserts and high mountains." Of her novel-in-progress she says, "It may help clear up a general ignorance about the Athabascans who have been called 'strangers of the north.'"

LUCI TAPAHONSO is of the Salt Water clan of the Navajo people. She is the author of *One More Shiprock Night* and *Seasonal Woman,* and she has been published in journals and anthologies including *The Remembered Earth.* A graduate of the U. of New Mexico's creative writing program, she lives in Albuquerque, New Mexico.

GERALD VIZENOR, teaching American Indian literature at the U. of Minnesota, is White Earth Chippewa. He is the author of *Earthdivers: Tribal Narratives on Mixed Descent* and *Wordarrows: Indians and Whites in the New Fur Trade.* He has finished a book of haiku poems and is currently working on a narrative history of the Chippewa. He lives in Minneapolis, Minnesota.

ANNA L. WALTERS, Pawnee-Otoe-Missouria, is author of *The Otoe-Missouria Tribe, Centennial Memoirs* and co-author of *The Sacred: Ways of Knowledge, Sources of Life.* Her work has appeared in *The Man To Send Rainclouds, Shantih, Voices Of The Rainbow, The Indian Historian* and other publications. She is the Director of NCC Press and she lives in Tsaile, Arizona.

SIMON J. ORTIZ is from Acoma Pueblo in New Mexico. He is the author of ten books of poetry and stories among which are *Going For The Rain, A Good Journey, Howbah Indians, The People Shall Continue, Fight Back,* and *From Sand Creek.* He co-edited the anthologies, *Ceremony of Brotherhood* and *Califa,* and was newspaper editor of *Americans Before Columbus* and *Rough Rock News* in the early 70's. Ortiz has been a college instructor in Native American studies, literature, and creative writing. His latest book, a short story collection called *Fightin'* is due to be published in late 1983. Currently, he is working on a two-part TV film series based on his short stories. He lives in Albuquerque, New Mexico.